RUSKIN'S CULTURE WARS

VICTORIAN LITERATURE AND CULTURE SERIES
Karen Chase, Jerome J. McGann, *and* Herbert Tucker, *Editors*

RUSKIN'S CULTURE WARS

Fors Clavigera
and the Crisis of
Victorian Liberalism

———— ❧ ————

Judith Stoddart

UNIVERSITY PRESS OF VIRGINIA
Charlottesville and London

The University Press of Virginia
H © 1998 by the Rector and Visitors
of the University of Virginia
All rights reserved
Printed in the United States of America

First published 1998

∞ The paper used in this publication meets the
minimum requirements of the American National
Standard for Information Sciences—Permanence
of Paper for Printed Library Materials,
ANSI Z39.48-1984.

Library of Congress Cataloging-in-Publication Data

Stoddart, Judith, 1961–
    Ruskin's culture wars : Fors clavigera and the crisis of Victorian liberalism / Judith
Stoddart.
        p.   cm. — (Victorian literature and culture series)
    Includes bibliographical references (p.   ) and index.
    ISBN 0-8139-1806-5 (cloth : alk. paper)
    1. Ruskin, John, 1819–1900. Fors clavigera.   2. Ruskin, John, 1819–1900 —
Political and social views.   3. Labor movement—Great Britain—History—19th
century.   4. Great Britain—Social conditions—19th century.   5. Liberalism—
Great Britain—History—19th century.   I. Title.   II. Series.
    HD8390.R93S76   1998
    306'.0942'09034 — dc21
                                                                              98-17583
                                                                                    CIP

To A. G. and A. G.

Contents

Acknowledgments

I WOULD LIKE TO thank the Bodleian Library, University of
Oxford, the Ruskin Foundation, the Ruskin Library, University of Lancaster, and the Ruskin Literary Trustees, Guild of
St. George, for permission to quote from unpublished materials in their Ruskin collections. Special thanks is due James
Dearden, now director of the Guild of St. George. As the cura-
tor of the Ruskin manuscripts formerly housed at Bembridge,
Mr. Dearden displayed incredible patience and generosity in
sharing with me the wealth of that collection.

Earlier versions of two chapters have appeared elsewhere.
Part of chapter 3 appeared as "Ruskin and the Cult of Community," *Victorians Institute Journal* 20 (1992): 231–59; sections of
chapter 4 appeared as "Conjuring the 'necromantic . . . evidence' of history: Ruskin and the Enlightenment Revival of the
1870s," *Nineteenth-Century Contexts* 18 (1994): 162–76. My
thanks to *Victorians Institute Journal* and to Gordon and Breach
Publishing Group for their permission to reprint portions of
these articles.

I owe a long-standing debt to Dinah Birch for starting
me on the labyrinthine labor of sorting through *Fors Clavigera*. Her forthcoming edition of the work will, I hope, make
Ruskin's letters accessible to those who do not have access to
the Library Edition and solve some conundrums even for those
who do. I would also like to express my gratitude to Cathie
Brettschneider for staying with this project through its various
permutations.

Above all, I am grateful to Clint and Anna, my two de-
lightful distractions, for their unfailing support and companion-
ship as I made my way through the Ruskinian maze.

Abbreviations

The *Works of John Ruskin* are cited in text by volume and page number.

BL	Coleridge, *Biographia Literaria*
CCR	*The Correspondence of Thomas Carlyle and John Ruskin*
CL	Coleridge, *Collected Letters*
CRN	*The Correspondence of John Ruskin and Charles Eliot Norton*
CWWH	*The Complete Works of William Hazlitt*
F	Coleridge, *The Friend*
LS	Coleridge, *Lay Sermons*
NH	Rousseau, *Julie, ou La Nouvelle Héloïse*
PR	*Weekly Political Register*
WTC	*The Works of Thomas Carlyle*

Introduction

IN 1870 DISRAELI announced the arrival of a turbulent decade. "It cannot be denied," he wrote in the preface to his collected works, "that the aspect of the world and this country, to those who have faith in the spiritual nature of man, is at this time dark and distressful." A "Teutonic rebellion" against the authority of Scripture and the challenges of natural science to a Christian worldview threatened the very foundation of social order, recalling the "Celtic insurrection of the preceding age." While religion faltered, a boom in national prosperity set materialism on the ascendant. "To those," Disraeli prophesied, "who believe that an atheistical society, though it may be polished and amiable, involves the seeds of anarchy, the prospect is full of gloom." [1]

The statesman's tone is leavened, perhaps, by the context; this preface appeared at the head of the satirical *Lothair*, whose parody of Catholicism was construed by a critic in *Macmillan's* as another nail in the coffin of organized religion. [2] Disraeli's dark predictions might also have been seen as the broodings of an ousted politician, forecasting anarchy under the new Liberal regime. But even Gladstone, Disraeli's successor as prime minister in 1868, was wary of the intellectual turn of the new decade. "I doubt whether any such noxious crop has been gathered in such rank abundance from the press of England in any former year of our literary history," he told the boys of the Liverpool Collegiate Institution in 1872, referring to Herbert Spencer's *Principles of Psychology*, David Friedrich Strauss's *Der alte und der neue Glaube*, and Winwood Reade's *Martyrdom of Man*. In such works the modern "disposition [was] boldly proclaimed to deal with root and branch," to break with the "patrimony" of the past, to cultivate the "delight of following free thought." But, he warned, that "free thought, of which we now hear so much, seems too often to mean thought roving and vagrant more than free; like Delos . . . drifting in the seas of Greece, without a root, a direction, or a home." [3]

Both Gladstone and Disraeli saw something more at stake in the moment than religious moorings. Their remarks register the tremors of a significant cultural shift, a critical reformation compared both by its advocates and by opponents such as Disraeli to the revolutionary fervor of the late eighteenth century. A young generation of intellectuals, who openly proclaimed their affiliations with the French *philosophes*, was mounting a challenge to all forms of established authority. John Morley's influential liberal manifesto *On Compromise* (1874) berated the English propensity to Gladstonian pragmatism and swept aside the statesmen's anxieties as the nostalgia of the old guard. "Every school of thought that has the smallest chance of commanding the future," Morley boldly announced, embraced "the right of thinking freely and acting independently, of using our minds without excessive awe of authority, and shaping our lives without unquestioning obedience to custom."[4] While Morley and Leslie Stephen, in his *Essays on Freethinking and Plainspeaking* (1873), rehearsed the arguments of John Stuart Mill for a new set of readers, the more conservative Walter Bagehot recycled the theories of Darwin to surprisingly similar purpose. If the survival of a species depended on variation in successive generations, Bagehot argued in 1872, it followed that variation of thought must be vital to its mental and moral success. The "peculiarity of arrested civilisation is to kill out varieties at birth . . . before they can develop"; only when the "chain of custom" was broken by a "government of discussion" could societies develop and improve.[5] In works such as Frederic Harrison's *Order and Progress* (1875), English Comteans proposed yet another theoretical model of social evolution predicated on the unrestrained development of public opinion.

Diverse political and ideological positions were suddenly converging in a widespread rebellion against settled intellectual, religious, and cultural convictions. The emerging radical spirit of the 1870s was succinctly embodied in the Metaphysical Society, founded in 1869. Conceived initially as a forum for exposing theological issues to methods of debate followed in scientific societies, its mission was expanded even before the first meeting to include all topics of discussion. The society secretary, James Knowles, proposed for its members a formidably ambitious agenda: "To form a complete library of mental and moral Science and speculation. . . . To compile a Dictionnaire raisonné of philosophical systems."[6] In 1877 Knowles tried to recreate something of the feel of the society debates in a "Modern Symposium" that appeared in his periodical, *Nineteenth Century*. There would be no editorial endorsements of particular positions; rather, the review would offer a sampling of leading opinions on topics of the day. Knowles firmly believed, as he wrote to Gladstone, that his role as editor was to be merely a coordinator, "*utterly impartial*," for "full and free discussion is the best way for arriving at and disseminating Truth."[7]

This format may have been conducive to mutual sympathy among Society members; it produced a very different effect in the impersonal pages of a review. Knowles had once lamented "the absence of any sort of kind of reports of the debates," but he came to feel that the "value & force & charm" of the meetings "were principally chiefly owing to this very absence of reporting & to the sense of mutual loyalty & confidence warranting quite open speech." The friendly debate that followed papers at the meetings was absent, however, in Knowles's journals, obscuring for the readers any unanimity among its members. One contemporary reader wondered what kind of leadership a periodical debating society could offer to a nation already unsettled by chaotic opinions. The "fine talk of the chosen *illuminati*," he charged in the *Saturday Review*, "is a mass of words with very little meaning. . . . [it] consist[s] of empty phrases to which all the parties can agree because they do not touch any of the points on which the cosignatories would be likely to differ." One of the original members of the Metaphysical Society used the pages of Knowles's *Nineteenth Century* to criticize this "diluting of essential principles," claiming that the attempt to maintain geniality and sympathy was impracticable in a world made up not of dinner companions but of people with real differences of education, circumstances, and motivation.[8]

According to Terry Eagleton, this void of critical content was characteristic of late Victorian discourse, with its Arnoldian commitment to disinterested truth. A nonpartisan criticism could "address itself to every sector of social experience only by a *kenosis* so complete" that it was left with "absolutely nothing to say." Committed only to an abstract inquiry after truth, this group of skeptical critics left themselves little discursive ground on which to stand. Certainly some members of the Metaphysical Society came to a similar conclusion. In 1878, after a five-year study, an elected "Committee on Definitions" was unable to establish a common vocabulary for Society debates. One contributor to the periodical "Modern Symposium," in response to an essay titled "The Influence upon Morality of a Decline in Religious Belief," complained that it seemed "difficult to discuss this question till it is settled, at least generally, what morality is influenced and what religious belief is declining." Another participant declined to "deal with a question very abstract and ill-defined," while a third felt that ambiguous wording had made the discussion "less pointed" and "less interesting than it might have been."[9]

The Metaphysical Society members, like other liberal intellectuals in the 1870s, had written themselves into a critical corner. In a decade that heralded the beginning of modern labor unions and the military offensives of an organized, nationalist Prussia, the leading lights of the English intelligentsia were unable to speak coherently to themselves, let alone to a disparate nation. The problem lay in part in the origins of the liberal model of authority. As another powerful editor in the period made clear, the new liberals saw themselves producing a domestic version of the French enlightenment. John Morley, at the helm of the *Fortnightly Review*, envisioned that journals such as his and Knowles's would continue the grand discursive enterprise of the eighteenth century, Diderot's *Encyclopaedia*. In place of "a systematic body of thought," Morley hoped the new reviews would provide what the *Encyclopaedia* had offered: "a sort of substitute for a philosophic synthesis" by "secur[ing] for a body of incoherent speculation an external look of system." Diderot's work had served as "a provisional rallying-point for efforts the most divergent," a meeting ground for ideas united only by a common appeal to rationality. Presenting such ideas through a widely circulated public forum, Morley hoped that the contributors to the *Fortnightly* would effect "a very considerable revolution in the intellectual habits of the time," involving "*le gros public* . . . in the radical discussion of propositions."[10] As Morley's remarks make evident, the new liberals patterned their ideal of open and free discussion after the late-eighteenth-century idealizations of the public sphere.

Yet such models had been based on the assumption of a homogeneous public. They typically relied on the "representative publicness" of those who participated in critical debate. The Second Reform Act of 1867, however, had challenged older notions of representation, partly enfranchising groups whose interests could not be assumed to be synonymous with those of the middle-class intellectual. The social theory within which a free exchange of opinion could function as meaningful political participation had been compromised. What Morley had billed as a program for "commanding the future" appeared to some contemporaries to be fatally tainted by liberal nostalgia.[11]

This janus-faced liberalism can be too easily summed up as a case of the bad faith of bourgeois intellectuals. The critical difficulty in which this new generation found itself was not simply the product of a concerted effort to produce "metaphors open-textured enough to conceal their class-roots," as Eagleton has charged. Rather, it was the symptom of a disabling paradox at the very heart of the liberal agenda. "We will not attack you . . . we shall not exterminate you; we shall explain you," ran the new generation's manifesto. Rational discussion would explain away entrenched authority and timeworn institutions. And yet it was only through meanings established by custom and use that rational discussion became possible. Gillian Beer has posed the problem slightly differently in her examination of nineteenth-century scientific discourse: "The enclosing within a community is a necessary condition for assuring stable signification."[12] In order to produce a vital political discourse, the writers of the 1870s had to appeal to the very conventional language that their critical program was designed to undermine. The alternative, as the Metaphysical Society discussions revealed, was for individuals to engage in an exchange of opinion that was "free" at the expense of meaningful communication.

John Ruskin, a member of the Society from 1870, observed with growing concern this intellectual impasse. Writing to C. E. Norton in November 1870 about the proceedings of the first meeting he attended, he regretted that the occasion had dissolved into witty jokes and pedantic discussions of minor points of logic. "I came back," he reported, "impressed more than ever with the frivolous pugnacity of the world,—the [Prussian] campaign in France not more tragic in reality of significance, than the vain dispute over that table" (37:25). Ruskin delivered three papers at Society meetings; each was an ironic commentary not only on previous papers, but also on the insularity of the proceedings. The first— a tour de force of philosophical speculation, punctuated with a host of non sequitur "therefore's"—concluded that it was "surely . . . not too much to expect of future schools of metaphysicians that they will direct mankind into methods of thought which will be at once happy, unerring, and medicinal" (34:111). In the face of political crises in Europe and class antagonisms in England, what was needed, in Ruskin's view, was not a speculative free-for-all but an authoritative explanation of first principles.

In 1875 Ruskin delivered his last paper at a Metaphysical Society meeting, enlarging on the contrast between his own vision of effective intellectual leadership and what he saw as the disarray of the assembled community. With a medieval metaphor, he emphasized the distance between the group's metaphysical debates and practical social guidance:

(16:161)

> *It has always seemed to me that Societies like this of ours . . . might be more useful to the public . . . by using their variety of power rather to support intellectual conclusions by concentric props, than to shake them with rotatory storms of wit; and modestly endeavouring to initiate the building of walls for the Bridal city of Science . . . rather than complying farther with the existing picturesque, but wasteful, practice of every knight to throw up a feudal tower of his own opinions, tenable only by the most active pugnacity, and pierced rather with arrow-slits from which to annoy his neighbours, than windows to admit light or air.*

The romance image must have suggested to some members a comparison between their gathering and the feudal society which was emerging in Ruskin's writings of the 1870s: the Guild of St. George. Ruskin had explicitly drawn the parallel in his monthly series of pamphlets, *Fors Clavigera* (1871–84), pointing to Society members by name. In the letter for February 1875, he had called the faith of both the Duke of Argyll and T. H. Huxley in "Enlightenment, and Freedom . . . and Science of the superbest and trustworthiest character," the "ruin" of England, "inevitable and terrible, such as no nation has yet suffered." His St. George's Company was engaged, by contrast, in constructive "raft-making amidst irrevocable wreck—the best we can do, to be done bravely and cheerfully, come of it what may" (28:263–64). In the January letter, William Connor Magee, then Bishop of Peterborough, had been accused of spouting empty eloquence and neglecting his pastoral duties (28:423–24). It was to the Bishop's Metaphysical Society paper that Ruskin responded in his last address to its members. Theoretical jousting between a bishop wielding Church doctrines and the scientifically armed members of the society, Ruskin stated, was far from a responsible solution to any real social problems.

Ruskin's model society as outlined in *Fors* would be governed not by speculation, but by an agreement "to work on a given system" (28:237). Those who joined his community would swear to a series of vows outlining fundamental principles; they would share the same reading matter and work at common tasks. In this political *hortus inclusus* (to use the title of a collection of Ruskin's letters published in 1887), signification would be contained by an openly acknowledged theory and praxis. Ruskin's frequent etymologizing in the letters of *Fors Clavigera*—as elsewhere in his late writings—seems an attempt to reassert the possibility of meaningful exchange, to fix key terms made slippery through contemporary debates. He took to task two contributors to Knowles's first nonpartisan periodical, the *Contemporary Review*, for their disagreement over the word *religion*, arguing that its derivation from the Latin *lictor* or *ligature* gave it a concrete history (28:718). Language use was not merely a matter of convention; it was the product of laws of evolution as fixed and regular as those outlined by Darwin. Ruskin's evolutionary etymologies need not be read as a "Lockean plea" for empirical truth, in John McGowan's words. For McGowan his "endless etymological ponderings" are evidence of a "hope that origins might be the clue to determinate meanings in a world that has become frighteningly indeterminate."[13] Ruskin's emphasis is not on regression but on historical mutability and variation; he tries to document meaning as it exists in specific physical and ideological conditions. The Metaphysical Society represented for Ruskin a community in which exchange was reduced to a series of non sequiturs; the ideal society he began to elaborate in *Fors* would provide an environment within which stable signification would be possible.

After Ruskin's criticisms in 1875, his presence was recorded at only one Metaphysical Society meeting.[14] He did continue to participate in Knowles's other forums, publishing papers first in the *Contemporary Review* and then in *Nineteenth Century* through 1881. But he was increasingly cynical about the benefits of free discussion. In 1865 he had criticized Mill's liberty of thought as little more than liberty of "clamour." True freedom of expression, he argued, should be conducted in the manner of a regulated "senate, in which men who deserve to be heard are heard, in due time, and under determined restrictions" (19:127). By the late

1870s, even the organized periodical forums seemed to add to the chaos of opinions, with contributors sounding off in all directions like "the last Cockney curly-tailed puppy who yaps and snaps in the *Nineteenth Century*" (29:246). The public was already convinced of its right to liberty of thought; what it needed was a standard of conduct and action in a period of transitional beliefs. "When I consider the quantity of wise talking which has passed in at one long ear of the world, and out at the other," Ruskin declared in *Fors Clavigera*, "without making the smallest impression upon its mind, I am sometimes tempted for the rest of my life to try and do what seems to me rational, silently; and to speak no more" (27:353).

Ruskin did, however, speak voluminously throughout the decade. In 1869 he was appointed Slade Professor of Art at Oxford; from 1870 to 1878, and again from 1882 to 1885, he drew large audiences with his sociopolitical expositions of art history. At the outset Ruskin was keenly aware that at Oxford he was addressing the clerisy. Discussing his position with the Regius Professor of Medicine, Henry Acland—who had been influential in securing Ruskin's appointment—he admitted that being "the best drawing master in the world . . . would be of no use *there*. Nor would I *be* a drawing master." For at a time when, as Ruskin felt, "we are on the edge of a revolution in all countries, of which none of us can know the issue," it was crucial to train the university men to "be armed for *any* issue" (36:593).

Doing so proved to take more than a series of well argued lectures. "I'm tired . . . and a little vexed," he wrote on returning to Oxford for his second term, "at finding the absolute neglect of all I have put in the young men's power, hitherto." A few days later he expressed how "sorry" he was "to find how absolutely necessary my personal presence is—how much depends on direct watching and sympathy." [15] If individual involvement was required to such a degree in teaching the educated, what did that imply about teaching the masses? Ruskin's experience at Oxford seemed to confirm what he had told C. E. Norton in one of their many arguments over Mill's theories of liberty: "a house . . . can be kept in order best by a Master," not by an open discussion of principles (36:591).

In 1870 the nation seemed to need to be kept in order. The outbreak of the Franco-Prussian War alarmed Ruskin, as it did many English observers. It "is very awful to me," he wrote to Norton, "being as I think all men's fault as much as the [French] emperor's; certainly as much Prussia's and England's" (37:12). Gladstone's policy of nonintervention, as Ruskin would characterize it in *Fors Clavigera*, demonstrated that the English lacked either the sense to determine which side was right or the courage to defend the party it supported (27:11). In August he told a Liverpool journalist of one positive step that might be taken to counter the European crisis. Tired of a government of many words and little action, alerted by the Prussian invasion to the vulnerability of an enlightened French people, the working classes could spurn the intellectual call to freedom of opinion and return to basic principles of order and authority. This "marvellous and ghastly war," Ruskin explained to his correspondent, "may perhaps render it possible to do what otherwise it would have been vain to think of yet . . . sift out . . . the great principles of government, which have made Prussia what she is, and ally a few of our workmen, who have self-command and sense, into a nucleus to be gradually enlarged for simple obedience to these laws among themselves, wholly careless and scornful of what is done above them by so-called governments, and neither troubling themselves to vote or to agitate for anything, but calmly to enlist, man by man, those who are worthy to join them" (37:15). Whether Ruskin already had a new project in mind here, or whether it suggested itself through his correspondence with the Liverpool journalist, this statement seems to be the germ of his "Letters to the Workmen and Labourers of Great Britain," *Fors Clavigera*, first published the following January.

From the start Ruskin's letters rejected theoretical musings on government reform. Opening with recent events in France and Prussia, his occasional correspondence continued throughout the series to resemble local rhetorical skirmishes rather than the dispassionate discourses of the liberal writers of the day. Like the martial rhetoric of his letter to the Liverpool journalist, the language of *Fors* was commanding, at times even jingoistic. In contrast to the deliberately cosmopolitan tone of writers who took the *philosophes* as their models, Ruskin adopted a nationalist stance, declaring in the first letter that he would "take no account of any other country but Britain" (27:23). Though in context this opening statement functions in part as ironic commentary on the insularity of politicians such as Gladstone, it lays at the same time the groundwork for a larger vision of nationalism in the letters.[16] Playing on the nonpartisan policy of editors like Knowles and Morley, Ruskin declared that his periodical publication would also be above party politics, but not as a means to impartiality. He would not adhere to a party line, which always entailed "sacrificing [one's] . . . opinions . . . or . . . having none worth sacrificing" (27:15). Rather, his end was to allow for a more decided partiality, to showcase his "clear and developed political opinions."

Ruskin distanced himself from the liberal periodicals of his day by announcing up front that he was "a violent Illiberal" (27:14). As the series unfolded, he made clear that unlike many of his contemporaries, he spoke not as an equal to what Arnold had called a "possible Socrates," but as a master, in an unmistakable voice of authority. The same personal presence that enforced his lessons at Oxford would now be turned to a wider public. Brian Maidment sees in this display of personality a response to the censorship Ruskin experienced in the 1860s when publishing *Unto This Last* and *Munera Pulveris* in periodicals: the epistolary pamphlets function as "an indictment of the appalling constraints which were created and sustained by the Victorian periodical press." In the context of the 1870s, however, Ruskin seems to be reacting rather to the *lack* of constraints of liberal forums. From the first letter Ruskin cuts himself off from the liberals' sense of shared enterprise, expressed by Morley's desire to secure "for a body of incoherent speculation" a formal "philosophical synthesis," [17] and by Knowles's community of seekers after Truth. Despite its periodical format—*Fors* was issued in monthly fascicles available for a yearly subscription—his one-man publication would not, like the journals of those editors, be a medium for a free exchange of ideas. While his contemporaries offered a speculative chaos, Ruskin pronounced only what was indubitably "true," with no intention of "competing for your audience with the 'opinions' in your damp journals" (27:99–100).

In the liberal model of the public sphere, discourse was seen as unconstrained by the material conditions of its production. The format of *Fors Clavigera*, in contrast, foregrounds the circumstances of its production. While writing, Ruskin is suddenly interrupted by a letter, a noise, or a scene out the window. As in letter 18, a single number of *Fors* might begin in one place on a particular day (Pisa, 29 April 1872) and resume at a different time and location (Lucca, 7 May; then Rome, 12 May). Unlike the epistolary form of his earlier letters to working men, *Time and Tide*

(1867), where each letter is a set essay on a given topic, the form of *Fors* dramatizes discourse as living process.

Ruskin explicitly addressed this discursive practice in references to the material production and circulation of *Fors Clavigera*. He explained in detail in the letters the cost and profit of printing a thousand copies of each number (the standard run in early years) (27:100), wrote of his private publisher (27:257), and rehearsed his scheme for the sale of the fascicles at a set price to booksellers (27:195). After the first three years of the venture, he decided that no free copies would be sent to the press for review; the letters "*must* be bought by every one who has it, editor or private person" (28:42). The market value of each number, he pointed out, was the price of "two pots of beer" (27:99), or for the reprinted annual edition, "a doctor's fee per volume" (27:257). Whereas other intellectuals envisioned the distribution of ideas through forums removed from market forces, Ruskin insisted on his letters as commodities, products implicated in the marketplace.

As many critics have pointed out, however, Ruskin's system of private distribution of *Fors Clavigera* had the effect of removing it from the market, paradoxically deemphasizing its status as an item of exchange: it acquired in Linda Austin's words "the negligible value of a commodity at the margin." As Austin explains it, the high price of the fascicles—sevenpence initially, then tenpence in 1874—combined with Ruskin's endlessly deferred explanations turned his letters into "unconsumable object[s] in a consumer economy."[18] Ruskin's rhetorical use of his publishing strategies to foreground the material circumstances of discourse seemed, in other words, to be frustrated by the practical effect of such a move. From the perspective of some readers, the private circulation of *Fors* made it seem as distant from political praxis as the works of the intellectuals it was meant to critique.

This view of *Fors* as a scarce commodity in the intellectual marketplace of the 1870s and 1880s has persisted in current criticism of the work. Jeffrey Spear tries to argue, somewhat obliquely, that its scarcity "may have contributed to its influence."[19] Unpublished sales figures for the first year's letters would seem at first to confirm that distribution of *Fors Clavigera* was not widespread. According to George Allen's records, 821 copies of the January 1871 number (of a printing of 1,050) had been sold by the end of the year; sales of the December number had dropped to 446.[20] By August of 1872, however, a second edition of 1,000 copies of the first number had been printed; a third thousand in January 1878; a fourth thousand in March 1885; and a fifth edition of 350 copies in July 1894. The first twelve letters had been issued in a second edition of 1,000 copies by 1874; all had run through four editions by 1889. A second edition of 1,000 copies each of letters 13–72 (1872–76) had been printed by 1877; letters 65 and 66 were reissued as well in a separate pamphlet entitled "Letter to Young Girls," which went through numerous editions through 1902. Starting with the January 1877 letter, the first edition run was 2,000. The last three letters, published in 1884, were issued in first editions of 3,000 copies; the March and October letters were issued in second editions in the late 1890s.[21]

The increase in sales throughout these decades help to explain the enthusiastic claim by Ruskin's publisher in February 1876 that "*Fors* is getting popular." The numbers are telling in contemporary context. In comparison to the sales of at least 2,000 copies of each monthly fascicle of *Fors Clavigera* through 1877, the average circulation of the monthly issues of John Morley's *Fortnightly Review* in the same period was 2,500 copies. Average quarterly sales of the *North British Review* were 2,000 copies; the *Observer* sold an estimated 3,000 copies weekly. Such comparisons do not take into account sales of annual bound volumes of *Fors*, which, according to Ruskin's publisher, rose steadily throughout the decade. "You would be surprised at the number of bound sets we sell now," he wrote in 1876, explaining his decision to "issue the full thousand per month of the current number [of *Fors*] besides the back ones."[22] Ruskin's idiosyncratic periodical circulated as widely as several other influential organs in the period.

A separate question is to whom it circulated. The *Fortnightly*, the *North British Review*, and the *Observer* had small, liberal upper-middle- to upper-class audiences. The subtitle of Ruskin's work—"Letters to the Workmen and Labourers of Great Britain"—seems to embrace a rather different readership. Ruskin's own descriptions of his intended audience remained somewhat vague. Workmen were, he explained at one point, "the providers of houses and dinners" (27: 187); a later note to the same paragraph broadened the definition to everyone "who must use their heads as well as their hands for what they do" (27: 187n). In the number for September 1880 he announced that this was "the first letter in *Fors*" addressed specifically to the Trade Unions, "to you as a body of workers separate from . . . other Englishmen" (29:398). All previous letters had been directed to "your existing Masters, Pastors, and Princes," but, he explained, he "had sign sternly given to [him] that [his] message to the learned and the rich was given, and ended" (29:400, 401). This apparent change in address must have surprised many of Ruskin's readers. He had, after all, rebuked the parish priests as well as the Archbishop of Canterbury, dismissed the works of the leading lights of Oxford and Cambridge, and scoffed at the country squires. His periodical had from the first aimed to cast a wider net than the intellectual gatherings he addressed in Oxford. Glancing back at nine years of his periodical venture, Ruskin seemed in this letter to elide the distinction between the voice of the Slade lecturer and that of the authoritative Master. His message and his audience in the Slade Lectures and in *Fors* before 1880, he now suggested, had been the same.

If Ruskin himself appeared to be somewhat uncertain about his specific audience, so were contemporary readers. In 1873 an Oxford student wrote to the professor to ask, as Ruskin paraphrased it for his cousin, "what I could possibly mean by writing such scholarly letters to working people." A *Guardian* reviewer predicted that "the working classes will be able to make nothing" of *Fors* beyond the occasional "direct onslaught on capitalists": "The illustrations which delight the cultivated eye, will be as much *caviare* to them as the text." This journalist's division of the cultured from the uncultured reader and of the aesthetic from the political Ruskin was reproduced without significant challenge in much subsequent criticism. In particular, such distinctions persisted in treatments that located Ruskin's late work in a narrowly defined radical tradition. *Fors Clavigera* has often disappointed those readers who would measure Ruskin's message to the working classes by the needs of a nineteenth-century proletariat as characterized by Marxist historians. Thus, E. P. Thompson speaks of "the pitiful impracticability" of Ruskin's rhetoric in *Fors*, arguing that while he "addressed the working men, it was not with any sense of identity of interest." Raymond Williams similarly faults the author of *Fors* for leaving his audience at a literary and political "deadlock" that was to be broken only by William Morris. The significance of Morris's continuation of Ruskin's social enquiry was, Williams writes, "that he sought to attach its general values to an actual and growing social force: that of the organized working class."[23]

Recent critics have effectively intervened in these disputes about Ruskin's grasp of his actual audience. P. D. Anthony directly takes on both Thompson and Williams by arguing that Ruskin was not aloof from working class needs, but he *was* concerned to diagnose an important "deficiency of Marxism" as it emerged in the period: Ruskin warned that "a proletariat schooled in capitalism's values will, if it acts politically, exaggerate capitalism's faults." In other words, Anthony contends, Ruskin deliberately does not form an "identity of interest" with contemporary working-class organizations. Jeffrey Spear, while crediting William Morris with completing the "social revolution" begun by Ruskin, reconsiders Ruskin's influence on labor leaders, and helpfully redirects attention to his broader educational aims to appeal to "the laborer . . . as he might be—as reading the letter[s of *Fors Clavigera*] might help make him." I have also argued elsewhere for the prefigurative nature of Ruskin's political rhetoric. Robert Hewison reads Ruskin's address to the workers not against a broadly defined set of interests but against specific labor issues in the 1870s, "which saw the first stirrings of the reawakened radical movements of 1848, expressed in the formation of political groups, charitable settlements and utopian communities."[24]

Such approaches to the vexed question of Ruskin's audience can correct too schematic readings of *Fors Clavigera*. The work does not fit easily into neat categories of class, nor into clear distinctions between aesthetic theory and political praxis. But even these more carefully historicized approaches cannot provide answers to the question of who *did* buy Ruskin's letters. There are no extant records of who bought *Fors Clavigera*. The membership rolls of the Guild of St. George do tell us about who subscribed to his practical schemes—a group of artisans, agricultural workers, small business owners—but not about the larger readership of his political pamphlets.[25] The readers' letters included in the "Notes and Correspondence" appended to each fascicle—from clergy, middle-class women, industrial laborers, newspaper editors, economists—provide a similarly selective picture of his audience. There is, in fact, no way of reconstructing at this distance who read Ruskin's letters.

What can be reconstructed is the way that Ruskin positioned *Fors Clavigera* within a significant discursive network. The contemporary publications most often referred to in the letters are the two papers that had reached unprecedented circulation levels in the early 1870s: the *Daily News* and the *Daily Telegraph*.[26] Ruskin uses clippings from these dailies to characterize by contrast his own publication. In letter 29, for example, where he quotes a *Daily News* article on the relation between England's real capital and the high price of coal, the opinion of the daily is made to stand for the opinion of a mass audience incapable of Ruskin's considered reasoning. The dialogue was continued in the following letter, where Ruskin reprinted the *Daily News* response to his attack. While their editor portrayed *Fors* as "a curious magazine of the blunders of a man of genius," Ruskin took the paper to task for selling "impulsiveness and rash splendour" to an undiscriminating "speculative public" (27:560, 561). The dailies rushed to print the latest news and hasty editorials; Ruskin took his time to craft what "the *Daily Telegraph* calls . . . 'utterances few and far between'" (28:444). His pamphlets offered, he argued, what had "cost me twenty years of thought" (27:99). Their relatively high price signified their value in a market dominated by "the 'opinions' in your damp journals, morning and evening, the black of them coming off on your fingers, and—beyond all washing—into your brains" (27:100).

For Ruskin, as for many other educated Victorians, cheap publishing made for a particularly dangerous combination of easy accessibility and lack of accountability by publishers answerable only to market demand. In 1855 a very public debate had surrounded the abolition of the newspaper tax, levied in 1819 as a means of controlling the growth of a radical press.[27] Cheap literature was synonymous for many in the period with immoral literature; through the 1870s and 1880s major periodicals continued to publish articles examining the social effects of inexpensive books and magazines.[28] Those who supported cheap newspapers in particular saw them as efficient vehicles of political enlightenment for the masses at a time when the "voice of the people" was increasingly influential in public affairs. With the abolition of the paper duty in 1861, the government's fiscal control over periodical papers effectively ended. In the next decade, daily papers became for the first time a mass-market staple.[29]

By creating in *Fors Clavigera* an ongoing dialogue with the dailies, Ruskin draws his letters into the debate about the political function of periodical publications. Ruskin left no doubt in *Fors* how he felt about "the wretches who have . . . the teaching of the people in their hands, through the public press" (28:641). His position was openly challenged by the *Spectator*, an exchange reprinted by Ruskin in letter 85 (Jan. 1878). Taken to task by the *Spectator* reviewer for "arraign[ing], if not the discovery of the printing-press . . . at least the inevitable result of that discovery," Ruskin responded: "There is nothing whatever of inevitable in . . . the power of saying a very foolish thing to a very large number of people at once" (29:321).[30] Profit-oriented publishers would do anything to increase circulation. Ruskin insisted that he cared about his message, not his sales. The work "must make its own way," he explained in connection with his decision to stop press advertisements of *Fors Clavigera*, "or stand still, abiding its time" (28:42).

Ruskin used the price of the fascicles to emphasize his difference from the quick political fix offered in the cheap dailies and weeklies. When a tradesman wrote to ask why Ruskin's set price for each letter seemed to put it "out of the reach of most of the persons it is meant for," Ruskin quoted a fourteenth-century Florentine law: "Eel of the lake shall be sold for three soldi a pound; and eel of the common sort for a soldo and a half" (28:40–41). In *Fors Clavigera* his readers received for their tenpence the best fruits of Ruskin's labors; for their penny, they could buy an illustrated paper "full of art, sentiment," and the latest police trials. He included in his letters plates of great art works worth, he argued, "all the illustrations in your *Illustrated News* . . . from one year's end to another" (27:512). The extra pence required to buy his periodical represented the superior quality of its contents. Ruskin could be trusted to provide only wholesome plates that would instill timeless truths, whereas "these illustrated papers do you definite mischief" with their indiscriminate mix of fine art, popular personalities, and sensational events. To set his fascicles apart from the cramped print and flimsy paper of mass-produced publications, they would be "decently printed on cream-coloured paper" with large margins for thoughtful notetaking (27:100).

The equation of price with moral value here was consistent with Ruskin's larger crusade to moralize the market system, outlined in *Unto this Last*, *Munera Pulveris*, and *Fors Clavigera*. Individual letters and annual volumes of *Fors Clavigera* would be relatively high priced, he maintained, so that buying them would require sacrifice. The effect of a disengaged criticism had been to polarize the act of reading: either it was presented as a rarefied, intellectual activity or as a mere act of consumerism, a mindless entertainment to divert the masses. The easy availability of works like the shilling Shakespeare created the impression that "merely to buy a book, and to know your letters, will enable you to read the book" (27:459). Discussing the value of his fascicles in relation to everyday purchases, Ruskin tried to politicize reading, to cast it as involving moral choice. He intended his work "for no one who cannot reach it" (28:40), he stated, a description meant to characterize not those without means, but those without the fortitude to forgo the purchase of "two pots of beer" for the cost of his letters (27:99).

Associated with Ruskin's morality of book buying was his campaign to reform book selling. *Fors Clavigera* was the first of his works to be distributed by his private publisher at a fixed price, with no trade discounts. When booksellers refused to carry his periodical on those terms, Ruskin trumpeted the fact in the pages of *Fors*. In the first of the "Notes and Correspondence" sections he called attention to his practice and cited a letter from an angry bookseller who said he would not sell Ruskin's letters, in fact would "decline to give any information how they are to be obtained" (27:257).[31] His "battle with the booksellers" was made to stand in *Fors* for Ruskin's distance from the improprieties of the literary market (28:531). Circulating outside a book trade where price signified the bookseller's profit, not the absolute value of texts, Ruskin's publication modeled an alternative mode of textual production and dissemination. As "the first producer" of his letters, Ruskin controlled the quality not only of the writing but of the ultimate product, "paper, binding, eloquence, and all" (27:100), and he determined its fixed value. His commodity would not be hawked by advertisement in the penny papers like the latest quack medicine (27:353). Rather, it would circulate within a community with shared values, passing "from friend to friend" (28:42). The "Notes and Correspondence" serve as a microcosm of such an audience, dramatizing a discursive community in which *Fors Clavigera* is debated, accepted, and translated into daily practice.

Maidment argues that Ruskin's inclusion of letters from readers as well as his reactions to them marks "a crucial shift from regarding the book as a kind of internal monologue describing the relationship between a sensibility and its external stimuli to a notion of the book as the exploration of the relationship between writer and reader."[32] This description of Ruskin's project, however, neglects the way he presents the contact between audience and writer. The exemplary display of reading and response in *Fors* is always filtered through the idiosyncratic personality of its instigator. In chapters 1 and 2, I argue that Ruskin's foregrounding of his process of mediation in the letters links him more closely to the condition of the dramatic monologue than to the open dialogic Maidment sketches out. Throughout *Fors* Ruskin emphasized the fundamental constraints of communication. His "Notes and Correspondence" sections provide a paradigm of exchange in an ideal society where discursive relations are tightly controlled.

Ruskin's insistence on his letters as an alternative moral center to the existing world of literary production had its drawbacks. The letters were, in a sense, predigested by the community of readers presented in them. They created a kind of self-enclosing hermeneutic rather like the self-sustaining community Ruskin envisioned for the St. George's Guild. In fact, they might seem to resemble Ruskin's critical portrait of the "feudal tower[s]" of private opinion—"pierced rather with arrow-slits from which to annoy his neighbours, than windows to admit light or air"(16:161)—erected by his liberal contemporaries. One Victorian reviewer suggested this resemblance in his discussion of the "quixotic" heroism of Ruskin as he appears in *Fors*.[33]

The paradox that Ruskin might reproduce in his peculiar publication the very discursive problem he meant to displace reveals his roots in a conflicted model of romantic authority. Ruskin's self-centered, self-dramatizing posture in *Fors* can be recognized as referring to a familiar tradition defined by an emphasis on the solitary voice. It looks back on the heroic individualism of the romantic man of letters, whose isolated stance was a response to the problem of situating authority in a rapidly changing society. With this precedent in mind, most modern treatments of Ruskin's late work leave him isolated as one of "the last Romantics." John Rosenberg's portrait of a tortured writer, for example, is powerful precisely because it represents Ruskin as the quintessential romantic genius.[34] Yet if Ruskin's letters recur to such a figure, they do so with considerable alteration. To cast *Fors Clavigera* as a Wordsworthian diatribe penned from the seclusion of the Lake District (much of the work was written at Ruskin's residence in Brantwood) is to miss the formal implications of the project.

The first chapter of *Ruskin's Culture Wars* locates Ruskin's letters in a divergent romantic tradition: the epistolary periodicals of Coleridge, Cobbett, and Carlyle. These very different projects explored the constraints and possibilities of individual authority in ways that considerably complicate familiar accounts of romanticism. Resiting Ruskin's pamphlets in this context makes it possible to see to what extent he is working within a set of conventions recognizable to his contemporaries. It also clarifies some crucial distinctions between Ruskin's earlier letters to working men, *Time and Tide*, and the more complex instance of *Fors Clavigera*. The later series reconsiders the authority of the confessional persona in a way that situates it at the fault line of debates in the 1870s. In *Fors* Ruskin does not simply rehearse well-tried arguments. He works out an unmistakably modern version of the self that is centered neither in Wordsworthian imagination nor in disinterested observation. The contingent self exemplified in *Fors* is the focus of chapter 2, where I elaborate its implications for our view both of Ruskin's political aesthetic and of the larger critical crisis of the period.

Far from presenting himself as a disinterested Arnoldian critic, Ruskin made clear from the outset that his letters would be personal, subjective, polemical. Although Arnold had taken him to task in the 1860s for his tendency to "forget all moderation and proportion, to lose the balance of one's mind altogether," Ruskin chose a format for *Fors Clavigera* that showcased such propensities.[35] He explained to one reader that "from beginning to end" *Fors* would be "full of all sorts of personality" (37:48). Not only did he speak in an idiosyncratic voice, he discussed throughout the series his private circumstances, his upbringing, his daily activities. Having been accused by Arnold of showing, "to the highest excess, the note of provinciality," Ruskin seems to have cultivated an entrenched parochialism at the very moment Arnold's ideal of sweet moderation had been adopted by many of his contemporaries.[36]

One reading of the relative critical neglect of *Fors Clavigera* in modern Victorian studies might be that Arnold was right. Ruskin really was, in the end, a writer whose lack of "fitness," "measure" and "centrality" made him marginal to the future of criticism. We should not be surprised that the recent revival of interest in *Fors Clavigera* coincides with a devaluation of Arnold's ideal of disinterestedness. The question may be less one of critical correctness than one of fashion. While Arnoldian standards dominated English studies, *Fors Clavigera* remained almost unreadable, at best a moving "literary curiosity." That was precisely the opinion professed by his liberal critics in the 1870s, who were themselves invested in a version of Arnold's urbanity. As Leslie Stephen put it in an early review, Ruskin, who seemed to be struggling "under the dominion of an excessive sensibility which bursts all restraints of logic and common sense," had turned out a series of letters marked by "weakness" and "futility." W. C. Brownell, in his 1902 survey of Victorian prose writers, succinctly articulated the Arnoldian rejection of Ruskin's diffusiveness, faulting him for an "arrogant and irresponsible mixing of genres in defiance of innate decorum." Some recent critics, on the other hand, have pointed to Ruskin's congeniality for "a critical outlook which seeks to substitute fresh clarifications for traditional genres." [37]

C. Stephen Finley has made a similar point about the critical fate of *Fors Clavigera*: "the work has no Victorian peers and has had to wait, as a kind of assault on the dainty sobriety of the high Arnoldian tradition, for the current generation and the contemporary critical climate to have its day." But Finley's insistence on the singularity of *Fors*—an insistence shared by other critics—involves, as this contextual study should bear out, a misprision similar to Brownell's. Dehistoricizing *Fors* leads quickly to characterizing it in the very terms used by Victorian Arnoldian critics. Finley reads it as an extended lyrical meditation, Ruskin's "private version of *King Lear*, raging, insistent, and—finally—insane." This does not take us much beyond Frederic Harrison's early assessment that *Fors* was the bathetic soliloquy of a once powerful mind: it was, he said, Ruskin's *Hamlet*.[38] While Harrison meant to denigrate *Fors* and Finley to praise it, both conjure it in terms of the romantic voice Arnold so famously regretted. Such readings miss Ruskin's radical revision of that lyrical voice, his attempt to reconfigure authority in a way that threatened the liberal program aggressively defended by several of his detractors, including Harrison and Stephen.

Ruskin's description of his method in *Fors*—projecting the "gesture of the moment" adopted "as the humour takes me" (29:197)—has seemed to endorse autobiographical treatments of the work. Rarely have critics acknowledged what Ruskin's statement explicitly emphasizes: that his discursive posturing in *Fors* belongs to a particular *cultural* moment. Ruskin's crisis of interpretation in the 1870s and 1880s was not merely personal; it was part of a larger crisis of political and social meaning. *Fors Clavigera* does not simply reject the Arnoldian position. It represents a considered alternative to a dominant strain of contemporary critical politics. The enlightenment model of authority represented not only by

Arnold but by a larger scientific and literary community was not yet recognized as canonical at the time Ruskin was writing *Fors Clavigera*. As that community's responses to *Fors* show, Ruskin was at the center of debates about what constituted critical authority. He remained a major cultural arbiter for writers such as Swinburne who were involved in a reformulation of Victorian criticism.[39] He also served as a pivotal figure for late century liberal theorists dissatisfied with purely rationalist models of polity. Chapters 3 and 4 of *Ruskin's Culture Wars* demonstrate how Ruskin's theories of nationalism and historicism posed a potent challenge to positivist accounts of the contemporary crisis.

To search for a coherent center or progressive logic to Ruskin's periodical letters is, then, to resist the force of his project, to read it through the very critical framework against which it reacted.[40] E. T. Cook's effort in the Library Edition of *Fors* to provide a compact *precis* of its contents runs to nearly fifty pages and considers the work under the conventions of six different genres (27 : xxxiii–lxxxii). John Rosenberg's elegant reading of letter 20 demonstrates that there are, indeed, some settled strains in Ruskin's vagrant patter; and Paul Sawyer's exposition of the recurrent myths in *Fors Clavigera* usefully highlights the personal preoccupations motivating Ruskin throughout the thirteen years of the work.[41] Yet searching only for unity in a set of discourses so deliberately occasional seems to beg a crucial question. Why, in a moment Ruskin felt to be plagued by a lack of order, would he attempt to intervene through a format whose defining characteristic is its diffusiveness?[42]

Looking at that question as the starting point for a critical strategy with which to address *Fors Clavigera* involves moving away from an effort to interpret the "meaning" of the work as a whole. As Edward Said says of recent work on Jonathan Swift, critics become preoccupied with producing "interpretations of a text, but not with asking if the text is a text or with ascertaining the discursive conditions by which a so-called text, may, or may not, have become a text." With their interruptions and endless deferrals of conclusions—in the very first letter Ruskin puts off the moral of his discussion, promising to reveal it "in the course of time" (27 : 26), promising again a year and a half later (27 : 317), partially revealing it in a letter of 1873 (27 : 580), and toying with it again in 1874 and 1876 (28 : 128, 646)—Ruskin's letters foreground the fact that they are anything but finished texts. As Maidment observes, the volumes of *Fors* read less as books than as "possible *discourses* or centres of activity and argument."[43] They dramatize what Ruskin saw as the inadequacy of conventional textual interventions in the changing England of the 1870s and 1880s.

The following chapters elaborate the circumstances of that crisis and dramatize Ruskin's "humours" as deliberate performances. The spread of Millite liberalism and the realignment of political groups in this transitional moment undermined entrenched forms of authority. By recreating the context of debate through art journals and working class periodicals, popular criticism, and intellectual history, I try to animate the sense of uncertainty and change in the period. Ruskin's periodical letters provide a special view of culture and politics in the 1870s and early 1880s. This book attempts to show how his cumulative text—published monthly over thirteen years—not only records but revises and redirects the preoccupations of the period. *Fors Clavigera* is more than a document by which we can understand what was involved in the culture wars of the late nineteenth century. With its experiments in form and perspective, its retreading of the boundaries between public and private experience, *Fors* exemplifies the vexed relations between textual and cultural politics. The ways in which those relations were negotiated by Ruskin and his contemporaries set the patterns for discussions of literature, history, and nationality in the new century.

I

Exemplary Citizens:
Cobbett, Coleridge, Carlyle, and
the Romantic Epistolary Address

FROM THE VERY FIRST letter of *Fors Clavigera*, Ruskin styles himself not as an active, socially minded Victorian sage but as a retiring romantic dreamer. When his garden world is disrupted, he cannot maintain his contemplative poise: "I simply cannot paint, nor read, nor look at minerals, nor do anything else that I like, and the very light of the morning sky, when there is any—which is seldom, nowadays, near London—has become hateful to me, because of the misery that I know of, and see signs of, where I know it not, which no imagination can interpret too bitterly" (27:13). Ruskin offers to interpret these signs less as a means of relieving misery than of absolving himself from any connection with it. "I must clear myself from all sense of responsibility for the material distress around me," he says, so that he can devote undivided attention to his Oxford art lectures.

It was a disclaimer he had used once before, in his earlier volume of letters to working men, *Time and Tide*. "I write," he had said in 1867, "not in any hope of . . . being at present listened to, but to disburthen my heart of the witness I have to bear, that I may be free to go back to my garden lawns, and paint birds and flowers there" (17:377). This statement represented an acute alienation, which he expressed in a January 1867 letter to C. E. Norton. "I have *no* thoughts," he confessed. "I am so puzzled about everything that I've given up thinking altogether.—It seems to me likely that I shall draw into a very stern lonely life, if life at all—doing perhaps some small work of hand with what gift I have" (*CRN* 99–100). Battles with the LaTouches that winter over permission to see Rose had left Ruskin feeling old and confused and unsure of his future. A few months later he admitted he had "been painting a little, and writing some letters on politics—but otherwise *I'm* all but dead" (*CRN* 102). The conjunction of his political letters with his personal uncertainty makes *Time and Tide* something more than "desultory discussions" of the 1867 Reform agitations (17:314). In these letters, Ruskin explores rhetorically the "lonely life." *Time and Tide* develops the erratic voice speaking from the margins that would shape *Fors Clavigera.*[1]

In a move away from the dogmatism of his earlier writings, Ruskin claims in *Time and Tide* that he "do[es] not care about influence any more, it being only my concern to say truly that which I know, and, if it may be, get some quiet life, yet, among the fields in the evening shadow" (17:377). Aloof from the turmoil of Reform, he seeks neither a voice in Parliament—which he tells his correspondent in *Time and Tide*, is "not worth a rat's squeak"—nor the power to sway "the balance of conflicting interests" (17:326–27). His views on law and government are those of a disinterested observer. Ruskin's detachment in *Time and Tide* is made to stand as a model of right rule, of "true legislation" as Ruskin defines it: "That every Man may be a Law to Himself" (17:324). Political power, Ruskin explains, lies in "honesty" and "resolution," not in forms of government. His private, contemplative life—which he pointedly contrasts to public agitation in letter 13—fosters the "patient purpose" and "peaceful strength" that are the hallmarks of the wise reformer. At the very moment of the passage of the Second Reform Act, when England seemed to be headed for a democracy of the masses, Ruskin affirms the virtues of political isolation.

Both Ruskin's rhetorical posture and his epistolary format link *Time and Tide* to a distinctive tradition of nineteenth-century political pamphlets. Beginning with William Cobbett's *Political Register* (1802–35) and including Samuel Taylor Coleridge's *The Friend* (1809–10) and Thomas Carlyle's *Latter-Day Pamphlets* (1850), this line of public reflection explored a middle position between the politics of engagement and detachment. In conversational productions that mixed current events with autobiography, the writers in each case attempted to authorize idiosyncratic reflection as exemplary originality, as personal perspective untainted by fallible systems and the chaos of modern life. Their epistolary salutations gestured the good faith of the writer isolated in the act of composition. Preserving the critical "innocence of the eye" advocated by

Ruskin (15:27), these pamphleteers experimented with a form that both evoked sociality and authorized self-reflexiveness.

Ruskin's self-dramatizing narrative of reform may be said to be underwritten by these texts, which explore the political ramifications of the lyric voice. His development of the "drama of his own bafflement" in *Time and Tide* turns personal pain to generic uses.[2] With their disinterested, contemplative speaker pursuing his "desultory" observations, these letters formalize the epistolary voice with which he experimented elsewhere in the 1860s.[3] Ruskin's confessions are presented as both spontaneous and paradigmatic: they model the utopic narrative of the new social order figured in *Time and Tide*. He speaks with the authority of the private man who knows "*his* business"; his contribution to a healthy society consists in his doing well his "right work" (17:376). In a society where worth would be calculated in moral and not economic terms, in which economy, indeed, would be based on moral value—every nation and every individual, Ruskin explains, "is fitted by its character . . . for some particular employments or manufactures" (17:318)—private effort would be seen to constitute public worth: "it would come to be felt that the true history of a nation was . . . of its households; and the desire of men would rather be to obtain some conspicuous place in these honourable annals, than to shrink behind closed shutters from public sight" (17:379–80). In Ruskin's ideal world, as in his self-referential letters, there would be no distance between public and private; the social order would simply be a peaceful "co-operation" of self-sufficient individuals "perfecting the manner" of their "own craft" in order to "enrich and complete [their] home" (17:317, 321). Thus, the insulated speaker is not, as might first appear, apolitical; rather, he becomes the type of the model citizen.

The opening installment of *Fors Clavigera* conjures the speaker of *Time and Tide* in different circumstances. The point of departure for Ruskin's new series of letters is Britain's nonintervention in the Franco-Prussian War. The alienated speaker becomes a cornerstone of the moral economy of *Time and Tide*; here he seems an impediment in a larger diatribe against political isolationism. The echo of the voice from *Time and Tide* quoted earlier—"I simply cannot paint . . ."—follows immediately on his disavowal of the advantages of an "insular position" (27:12). The title later given the letter, "Looking Down from Ingleborough," would seem to describe the kind of centered, domesticated perspective applauded in *Time and Tide*.[4] In fact, the paragraph to which it refers mocks that perspective as intellectual "little Englandism." As he translates the Franco-Prussian War into "narrow and homely" terms for his readers—making it into a slightly ridiculous reenactment of the Wars of the Roses—Ruskin turns the event into an allegory of self-interest (27:23).

Ruskin the detached dreamer becomes in this context part of a series of examples of "ineffectual" posturing (27:12). His unmistakable echo of *Time and Tide* might be read here as the prelude to a deliberate departure. The voice I used in 1867, Ruskin signals, is not the voice I use now. This time, when I step out of my isolation, it is more than a conventional gesture. That was the isolated romantic critic; this is the Victorian sage who has rejoined the world. Ruskin's revisions to early drafts of the letter, which flesh out the recognizably contemplative voice, might seem at first to support such a reading. Expressing his disapproval of social circumstances in manuscript drafts, the speaker says twice that he cannot "stand it any longer"; in the printed version, he vows instead that he "will put up with this state of things, passively, not an hour longer"; he "will endure it no longer quietly" (27:13).[5] The published text, so the reading might conclude, emphasizes the change from passive observer to the pragmatic Ruskin, founder of the Guild of St. George, pioneer in bookselling.

Yet Ruskin never quite relinquishes that other voice. The plangent strain of the private, alienated writer is heard again and again in *Fors*. "I don't suppose any man," he lamented as he began the fourth year of his pamphlets, "with a tongue in his head, and zeal to use it, was ever left so entirely unattended to, as he grew old, by his early friends" (28:15). In an overt reference to a passage from *Latter-Day Pamphlets*, Ruskin locates himself squarely within the confessional epistolary tradition he appears to have abandoned at the outset, with an appeal not to Carlyle's message but to his marginality (28:22). Six years later Ruskin admits that the potentially "useful" messages in his letters are "scattered" by the vagaries of "personal imagination" (29:384–85). But, he explains, he has always been prone to be "dilatory, dreamy . . . busying himself . . . rather with the things that amuse him . . . than with . . . wider cares" (29:395).

Noting the persistence of this contemplative voice, most modern critics have considered the letters as sustained lyrical utterance. In their often eloquent treatments, beginning with John Rosenberg's, these readers have recuperated Ruskin's letters for current criticism precisely by situating them within the familiar terms of the greater romantic lyric. Harold Bloom offers a particularly compelling formulation of this view in his distinction between the "achievement" of Ruskin's early works and the "grandeur and ruin" of his efforts of the late 1860s and 1870s: "Ruskin's rejection of Romantic mythopoeia as the Pathetic Fallacy shows a . . . distrust of Wordsworthian self-consciousness, but the later Ruskin put such distrust aside. . . . The aesthetic tragedy of Ruskin is that [his late] works . . . are giant Pathetic Fallacies." In this picture of his career, *Fors Clavigera* does not mark a departure from a confessional tradition. Ruskin's apparent critique of that tradition in his first letter might thus be glossed as a failed resolution at independence, a last effort to continue the "searching criticism of Romanticism from within, for the sake of saving the Romantic program . . . from extinction through excessive self-indulgence."[6]

The wayward, confessional narratives of *Fors Clavigera* would turn out in this view to be a kind of Ruskinian misreading of *The Prelude*. There are several problems with moving to such a conclusion. It collapses the perspective of the writer of *Fors* and the writer of *Praeterita*, Ruskin's autobiography that incorporates a number of the confessional digressions first printed in *Fors*. The genealogical relationship between the two texts is important for recognizing their difference. In *Praeterita* autobiographical fragments from *Fors* are recollected, in the double sense of the term: they are collected, along with new material, from the earlier work, and they are presented from the point of view of the elderly author sitting in his childhood nursery. It is indeed a Wordsworthian revisiting, as the writer "summon[s] . . . long past scenes for present scrutiny" (35:11). Despite its resistance to the topoi of romantic *Bildung*, *Praeterita* does present, as Paul Sawyer convincingly argues, an "intuitive unity."[7] In contrast, as readers have long noted, there is no tranquil, unifying perspective in *Fors*. In letters that start, stop, move without warning from present to past tense, autobiographical fragments are simply another digression.

Moreover, to turn *Fors* into unmediated autobiography, as many critics have done, is to conflate voice and author, to read political prose as unproblematized lyric poetry. By characterizing the lyric self as self-conscious posturing in the first letter of *Fors*, this late Ruskin reveals more in common with the critic of pathetic fallacy than most accounts suggest. The speaker of *Time and Tide* openly invokes the authority of the isolated romantic speaker; here Ruskin uses his format to question the very assumptions that would seem to authorize such personal interventions. As Cobbett and Coleridge had already discovered, an epistolary format estranges the conversational voice of the lyric poem by calling attention to conversation as convention. For both writers foregrounding discursive convention was the first step in claiming an authority that might be more than personal. Cobbett's individual speaker becomes the exemplary political participant, well versed in social codes. Coleridge, responding in *The Friend* to Cobbett's influential example, attempts to theorize a link between lived experience and fixed systems. He overtly distinguishes his epistolary practice from the limitations of lyric voice as it had come to be understood in the early nineteenth century. Cobbett and Coleridge stake out monologic positions that represent, not pathetic delusion, but what Ruskin deems by contrast "the ordinary, proper, and true appearances of things" (5:204). At the same time, both positions are firmly grounded in individual "contemplative fancy." Although to very different ends, they mediate in important ways Ruskin's early distinction between true and false perceptions. And they do so in a form that exemplifies such mediation, that calls attention to the transformation of spontaneous utterance into studied composition, of confession into deliberate self-presentation.

Read against this subgenre of romantic prosaic epistle, Ruskin's "trivial and desultory talk" (29:384) in *Fors Clavigera* looks conventional, not spontaneously confessional. In what follows I elaborate the legacy of those earlier examples of epistolary political pamphlets. Ruskin's "self-created, self-dramatizing, didactic dialogues" are not the radical experiment some critics would make them.[8] But neither are they simply a reversion to an already tested formula. The challenge in *Fors* to the authority of the persona adopted uncritically in *Time and Tide* clearly distinguishes his series of letters to working men. As I argue, the use—and misuse—of that persona had particular public resonance in the early 1870s. Late Victorian readers had employed Cobbett's and Coleridge's romantic productions to characterize specific sides in debates about authority. As Ruskin renegotiates his early theories of perception, the form of *Fors Clavigera* allows him to occupy and significantly to alter familiar ground.

Carlyle, attempting a similar turn at midcentury in *Latter-Day Pamphlets*, concludes that individual authority simply collapses under the weight of pathetic misperception. Ruskin's critics would try to assimilate his case to Carlyle's, prompted, no doubt, by Ruskin's own citations in *Fors* of that sage's splenetic project. Like many modern readers, certain of his contemporaries dismissed *Fors* as an unfortunate pathetic fallacy. These interpretations were in some cases deliberate misreadings of Ruskin's extension of the personal periodical project. *Fors* does not despondently return to Carlyle's ironic treatment of the form. Exploiting the tensions between Cobbett's experiential, fragmented accounts and Coleridge's efforts at collected observation, Ruskin works out a position in which contingency *is* collective wisdom. His epistolary campaign would push to its epistemological limits the discursive revolution registered by Cobbett at the beginning of the century.

When William Cobbett launched the *Political Register* in 1802, he recognized a subtle change in the terms of public debate. The exclusive dialogue of eighteenth-century literary and political coteries had been interrupted by outbursts from both the working and middle classes during the depressions of 1795 and 1800–1801. After the turn of the century, discussions of national policy had to be framed with wider reference to public morale.[9] Although Cobbett's epistolary periodical specifically addressed those with political power, it did so in plain terms, exposing the actions of "gentlemen of rank" to general scrutiny. The open letter at the head of each week's *Political Register* embodied, according to Raymond Williams, a shift in political process at the turn of the century "from attempts at private influence, in correspondence within a ruling class to persons in power, to attempts at public influence, within the same limited circle by a quasi-personal form of address."[10]

In 1816 Cobbett announced in his publication that it was time to break out of that prescribed circle of power. The "System," as he labeled a network of politicians, fundholders, moneylenders, and the press, had conspired to deceive the public about the source of their economic distress. Through caricatures of shifty tradesmen and unruly workers, the partisan press diverted attention from heavy indirect taxation. Personal vice, not economic policy, was made to seem the root of public unrest. In Cobbett's view, this effort to "turn [people's] eyes" did more than preempt a possible political alliance between working men and tradesmen: it authorized resolving tensions by force, not reform (*PR* 31:407). Such a scheme radically undermined the notion of polity as social contract.

Cobbett vowed "to lay before [the people] a perfect knowledge of the real causes of their sufferings" (*PR* 31:407). No longer would he speak only to the political elite. He aimed to enlarge the public sphere, in an effort to "unite [the classes] in the cause of their country, and to preserve the tranquility, and to restore the happiness of that country." Published in a new cheap format, his periodical would be recast as "a Letter to the Labourers and Journeymen of the Kingdom." Working out of the conventions of epistolary exchange, Cobbett offered rational conversation as a model for political participation.

His first "Address to the Journeymen and Labourers" was published on 2 November 1816 as a separate broadsheet selling at 2 pence and as a section of the regular weekly 1-shilling issue of the *Political Register*. The cheap *Register* circulated rapidly through its intended audience, selling 44,000 copies by month's end; by the end of the year its circulation had swelled to 200,000.[11] Not only was the working-class reader addressed as an equal—"Friends and Fellow Countrymen," Cobbett began (*PR* 31:433)—he was appealed to as the motive force in national life. It was "the lot of mankind," Cobbett admitted, "that some shall labour with their limbs and others with their minds." But that was merely a practical division of labor, not a natural class hierarchy. "We are all equally interested in the peace and happiness of our common country," he argued, and it was the majority of the people, not the minority in power, who could act on that interest (*PR* 31:435).

The implication that government should involve the conscious consent of all citizens set off alarms in a country still haunted by the specter of the French Revolution. A few months after the appearance of his cheap edition of the *Register*, Cobbett fled to America under threat of government prosecution. Other journalists preached reform to the workers, but his conversational style posed a particular threat to established codes of public discourse. The London press responded in kind. The *Political Register* was challenged by counterpublications, the most influential of which was the *Anti-Cobbett*—coauthored, rumor had it, by Canning, Gifford, and Southey. They adopted the epistolary format of the *Register* only to challenge its political propriety. The *Anti-Cobbett* characterized its namesake as a sort of popular Valmont, exploiting the courteous conventions of letter writing for personal gain. Written in a "style . . . evidently intended to mislead the ignorant," the *Political Register* had appealed to "the candour and simplicity of your hearts," the *Anti-Cobbett* told its "good Friends" of the working and middle classes. As his title suggested, Cobbett was driven by crass political motive; their *Patriotic Register* was inspired by the noblest, most disinterested motives. Through its appeal to a more conventional rhetoric of "King and country," the *Anti-Cobbett* would teach its readers to distinguish the voice of "a seditious, selfish Bully from a true Friend of the People." [12]

Cobbett had created a kind of populist *Spectator*, refashioning general public address as familiar conversation. The appeal of such an approach was that it personalized a subject with which most of his readers had felt little connection. As an architect in Hull wrote to Lord Sidmouth (one of the *Register*'s most persistent opponents), even "women, who never could talk on politics are now warm for Cobbett." [13] Here, as in his *Grammar of the English Language* (1818), the conversational format eases the reader into what appears at first a formidable subject. And here, too, the matter at hand is shown to be a set of codes and conventions that can be acquired by the diligent reader. Much of the *Register* is devoted to explaining in common terms political and economic vocabulary. It functions as a popular primer for an audience just beginning to recognize themselves as citizens.

More importantly, it explains not only what such codes mean, but how they operate. In the *Grammar* the author's letters are designed to draw the reader in and to present him or her with a practical model of the civilized art of communication. In the *Political Register*, Cobbett's accessible format exemplifies proper civic behavior. As in his public letters, political discourse should be pronounced openly, not crafted behind closed doors, as the government's had been: "I advise my countrymen to have nothing to do with any *Political Clubs*, any secret *Cabals*, any *Correspondencies*; but to trust to *individual exertions* and *open meetings*" (*PR* 37:220). While his tone was often passionate, Cobbett's diatribes in the *Political Register* were framed within the polite codes of epistolary exchange. He bragged that his exemplary conduct had dissuaded workers in Sheffield from "proceeding to any serious acts of Riot, to which they were frequently incited by disorderly persons" (*PR* 31:773). For Cobbett, leveling the political playing field meant publicizing and enforcing existing rules, not rewriting them.

His dual aims of democratizing the public sphere and promoting a sort of political correctness have frustrated critics who try to align Cobbett with a particular ideological perspective.[14] In fact, the impulse of the *Political Register* has little to do with partisan politics. Cobbett was invested in a particular idea of the relation between the individual and society; his party loyalties shifted as he judged those in power against it. In a vocabulary of rights derived from Paine, Cobbett elaborated as early as 1796 a familiar version of social contract. Protection by the state formed the "birthright of any individual subject"; citizens, in return, must not "alienate that allegiance which is the right of the state."[15] The cheap edition of the *Political Register* was supposed to repair what Cobbett saw as a breach in this ideal of social reciprocity under a repressive postwar government. His appeals to the ruling class had failed. In the *Register*, he sought to promulgate more widely his social theory in order not to democratize government but to increase the pressure on those in power. If all citizens learned to recognize and demand their rights the authorities would be forced to act honorably. "I . . . see no necessity for any one *new establishment*," he explained in 1816. "Our excellent *form* of government; our excellent modes of carrying on the business of a nation, leave us *nothing new* to wish for" (*PR* 31 : 385). To instruct the civically illiterate in the ways of "our forefathers, who well understood" the language of "duties and . . . rights" might seem a conventional move.[16] But in terms of the enlightenment social theory Cobbett echoed, polity *is* convention. The atomistic contract theory of the seventeenth and eighteenth centuries locates the origin of community in consensual bonds. The particular forms of government mattered less to the writer who alternately championed republicanism and monarchy than the process of agreement behind them. Seeing ourselves as social beings meant recognizing the arbitrary arrangements by which individual desires were subordinated to "the peace and happiness of our common country" (*PR* 31 : 435).

Paradoxically, the *Political Register* makes the case for this common cause in a highly idiosyncratic style. While stressing the importance of "an uniformity of sentiment as to public matters" (*PR* 31 : 435), Cobbett displays a Swiftian spleen, excoriating public figures by name, even at times railing against his readers. Unlike other political writers who could be aligned with a recognized position, he styles himself a "*self-dependent politician*" who "scorn[s] to follow any body in matters of opinion." As

E. P. Thompson puts it, Cobbett's insistence on his status as outsider untainted by the "System" set a fashion for the "political protestant . . .
owing deference to no authority but that of his own judgement and
conscience." [17]

That appeal to internal authority had considerable contemporary
resonance. In his 1821 *Table Talk*, Hazlitt approvingly noted Cobbett's
shedding of "all ties and shackles on his understanding" (*CWWH* 8:57).
The "most powerful political writer of the present day," Cobbett relied on
personal observation, not abstract doctrines, to carry his points: "He does
not view things on a large scale . . . but as they affect himself, close, pal-
pable, tangible." In a style "strip[ped] . . . quite as naked as anybody would
wish," he turned to "himself . . . as the best possible illustration" of the
topic at hand (*CWWH* 8:56, 53). This assessment of Cobbett's peculiar
authority echoes at several points Hazlitt's descriptions of Wordsworth's
originality. Wordsworth, too, had thrown off the shackles of tradition,
making himself "his own subject" (*CWWH* 5:156). Like the writer of
the *Political Register* who tempted the reader to "draw our chair to the
fire" to hear something "good, manly and simple," Wordsworth the
"homely" poet "delivers household truths" (*CWWH* 8:53, 11:86). Lack-
ing the "constructive faculty" of a systematic thinker, Wordsworth's
achievement lay rather in his ability to translate personal perceptions into
a "vernacular" idiom. Wordsworth the poetical protestant "chooses . . .
to owe nothing but to himself" (*CWWH*, 5:156, 11:88).

Hazlitt's account convincingly draws Cobbett's periodical into a
larger discursive revolution and makes his declaration of independence
seem formulaic by 1816. The ongoing tales in the *Political Register* of
the author's childhood, travels, aspirations, and disappointments also, in
Hazlitt's telling, assimilate to a potent confessional tradition. As in other
contemporary discourse, the confessions in the *Political Register* point to
the importance of lived experience over abstract philosophical systems. In
a series of pamphlets championing, in the words of Paine's famous rejection of Burke, the "right of the *living*" over the "manuscript-assumed authority of the dead," the life of William Cobbett, self-educated plough-
boy, dramatized the political potential of everyman. [18]

Whereas the romantic valuation of lived experience had, at bottom,
a Rousseauan impulse, Cobbett's self-display works to a radically different end. For the self-educated writer, the challenge is not to shed social

conventions but to master them. The tales of his rural childhood demonstrate his populist roots, but they offer no special wisdom. It is his distance from those illiterate beginnings that illustrates the political message of the *Register*. Cobbett shows by example how anyone who can read his newspaper can learn to be a "man of . . . weight in the world" (*PR* 34:261). His goal is not to remake society from the inside out, as it were: for him, there is no primal imagination by which to judge human institutions. The self and society work on purely rational laws. In letters "addressed directly to the understanding and the reason," Cobbett vows to make possible "a perfect knowledge of the real causes" of happiness and misery (*PR* 7:1, 31:407).

The digressive, personalized politics of Cobbett's serial "Address to the Journeymen and Labourers" clearly anticipates the manner of Ruskin's "Letters to the Workmen and Labourers of Great Britain." Like Cobbett, Ruskin will use autobiographical example to model civic behavior. His wayward speaker, too, illustrates how individual will must be subordinated to the rules of community. But Ruskin's equally fragmented, experiential tales do not offer the promise of political enlightenment. The political conventions easily legible for Cobbett become tangled in conventions of representation for Ruskin. Where Cobbett reads individual and social progress, Ruskin discerns immutable figures caught in labyrinthine discursive codes. Ruskin's idiosyncratic speaker is less sure than his predecessor of his independence and rational control over public events. If Cobbett claims to reproduce political reality in the texture of his letters, Ruskin will expose the makeshift nature of such a production. He exploits Cobbett's familiar form in order to reinstate individual authority on quite different epistemological grounds.

In *The Friend* Coleridge had made a similar attempt to redirect Cobbett's line of political engagement, an attempt which would have somewhat different implications for Ruskin's later project. Coleridge's insistent attacks on the *Political Register* indicate how successfully Cobbett had characterized the role of public commentator. His display of exemplary knowledge infuriated Coleridge. In his second Lay Sermon of 1817, Coleridge denounced those who through periodical "implements of irritation" manipulated popular sentiment (*LS* 147).[19] "The corruptions of a system," he claimed, "can be duly appreciated by those only who have contemplated the system in that ideal state of perfection exhibited by the reason" (*LS* 156). In his appeal to actual experience, Cobbett had reduced reason to pragmatism, or in terms Coleridge took pains to distinguish in his 1816 *The Statesman's Manual,* he had confused reason with the inferior power of understanding (reprinted in *LS* 19n). Cobbett's periodical, Coleridge had written to his friend Daniel Stuart in 1808, purveyed empirical observation as political wisdom: it was "the careless passionate Talk of a Man of robust common sense, but grossly ignorant and under the warp of Heat & Prejudice" (*CL* 3:142).[20]

Coleridge tried to counter such journalistic bravado in *The Friend.* That Cobbett was a prime example of the "political provocatives" Coleridge attacked there is clear from his continual references to the *Political Register* in the planning stages of *The Friend* (*F* 1:74). The price of the new work, the method of its circulation, the trim size, and the quality of the paper were determined in relation to Cobbett's practices.[21] As Coleridge described it, the aim of *The Friend* was, in part, directly to counter the influence of the *Register.* Cobbett "applies to the Passion" through "calumnious Personality" reacting to "Events of the Day," Coleridge charged. He vowed to "abstain as from guilt" from such methods: "to strangle these Passions by the awakening of the nobler Germ in human nature is my express and paramount *Object*" (*CL* 3:141).

Despite Coleridge's declaration of detachment, *The Friend,* like the *Political Register,* drew significantly on "Passion and Personality." Coleridge's voice in his earlier periodical effort, *The Watchman* (1796), was that of an interested observer of current public affairs. By contrast, *The Friend* provided commentary on his own experiences and conclusions. "The warmth of my feelings . . . ha[s] led me on to an extent that compels me to defer the investigation of the great Theme," he apologized in his second essay, explaining it was "sometimes an Author's duty to awake the Reader's indignation by the expression of his own" (*F* 2:36, 33). This justification diminishes his proclaimed distance from Cobbett's confessional style. So does his response when challenged about the fragmentation of his numbers. "The error of running one number into another I shall avoid as much as possible," he replied, "& yet how often does Cobbett break off and recommence" in the *Political Register* (*CL* 3:232). Like Cobbett he was willing to interrupt argument with personal anecdote. Coleridge seems truly to be, as he says in a characteristic confessional moment, "the biographer of my own sentiments [rather] than a legislator of the opinions of other men" (*F* 2:9).

This statement links *The Friend* to Coleridge's more familiar production, *Biographia Literaria*. The periodical can be seen as a first run of Coleridge's later effort to distinguish "the unified essential self" from "the accidents of historical contingency." [22] Reading it this way makes sense both of Coleridge's determination to take on Cobbett and of the apparent similarities of the writers' periodical letters. In the *Biographia* Coleridge sought to reverse the contemporary valuation of "observation" over "meditation." To transcribe empirical experience was to produce "technical artifices" (*BL* 2:83). Only through "*genial* discrimination" could particular observations be subsumed under general principles. In an influential account of Wordsworth's poetry, Coleridge argues that what appeared to some readers an unmediated reflection of lived experience was in fact a product of contemplation. Wordsworth's genius was not simply mimetic: he elevated personal experience by "meditative observation" (*BL* 2:144). Coleridge tries to preempt precisely what he would have seen as Hazlitt's misreading of Wordsworth's authority as a kind of poetic sensationalism. That Hazlitt could later assimilate Cobbett to that authority suggests how damaging his example must have seemed to Coleridge's campaign against unreflecting empiricism.

Coleridge does with Cobbett in *The Friend* what he does with Wordsworth in the *Biographia*: he resituates a familiar point of view in an altered philosophical landscape. From the first sentence of the prospectus, Coleridge bases his claim to be heard on individual attainments—his own "Study, Reflection, Observation"—not on political connections (*F* 2:16). He, like Cobbett, announces his incorruptible independence, insisting in the first number that he will "stand aloof from the crowd" and "dissent from the opinions of great Authorities" (*F* 2:10). To that end he rejects the "masquerade" of anonymity practiced by the leading journals of the day, determining instead on speaking conspicuously "in my own person" (*F* 2:32). As the title of his periodical suggests, he intends in his mode of address to "avail myself of the privileges of a friend," "waiving the ceremony of a formal introduction" to his reader (*F* 2:6).

Coleridge invokes in his first two numbers the easy familiarity and idiosyncratic judgment that were the trademarks of Cobbett's style. He, too, conforms to the profile of the new romantic man of letters whose authority, as Marilyn Butler has described it, derives from moral sincerity, not birth or connections. [23] But in the third number of *The Friend*, Coleridge carefully distinguishes sincerity of manner and of purpose.

While other writers justified their familiar address by "mere veracity, by open-heartedness," his appeal to the reader is based on "*moral*," not "*verbal* truth" (*F* 2:41, 42). The "Demagogue" depends on "bold, warm, and earnest assertions," on "arguments built on passing events": he practices a mere journalistic "*veracity*," calling it literally as he sees it (*F* 2:46). Coleridge's full description of the demagogic style here closely parallels contemporary descriptions of Cobbett's methods in the *Political Register*. Coleridge, on the other hand, depends on "*Simplicity*," telling the whole truth behind particular circumstances. Unlike "our hurrying Enlighteners" who are driven by "the activity of their passions," he patiently explains first principles. Other journalists may be earnest: he is "earnestly sincere" (*F* 2:45, 47, 43).

As Coleridge makes clear, *The Friend* is not to be read as the table talk of a representative man speaking to men. Cobbett's style of thinking on his feet evinced presumption and ignorance, not exemplary rationality. Only the "Few" who had served "an apprenticeship from Infancy" to "the process of Thought" should speak to "the Many" (*F* 2:52). Quick wit came cheap; true wisdom cost the labor of a lifetime. In contrast to Cobbett's picaresque tales of rubbing along in society, Coleridge casts his "biography" in the form of a paper trail. He details encounters with authors and theories, not highwaymen and newspaper taxes. Where Cobbett authenticates his claim to be everyman, Coleridge provides a pedigree of his political principles.

His variations on Cobbett's epistolary format reinforce such differences. Like Cobbett, Coleridge relies on appeals to the reader to create the effect of direct correspondence. But while the prospectus of *The Friend* takes the form of an extract from a letter, the regular numbers appear without salutation or closing signature. Coleridge's essays are not to be understood as a mutual correspondence. If Cobbett suggests that anyone can learn the conventions of social conversation, Coleridge argues for the priority of the thinking few. As his use of certain epistolary conventions shows, he, too, knows the rules of the "intercourse of . . . public life." But to analyze conventions, not simply to master them, requires critical distance. Writing from the privileged perspective of "deep retirement," Coleridge can pronounce "in calmness on the present age" (*F* 2:28).

Coleridge deliberately plays on epistolary conventions to produce a

kind of hybrid confessional essay. Neither pat theoretical treatises nor
unpremeditated conversation, his pamphlets attempt to conflate the distinction between theory and praxis. Genuine theory *is* process, as the
biography of his sentiments is meant to reveal. In *The Friend* Coleridge
tries to exemplify the "long, difficult, winding" path to "knowledge,"
which, like his self-reflexive discourses, "oftentimes return[s] upon itself"
(*F* 2:268).[24] He attempts to essentialize lived experience in a way that
would mediate Burke's "manuscripted authority" and Cobbett's insistent
pragmatism.

Again, this move anticipates a crucial argument of the *Biographia*.
There Coleridge demonstrates that Wordsworth's apparently confessional
style is artfully contrived. Too often, he says, when we read lyric poems
"we refer them to a spontaneous energy rather than to voluntary effort"
(*BL* 2:34). In *The Friend* Coleridge shows that spontaneity divorced from
reflection amounts to crude empiricism. In the "turbulent heat of temporary fermentation" we respond to the evidence of our senses; we remain in the world of "facts which subsist in perpetual flux" (*F* 2:7,6).
Writers like Cobbett who relied on observation displayed a sensibility
that "exist[s] in fragments" (*F* 2:41). Such improvised reactions to local
circumstance—what Hazlitt calls, echoing Coleridge's terms, Cobbett's
display of the "first concoction, fermenting and overflowing" of his ideas
(*CW* 8:57)—prefigured the compromised characters of the Victorian
dramatic monologues, not the composed authority of the "permanent
Self" of the romantic lyric (*F* 2:101). In *The Friend* Coleridge claims that
authority for the political journalist, whose task is to report "the Principles of Truth, which belonging to our permanent being, do not lie
within the sphere of our senses" (*F* 2:52).

That Coleridge could not command such authority in a format
composed of periodical fragments is evident. In the 1812 rifacimento, he
generally deleted the first-person pronoun, presumably to distance more
decisively essential principles from personality. Whereas Cobbett's conversational tone helped to exemplify his pragmatic politics, Coleridge's
adaptation at times undermined his theoretical ideals, as his apologies in
the first numbers show. He never found a form that could sustain his
notion of a transcendent yet situated self who negotiates empiricism and
idealism. To interpret the lyric voice as a theoretical abstraction of everyday experience meant doggedly denying its contingency, as he did in the

case of Wordsworth. Yet such a denial risked conflating critical and social detachment. Cobbett's political epistles, unlike lyric poems, insisted on the inherent sociality of the speaking self. That Coleridge hoped to graft the authority of the isolated self on Cobbett's example of rooted individualism is evident in *The Friend*. The logical contortions of the resulting hybrid are paradigmatic of the condition of the modern self as Charles Taylor describes it: "constitutionally in tension" between "a stance of disengagement from one's own nature and feelings" and an effort at "expressive self-articulation." [25]

The interest of Coleridge's uneven production is precisely that it embodies this tension not just thematically but formally. It exploits—even if at times unwittingly—the paradox of engaged detachment that underwrote romantic authority. Adopting a vehicle that circulated "as a Newspaper, and with the Newspapers" (*CL* 3 : 165), Coleridge attempted to build a constituency for the alienated observer. That entailed, at one level, enlisting subscribers to what was still a fairly new romantic experiment, as Coleridge struggled to do for his periodical. In *The Friend* he links this sense of constituency with its broader political meaning. Those who subscribed to his pamphlets were to understand that he was speaking not just to them but for them. The personal voice was to be read, as was the editorial "we" of the newly powerful newspapers, as the vox populi. For in a society defined in terms of markets and individual rights, the position of the private individual *was* representative. Coleridge's notion accords with Jürgen Habermas's description of the transformation of the social structure in the early nineteenth century: "The bourgeois public sphere may be conceived above all as the sphere of private people come together as a public." [26] The public/private split on which most modern accounts of romanticism hinge was effaced in Coleridge's telling. Even those who lived in the "deepest retirement" fully participated in the public sphere through newspapers, the forum in which "intelligent Men now converse with each other" (*F* 2 : 290, 28). In Coleridge's private periodical, the individual voice is not asocial: it is the very foundation of the public sphere he takes pains to define and defend in *The Friend*.

This exemplary isolated speaker closely resembles the Ruskin of *Time and Tide*. Distant from political turmoil, he speaks to readers seeking to understand their new stake in postreform government. In this renegotiation of public and private relations, the letter writer represents

rational engagement removed from the political fray. The varied mani-
festations of Ruskin's early letters to working men suggests the perme-
ability of the public sphere outlined by Coleridge. Originally part of a
private correspondence with Thomas Dixon, his epistles were reprinted
first in newspapers and later in a discrete volume. The etiquette of individual communication is made to illustrate, according to Ruskin's 1867
preface to *Time and Tide*, the "honesty of exchange" in public life (17:
313). While Ruskin retains many of the signs of the original correspondence—the personal address, the closing salutation, and, unlike Coleridge in his rifacimento, the first-person pronoun—he can omit "passages of merely personal or temporary interest" without damaging the
composed authority on which the work rests (17:314). The private individual writing from his position of detachment represents Ruskin's ideal
participant in public debate.

But in *Fors* Ruskin reengages the epistolary speaker in what Coleridge had dismissed as "arguments built on passing events." His manner
appears to be similar to that of Coleridge's demagogue, hurried by "the
activity of [his] passions" (*F* 2:46, 47). And yet if his style in this later
production resembles Cobbett, like Coleridge he berates the modern
journalistic temper and claims to offer considered political truths. This
might seem simply to replicate Coleridge's own formal gymnastics in *The
Friend*, where he tries unsuccessfully to mediate empiricism and reflection. Ruskin, however, deliberately keeps both positions in play. He not
only refuses to rest in the privileges of "deep retirement": he uses his own
passionate displays to at times satirize its apparent prerogatives.

The detached observer in the opening letter of *Fors Clavigera* is compromised, as I argued earlier, by Ruskin's political commentary there.
His critique of national and intellectual isolationism shows the artistic
dreamer to be little better than a poetic little Englander. Disengagement,
in a larger climate of political nonintervention in the early 1870s, signaled
either an inability to judge at all, or a failure of nerve to speak the truth
(27:11). Despite this apparent rejection of "ineffectual" romantic contemplation (27:12), Ruskin frequently portrays himself in this familiar
pose. Such a move verges on a parody of romantic authority in the manner of the Victorian dramatic monologue. Like the pilloried Simeon
Stylites, Ruskin the grumpy sage invites the kind of mocking that a *Punch*

illustrator later practiced in his "Fancy Portrait" entitled "Mr. Narcissus Ruskin." The cartoon portrays the author of *Fors* gazing at himself in a pool: the caption reads, "Who is it that says most? Which can say more, than this rich praise,—that You alone are *You!*" [27]

To suggest that Ruskin deliberately leaves himself exposed to such caricaturing—that he can even be seen, in the first letter, to preempt it—appears to dismiss a crucial strain in the letters. The decidedly unironic voice of the Master of the Guild of St. George, who must be "implicitly trusted" so that he can "act undisturbedly" (28:648), might be said to reinhabit the narrow perspective criticized in the opening of *Fors*. But, as I argue in more detail in chapter 2, the epistolary method does constantly disturb and disrupt the Master's reflections. Like the improvisational characters of Victorian dramatic monologues, Ruskin the letter writer must constantly adapt to the circumstances in which he finds himself, as well as to the implied demands of his audience. The form cuts short lyric utterance, displaying in place of steady reflection the individual's struggle to "contend with the difficulties arising out of his present position, gradually modifying it" (28:643).

What Ruskin produces in *Fors Clavigera* is a format that embodies the problems of exemplary individualism in the late nineteenth century. In a climate of political and intellectual crisis, it was no longer easy to discern, in the words Ruskin quotes from Thomas Carlyle's epistolary pamphlets, "Who is best man" (27:248). Carlyle had already demonstrated the potential for misreading the personalized address so powerful in the case of Cobbett and Coleridge. In the wake of European revolutions and Chartist agitations, every "stump-orator" claimed that his was a representative voice. "Vox is the God of this Universe" Carlyle claimed, at a time when the argument for universal suffrage turned on the worth of individual utterance (*WTC* 20:192). Written in the wake of Chartist agitation and the series of European upheavals in 1848, Carlyle's postrevolutionary periodical, *Latter-Day Pamphlets* (1850), takes as its theme the implications of romantic individualism gone public. Citing and applauding Carlyle's work in *Fors*, Ruskin forges a dangerous alliance. Carlyle's notorious instance of the political periodical would seem to have preempted a return to the form two decades later, even on the part of the most devoted disciple. For Carlyle had concluded that, in a jesuitical age, when everyone professed a self-satisfied sincerity, the only way to restore social order was to ironize the romantic project and, ultimately, to shut it down.

To this end Carlyle revives the epistolary periodical, if only finally to undermine its discursive viability. Readers have questioned Carlyle's choice of format, attributing it to an unfortunate lapse of critical control.[28] Carlyle's letters, on the other hand, indicate a very deliberate return to the subgenre as used by Cobbett and Coleridge. In response to contemporary political crises he determined to write his own periodical publication called "two-penny Trash," the derisive nickname given to Cobbett's cheap edition of the *Political Register.*[29] The apocalyptic title under which his pamphlets were published highlights the impasse to which the romantic epistolary venture had come. By the time Carlyle was writing the work, the political epistle was no longer the form of the few but the habit of the uncritical many. Access to print had become so easy that anyone, under the sway of "any vote, idea or notion," could now "take a pen, and therewith autocratically pour forth the same into the ears and hearts of all people" (*WTC* 20:221).

Carlyle savagely mimics that pouring-forth in order to show its fatuity. In the process, he also exposes the fatuity of his own voice in the pamphlets. He presents himself again and again as a foolish, garrulous old man unable to intervene effectively. The isolated sensibility that had marked the authenticity of Cobbett's and Coleridge's projects is here shown as simply outmoded: "isolated men, and their vague efforts" had little to do with modern democracy (*WTC* 20:36). While a new generation was potentially "in the happy case to *be* something and to *do* something," Carlyle lamented, he could merely continue "eloquently talking about what was done and might be" (*WTC* 20:213). Carlyle writes strong heroic authority, including his own, into the past, as something to "look back on . . . with pity and incredulous astonishment." For "to publish the secret of [one's] soul in words," says the author of the mock autobiography, *Sartor Resartus*, should be regarded as "ignoble." If Coleridge worried about the distinction between "verbal truth" and a reflective representation of individual experience, Carlyle argues that *any* verbal translation of experience "obstruct[s], and will in the end abolish, and render impossible" essential truth (*WTC* 20:196). As Coleridge's several revisions of *The Friend* had shown, distilling general from personal revelation was at best difficult. In *Latter-Day Pamphlets* Carlyle suggests that it is simply futile. Here, as in *Sartor*, to represent through language means always to *mis*represent the "facts" of "veridical Nature." The mark of "divine prophecy," on the other hand, is its "intrinsically . . . silent nature" (*WTC* 20:193, 196).

The title of Carlyle's publication takes on a second meaning in this context. Not only does it express a crisis: it marks Carlyle's contribution as merely the latest in a series of failed efforts. Near the end of his last pamphlet he mocks those who, still reading, are waiting for the revelation of a "new religion." Instead of a revelation, Carlyle finishes his work with the "great waste ocean-voice" of "ennui" (*WTC* 20:333, 336). His readers are awash with "vocables," his among them. In *Sartor Resartus* Carlyle's use of a number of fictional speakers acts out a Millite notion of truth as the sum of multiple perspectives. Here the fictional speakers—the journalist Crabbe, the Prime Minister, the Professor—simply add to the "inarticulate . . . voice[s] of Chaos" in a democratic age (*WTC* 20:5).[30] There is no final resolution in *Latter-Day Pamphlets* precisely because Carlyle argues that the search for truth can only begin outside the text. "Inarticulate work," not words, would help individuals move toward "inarticulate Veracity" (*WTC* 20:195).

Coleridge tried to counter what he saw as Cobbett's fragmented observer with the composed lyric self. Carlyle shows that considered reflection—including his own—can too often turn to intellectual rigidity, to the pose of "the mature man, hardened into skeptical egoism," who "knows no monition but that of his own frigid cautions, avarices, mean timidities; and can lead nowhither towards an object that even seems noble." The modern condition *was* fragmented, as Coleridge had feared; that was the "inevitable fact" of the age (*WTC* 20:8). Cobbett, whom Carlyle characterized elsewhere as a great "improviser" of "ever-fresh denouncements," at least had represented the protean spirit of democracy.[31] For democracy was not a drawing-room drama, rather a "drama full of action, even fast following event" (*WTC* 20:10). The sage's monologue at the end of the pamphlets drones on, but the real action has moved offstage, outside the text.[32]

Unlike Carlyle's pamphlets, *Fors Clavigera* does not end in a broadly deconstructive moment. Carlyle's insistent probing of the problems of representation proves in Ruskin's letters to be a step toward rehabilitating, not demolishing, personal authority. Where Carlyle worries about linguistic corruptions of essential truths, Ruskin will emphasize the process of mediation. If for Carlyle the epistolary pamphlet foregrounds all too clearly that process, for Ruskin it offers a means of reuniting work and words. The way we act is revealed in *Fors* to be always contingent on the forms through which we speak. We cannot act, Ruskin suggests, outside the fragmented frameworks of convention. Political participation is inevitably linked to the spectacle of self-representation. Carlyle proclaims the irrelevance of isolated reflection to the conduct of a society; Ruskin makes the constraints and political delusions of the monologic condition exemplary of the drama of communal life.

Ruskin reconstructs the significance of the romantic epistolary example at a moment when the myth of the "permanent self" on which it depended had been debunked. New scientific theories about the nature of perception and knowledge denied the existence of a stable, judging consciousness. "Character," says the modern-minded Mr. Farebrother in George Eliot's *Middlemarch* (published in the same years Ruskin began *Fors*), "is not cut in marble—it is not something solid and unalterable. It is something living and changing."[33] Cobbett had already demonstrated how well the epistolary periodical dramatized self as process. Late-nineteenth-century thinkers had pushed the empirical theories out of which Cobbett worked to their logical limits. Impressionism and Paterian aestheticism render experience as a series of discrete perceptions in a way that has much in common with the disjointed method of *Fors*.

With *Fors Clavigera* Ruskin intervenes in this contemporary rethinking of artistic authority. His impressionistic tableaux foreground new understandings of perception and truth. Whereas in *Modern Painters* he could present a clear, Coleridgean distinction between the "true appearances of things" and the "extraordinary, or false appearances, when we are under the influence of emotion" (5:204), the epistemological stakes had been raised since Ruskin had worked out this formulation of the pathetic fallacy. Empiricism and subjectivism had been inextricably linked in modern scientific writings: as the mathematician W. K. Clifford argued, "We can have no experience to know that some of our sensation is not supplied by ourselves."[34] The problem now was to reimagine the authority of individual experience that might or might not correspond to an external truth. The epistolary periodical, with its focus on singular perspective, was peculiarly suited to exploring that problem.

Beginning where Carlyle's *Latter-Day Pamphlets* ended, Ruskin showcases the limitations of personal perspective. His method ironizes settled understanding. The paradoxical upshot of *Fors Clavigera*, as I demonstrate in the next chapter, is that seeing character as process makes constructions of the self more, not less authoritative. For it was the effort to construct, to make representations, that marked the moral truth of human experience in the post-Darwinian era.

II

⎯⎯⎯⎯⎯⎯⎯⎯⎯⎯⎯⎯⎯⎯

Ruskin's Figurative Perceptions and
the Politics of Representation

WHEN RUSKIN LAUNCHED *Fors Clavigera* in 1871, his stature as a major
Victorian sage had been officially confirmed. His appointment to the first
Slade Lectureship in 1869 had given institutional sanction to his views on
art. From 1869–1878 he lectured at Oxford to capacity crowds; as the
audiences grew, he was obliged to deliver many lectures twice. In 1872,
when his cousin Joan Severn wrote to tell him of Scottish interest in his
writings, he could point out that "now, as far as my own power is concerned, I hear enough."[1]

Nor was his following merely academic. A popular book of 1870
had celebrated Ruskin as "one of our greatest modern teachers," the defining voice of "the politics of the future."[2] With such recognition, Ruskin was able to capitalize on the moment through a "propaganda effort"
reaching beyond the university setting.[3] His newest letter campaign, *Fors
Clavigera*, would go forth as the work of the Oxford Slade Lecturer, a far
cry from the anonymous "Graduate of Oxford" who had penned *Modern
Painters*.

Fors Clavigera sounds familiar Ruskinian themes: the moral landscape
of art, capitalist idolatry, the epistemological limits of empiricism and rationalism. Its formal variations on these themes complicate positions that
often seem predictable and dogmatic in his other works of the period.
Unlike his lectures, for example, his pamphlets shift the focus from what
is communicated to how it is conveyed. The epistolary address foregrounds communication as representation not presentation, as mediated,
not immediate linguistic performance. As one critic has noted in an important distinction between the dramatic epistle and monologue, the
epistle presents the "composing mind," not the "improvised conversation

which dramatic monologue purports, as 'non-writing,' to be."[4] And that shift from the seeming transparency of speech to the opacity of writing calls into question, in a way new in Ruskin's work, his positions on perspective, on means of knowing, and on imaginative as opposed to empirical observation.

In other words, in *Fors Clavigera* Ruskin adopts a form that disrupts the kind of established authority he had so recently achieved. Instead of presenting coherent treatises from a settled perspective, *Fors* moves disjointedly through constantly shifting, idiosyncratic viewpoints. Rather than presuming on individual authority, the letter form as Ruskin uses it here calls into question the premises of any such authority. The imperial cogito at the heart of enlightenment and romantic ideology is unceremoniously deposed. "Your faithful friend, John Ruskin," who signs each letter, bears only a casual relation to the reliable figure underwriting nineteenth-century sage discourse. Continually thrown off course by the vagaries of chance or "Fate," embroiled in local battles with a newspaper writer or a correspondent, this speaker's performance is always contingent. The "faithful friend" does not, as in Victorian realist novels, provide an overarching narrative to distill the truth of such performances. In his confessional letters Ruskin never establishes a sagelike perspective, a perspective that would make personal opinion and revelation count as more than narcissistic indulgence.

Some contemporaries did see *Fors Clavigera* as a protracted exercise in Ruskinian egoism. One of the earliest notices of the work remarked on the author's "rather childish pride in exhibiting the width and depth of the distinction between himself and his neighbours." Rather than appealing to common points of reference, he "ostentatiously exhibits his most amazing caprices."[5] Ruskin did little to defend his publication against such charges of solipsism. In an 1872 letter, he asserted that *Fors* was directed to "persons who wish to know something of me . . . and from beginning to end will be full of all sorts of personality" (37:48). Given the cultural circumstances in which the work was published, Ruskin could not have doubted how this cultivation of personality would be received. The impressionistic manner of *Fors* places it at the fault line of literary and scientific debates about the nature of intellectual authority in the 1870s. As new movements in biology, physiology, and psychology revealed individual perception to be "eminently inconsistent and relative," some critics reconfigured authority in terms of scholarly and institutional consensus, not of personal privilege.[6] At Oxford in particular, battles raged over the merits of disinterested research. Both the charismatic leadership of a Jowett and the dilettantish sensationalism of a Pater had been called into question.[7]

As his frequent attacks on empiricism, evolutionism, and materialism in *Fors Clavigera* would make clear, Ruskin did not accept the scientific and philosophical premises behind the emerging ideas of consensual authority. Nor did he make common cause with the versions of heroic individualism propagated by the opposing camps. Like the Carlyle of *Latter-Day Pamphlets*, Ruskin dreaded the social consequences of radical individualism, especially in the wake of ballot reforms and working class organization. Given the altered political climate, advocating as he had in *Time and Tide* that "every Man may be a Law to Himself" would invite misapprehensions about the social vision he was sketching out (17:324). The model community in *Fors Clavigera* operated on fixed principles that constrained personal liberty. Instead of rational consensus, Ruskin would advocate an authoritarian nationalism in which individual will was subordinated to communal sentiment.

The egoistic persona of his pamphlets seems to contradict this larger political vision. In practice, Ruskin's paradoxical performance dramatizes the delusions of self-will. The letter writer pursuing his course as "the humour takes me" comes to illustrate the impossibility of independent action (29:197). If Ruskin plays the passionate prophet, he does so in a manner that undercuts the role's viability, at least as that role had been characterized in recent debates. As the response to his Slade lectures indicates, the polarization between critical detachment and solipsistic reflection was still in process. Ruskin exploits his public part to align both positions with an untenable extreme, an extreme embodied by the wayward speaker continually checked by the disruptive world. Disengagement, whether of the imagination or of reason, is shown to be a delusion. In *Fors Clavigera* Ruskin recasts contemporary debates as quibbles over a distinction without a difference. The observation of sage or scientist he presents as similarly constrained.

Ruskin was well aware when he began *Fors* that he had been cast by some observers as a dated romantic sage out of step with new scientific and aesthetic thinking. His appointment as Slade Lecturer at Oxford had

played to mixed reviews. To some onlookers it was a welcome confirmation of his vital influence on modern art. To others it seemed a desperate effort to prop up high-Victorian aesthetic theory at the very moment of its demise. The *Saturday Review* professed the latter opinion. It
dismissed Ruskin's inaugural lectures as the blustering of an outdated sage
ensconced in a sinecure. A few years earlier, said its reviewer, Ruskin's
"influence on art in England was sufficiently considerable to be dangerous." But even a named professorship could not restore him to the position of "the infallible prophet" he had enjoyed in "the good old pre-
Raffaelite times." Despite Ruskin's tendency "to talk as if he continued to
believe in his own little papacy," it should be clear to modern undergrad-
uates schooled in French realism and emerging impressionism that his
ideas were nothing more than "a bit of British eccentricity unworthy of
serious attention." [8]

The *Academy* also portrayed Ruskin as out of fashion. It judged his
moral aesthetic by the catch phrases of *l'art pour l'art* movement. The
genuine work of art was a "perfection of sensual pleasure," nothing more.
All value was extrinsic, a projection "by the beholder," not, as Ruskin
seemed to argue, an inherent property of a work. The real interest of
Ruskin's bombastic opinions, according to the reviewer, lay in their contradiction of his own theories. His heated rhetoric demonstrated that it
was in "moments of explosion" and "excess"—not in studied displays of
dispassionate "goodness"—that art, like his lectures, conveyed the "most
fervid glow of human beauty." [9]

At issue for these reviewers is not so much what Ruskin says. As they
point out he covers familiar terrain. Rather, what looms large is Ruskin
as ceremonial figurehead, as sanctioned representative of a version of
critical authority that neither reviewer accepted. Both readings focus primarily on Ruskin the personality, the charismatic head of "an intellectual
autocracy." For the *Saturday Review* critic Ruskin stood as a "representative man" of an old guard whose "naive" emotional rhetoric was "super-
fluous" to rational society. [10] The reviewer in the *Academy* lumps Ruskin
with the aesthetes of the 1870s, for whom, in this telling, artistic authority was a matter of individual pleasure. His passionate appeals might indeed be momentarily stirring, but they were ultimately irrelevant to the
larger ethical and political concerns he claimed to address. He was in the
end a local colorist with illusions of grandeur.

To characterize Ruskin as a compelling eccentric was to cast him in a recognized role in the contemporary critical scene. He could not be counted with the skeptical pragmatists of the *Saturday Review*, whose position might be summed up by Leslie Stephen's call to "dispers[e] the old halo of erroneous imagination" through an "unflinching" commitment to reason. Nor was he one of the disciplinary experts who published in the pages of the *Academy*, a journal founded by one of the leading figures in Mark Pattison's movement for endowed research at Oxford, Charles Appleton. The *Academy* aimed to exemplify the value of scholarly consensus "by bringing together a body of *skilled and authoritative* opinion." [11] Its reviewer of Ruskin's lectures, E. F. S. Pattison—who was herself a professional art critic for both the *Academy* and the *Saturday Review*, as well as the wife of Mark Pattison—casts Ruskin not as authoritative specialist but as feverish amateur. [12] In the new "Age of Reason" he was something of a gothic survival, a reminder of the fashion for personal "caprice." [13]

The reviews of Ruskin's inaugural lectures at Oxford gave occasion for the still-fluid distinctions between competing versions of cultural authority to be firmed up. If in Mark Pattison's telling the nineteenth century split into two periods, a prolonged "romantic . . . reaction" to the enlightenment and a rationalist revival beginning in the late 1860s, Ruskin could be made to stand for the excesses of an old school dismissed by "the sovereign reason." [14] Like the Carlyle of John Morley's 1870 essay, he seemed "to prefer effusive indulgence of emotion to the laborious and disciplined and candid exploration of new ideas" essential to the "true renovation of England." In this disjunction of affect and effect, of pragmatic reason and unrestrained emotion, Ruskin was branded the last of the romantic sages. As Stopford Brooke put it in his review of Ruskin's early lectures, the Professor, with his "acute sense of beauty," lacked the intellectual "iron nerve" that would make sense of the political and philosophical issues he broached. His attempt "to play his part in that battlefield" had the predictable result that "would follow on sending a poet like Shelley into one of the war hospitals. He ceases to be able to write poetry and he kills the patients." [15]

The opening letter of *Fors Clavigera*, begun in 1870, might be said to lead off with such a critical scenario. Ruskin the romantic dreamer, as he portrays himself there, faced with the economic and political casualties of modern England, cannot sustain his creative activity. His critique in this letter of the "ineffectual" artistic sensibility mimics the attacks on his own performance as Slade Lecturer. This inaugural moment in *Fors Clavigera* provides more than a vague allusion to romantic tradition. Ruskin's self-portrait calls into play the contemporary criticism that had defined that tradition—and Ruskin's place in it—in a decisive way.

In *Fors Clavigera* Ruskin cultivates the character of isolated eccentric, exploring, as Coleridge and Carlyle had before him, the implications of romantic individualism gone public. His choice of format—a series of confessional letters, sold only by an obscure publisher because, as a printed advertisement in each number explained, "the Author wishes to retain complete command over their mode of publication"—drew further attention to his self-conscious display of personality. If the battle lines were drawn between "strong individuality" and disinterested intelligence, between "self-indulgent mannerisms" and "rational discipline," Ruskin leaves no doubt in his new publication to which camp he belonged.[16]

Although it is fruitless to speculate on whether Ruskin consciously drew on the existing examples of the epistolary format, it is certainly the case that those precedents had been loaded with an ideological baggage of which he could hardly have failed to be aware.[17] Both Carlyle's and Cobbett's periodicals had been made to figure prominently in the current critical campaigns. Three recent studies of Cobbett had reconsidered the journalist's example for a new generation of radical empiricists. As one writer suggested, the *Political Register* was a salient reminder of the potential power of skeptical enquiry. But while Cobbett's ruthless exposure of "persistent fallacies" was entirely admirable, he had turned the pursuit of truth into something "violently personal." His overwhelming "egotism," another critic remarked, caused the "veerings about" in his reasoning that kept him from joining the greatest rank of English political writers. The epistolary format of the *Political Register*, although an excellent vehicle for conveying empirical experience, allowed the self-educated writer to indulge his idiosyncracies.[18]

Carlyle's *Latter-Day Pamphlets* too had been made to stand for skepticism contaminated by self-indulgence. Carlyle's "poetic temper of criticism . . . needs to have special safeguards," John Morley remarked in 1870. In his political pamphlets there was no check on his "childish" habits of reasoning. He ignored "the central division between object and subject" that would lend "intellectual precision and definiteness" to his thinking. As a result, his social analysis was "effectually veiled by purple or fiery clouds of anger, sympathy, and sentimentalism." Even Arnold lamented Carlyle's display of pathetic fallacy. The *Political Register, Latter-Day Pamphlets* and Ruskin's economic works of the 1860s, he argued, showed the limitations of criticism "blackened" by a too-emotional investment in "political practice." Their ineffectualness proved the need for a "more free speculative treatment of things." [19]

To write an epistolary periodical in the manner of Carlyle and Cobbett was thus to write in a form whose political and intellectual commitments were a matter of public record. It signified a type of reactionary romanticism, a sentimental corruption of the enlightenment faith in rational inquiry. As one writer commented in 1868 of *The Friend*, at a time when "intellectual radicalism has once again become a fashion," the "defects" of such an enterprise demonstrated how "searching for fundamental principles" can too easily lead to a "morbidly introvertive turn of mind." [20]

The reviewers of *Fors Clavigera* did not miss the implications of Ruskin's formal statement. His thinking, Leslie Stephen commented, did not take a "systematic form": the personal letters "give free vent" to his "unusual if not morbid sensibility." Ruskin displayed a dogged "determination to see things for himself." [21] The implied perversion of Arnold's charge to the critic "to see the object as in itself it really is" is unmistakable. So is Stephen's echo of the martial metaphor Arnold uses to characterize Cobbett's and Carlyle's fatal incursion into the "field of political practice." [22] Ruskin, Stephen noted, appeared "content to be a brilliant partisan in a random guerilla warfare" rather than a first rate critic. Although *Modern Painters* had "done more than any other [book] of its kind to stimulate thought and disperse antiquated fallacies," Ruskin now showed symptoms of the very disease he had so acutely diagnosed there. Invoking Ruskin's own description of the pathetic fallacy, Stephen regrets that in *Fors Clavigera* "the shock" of modern life has debilitated Ruskin: it "seems to throw him off his balance." [23]

Other critics recognized the discursive position Ruskin staked out with his epistolary pamphlets. The *Saturday Review* complained that he deliberately catered to a popular "crav[ing] for personal knowledge" of literary celebrities. Ruskin "must be quite aware" that he was "already a man of sufficient mark to make it a subject of considerable interest to a large circle to know whether he takes sugar in his tea or likes cats." His anti-intellectual, "self-satisfied" style made it "impossible to judge of Mr. Ruskin on ordinary grounds of criticism, literary or moral."[24] The *Spectator* remarked that Ruskin's presentation did not exemplify the "operation of a law," as Arnold's more orderly essays did. He said "nothing to which the sharpest critic would object if he had said it in an autobiography to be published posthumously," but his personal tone seemed misplaced in a purportedly political work.[25] As H. D. Traill noted in the last year of Ruskin's serial, his penchant for confession and logical "unexpectedness" directly recalled *The Friend*, whose readers despaired "of the survival of any sense of theorematic unity."[26]

Ruskin's display of personality was thus read in terms of what was becoming a completely conventional dichotomy. In *Fors Clavigera* Ruskin writes himself into one side of this critical divide—the side with which he had already been aligned in early reviews of his Slade lectures. But if he adopts the role of the sentimental egotist rather than that of the disinterested critic, he does so, ultimately, to reveal their shared characteristics. To insist on either empirical observation or affective experience, on either the primacy of the cogito or of the imagination, was to presume in each instance on a center that would not hold. For both positions were derived from the Lockean view of self, from what Charles Taylor has termed the notion of the "punctual" self "defined in abstraction from any constitutive concerns." Both positions, as they had been formulated in contemporary debates, implied the ability to step outside existing interpretive frameworks, either by means of a morally neutral position grounded in sensual perception, or by means of an expressivist turn inward.[27]

Ruskin attempted to unravel this common thread in aesthetic, philosophical, and political discourse of the period. Radical individualism, he suggests in *Fors Clavigera*, is a fundamental delusion. Through a rhetoric and format in which eccentric individuality seems everywhere in evidence, he sets out to illustrate the "law of Fate" by which individuality is in fact circumscribed (27:46). There was no Coleridgean "permanent Self" to adjudicate disparate experiences (*F* 2:101). Instead of the essentially aestheticized individual of Millite liberalism who operates in a private sphere unconstrained by ideological imperatives, Ruskin presents in *Fors* a self inextricably implicated in society. For the individual, as for the artist in Ruskin's version of the aesthetic, there is no disinterested position: art, he argued throughout his writings, is inherently moral, political, ideological. "You had better cease to talk of" foundational independence, Ruskin warns in *Fors*, "for you are dependent not only on every act of people whom you never heard of, who are living round you, but on every past act of what has been dust for a thousand years" (27:50).

What appears to us a unique point of departure is, Ruskin suggests through the image of the labyrinth, rather part of a "single path or track, coiled, and recoiled, on itself" that "has ruled all minds of men to this hour" (27:407, 400). We are always situated within this "imaginary maze," this network of images and values constructed by generations before us. The "spectral" walls of this inherited interpretive framework determine our "figurative perceptions" of experience (27:408, 29:54). Although we can reorient ourselves within the maze, we can never entirely escape it. In the terms of a slightly different metaphor, we are caught in "webs of interlocution": we can only define individual perspective *in relation*, "through conversation in a broad sense" that situates us within already meaningful frameworks.[28]

What seems to us most private—our opinions, our sensual perceptions, our conceptions of ourselves—is in fact dependent on this larger cultural conversation. In letter 28 Ruskin returns to the image of the labyrinth to explore the political ramifications of such a notion. His readers, Ruskin acknowledges, were well schooled to demand the "ultimate privileges of Liberty" (27:522). But while they clamored for the right for "every man" to define "his own place," they neglected to notice that their places had already been defined for them (27:507). Declarations of independence were meaningless in an economic and political framework in which his readers functioned as "serfs" (27:515). To deny one's entanglement in this social labyrinth was not to be free but to be trapped within codes of which one remained unaware. In terms of the myth of Daedalus's labyrinth as Ruskin explains it, such a denial leaves us wandering aimlessly without the benefit of Ariadne's clue—in this letter, a knowledge of the historical evolution of the ideas of serfdom and freedom. But "if the spider, or other monster in mid-web, ate you," Ruskin warns, "the help in your clue . . . would be insignificant" (27:408). Not to define oneself in terms of the existing conversation was literally not to signify: it was to risk being swallowed up by others' representations. To operate as though individual opinions function "independently" of a larger cultural "truth, which is above opinion," and to ignore the "public interest, which is above private," is to be an "idiot" (27:521). It is, in effect, to use an idiom incomprehensible by a larger community.

Ruskin's epistolary address points to the way in which our tales of self must always be oriented within this common discursive space. What he writes is not a lyrical monologue, but a letter which implies participation in an ongoing dialogue. The isolated monologic condition, as some Victorian poets had shown, was a romantic mirage. The speakers of dramatic monologues are often, at best, pathetic in their efforts to defend their autonomy. At worst, as in the case of the hero of Tennyson's *Maud*, the attempt to act out this self-delusion results in a kind of "idiot gabble" (l. 279), where meaning grinds to a halt.[29] Such a disruption of meaning is precisely the way that Ruskin represents the hiatus in his monthly letters from 1878 to 1880. The series stopped, he explains, because he "went mad," but not, as his doctors had diagnosed it, from "overwork" (29:386). In fact his madness was a product of a communication breakdown: his readers had "stopped their ears" and "the solitude at last became too great to be endured" (29:387). To fall outside the general conversation was to have an identity crisis: not to be heard was not to exist in the terms of "common humanity" (29:384). The opposite of egotistical madness was not rational disinterestedness—which simply perpetuated the myth of autonomy—but "common sense," the ability "constantly to perceive truths to which self-indulgence renders us blind" (29:534).[30]

In this view of the constitutive self, what becomes important is not critical originality, as it was on both sides of the current debates about authority. Rather, what matters is "What sort of creatures you think yourselves": in other words, how you configure yourself *as* self in terms of a vocabulary comprehensible to "those you call your best friends" (27:508). What makes us distinctively human, what makes us recognizably "sane" and not part of an unchartable moral territory, is not the actual existence of a rational or imaginative center of identity. Instead, it is the fact that we act *as if* such a center existed. The self is, itself, a metaphor, a way of representing as a coherent whole what might otherwise appear as disjointed perceptions and utterances. "The best that I can make of myself," Ruskin says, may "be a faithful sign-post" (27:558). That is, what matters for the way we act in the world is, as it were, how we bill ourselves.

Writing his pamphlets in the form of a letter dramatized this kind of self-representation. Unlike a political essay, a political epistle does not appear as reportage or disinterested commentary. Rather it presents events as they are constructed in the mind of the signatory. Indeed, a letter is read by its recipient as standing for the signatory: as Daniel Harris puts it, the letter "present[s] the writer *as* his completed writing, the metonym of himself." The autobiographical byways and confessional moments in *Fors Clavigera* record the attempt to "think oneself." This means not thinking *for* one's self, as Ruskin makes clear when he repeats throughout his letters that what he gives is not original opinion. It entails the effort to present one's self *to* one's self, as well as to others, to imagine one's self as the "Author of this book" whom Ruskin lists in the index to *Fors Clavigera*.[31] Ruskin models the attempt to construct the self as a subject of discourse, in the dual sense: as a thing which can be talked about through discourse, and as a thing which is constituted by discourse.

As Ruskin's images of webs and labyrinths would indicate, the upshot of this argument is a constrained view of authority. "Whatever is dictated in *Fors*," he writes, "is dictated thus by common sense . . . common humanity . . . not by me" (29:384). His words are "not the command of private will, but the dictation of necessary law" (28:649). We are right, then, to read each letter as a metonym, but not for a unique consciousness. Instead, the individual, and individual utterance, is itself a metonym of a larger network of representation. This begins to sound something like Coleridge's attempt in *The Friend* to distinguish "Principles of Truth" that are part of our "permanent being" from the vagaries of personality (*F* 2:101). But where for Coleridge digression marked the failure of his epistolary project, the unwelcome intrusion of the spurious self, for Ruskin such intrusions become the point of the exercise. It is precisely where we let go of the illusion of authorial control that we come closest to some kind of truth. To attempt to essentialize lived experience as Coleridge had done was to deny the way in which perception is inevitably implicated in a common fund of representations. There *is* only spurious self: we can only pose as the authors of a system of thought that in fact authorizes us.

The recognizably modern version of self proposed here—histori-cally contingent, locked in by subjective experience—does not lead in *Fors* to a relativism of the sort associated with the aesthetes of late cen-tury. Nor does it lead to the scientific view of knowledge Ruskin op-poses in *Fors*: that the best approximation at truth lay in collecting a se-ries of discrete experiences, in amalgamating the opinions of specialists in discrete fields. In a paper delivered to the Metaphysical Society in April 1871, Ruskin had pointed to the epistemological inconsistency of such a view. To argue for a dialectical synthesis of individual perceptions was to posit a type of transcendental empiricism. The artist, he claimed, not the scientist, was the only uncorrupted empiricist: he is "incapable of conceiving anything at all, except as a phenomenon or sensation . . . that which is not an appearance, or a feeling . . . is to him nothing. . . . No quantity of the sternest training in the school of Hegel, would ever enable him to think the Absolute. He would persist in an obstinate refusal to use the word 'think' at all in a transitive sense" (34:107–8). In *Fors* Ruskin tries out this committed pursuit of sensationalism, of particularism with-out synthesis. Such a commitment, he suggests, need not involve an abro-gation of "common truths" (28:107).

If Ruskin's history as related in *Fors Clavigera* is hardly everyman's, the effort to represent it, to make it meaningful, is. For what is "assuredly true,—inevitable,—trustworthy to the uttermost" (28:107) is not to be found beyond individual experience, but in the means by which we re-cord and communicate it. Despite what materialists like Huxley pro-fessed, sight was not "altogether mechanical," Ruskin asserted in an Ox-ford lecture of 1877 (22:512). The way we represent what we know is integral to what we know: we have no raw experience, only "figurative perceptions" (29:54). Individual observation is always constructed out of a common heritage. Language and art are not spurious embellishments of human experience. They are its very substance.

To claim, as Mark Pattison had in promoting at Oxford the liberal scientific view of truth, that "modern societies are regulated more and more by knowledge, and less by tradition," was to pose a false opposi-tion.[32] All constructions of knowledge were constrained by tradition. The true "man of science," Ruskin argued in an Oxford lecture of 1872, did not search for "the arrangement of new systems, nor the discovery of new facts," but recognized his "submission to an eternal system, and the proper grasp of facts already known" (22:150). In *Fors Clavigera* he would show that the myths running through the letters are more "factual" than the experiments of contemporary scientists. They record the inherited structures of thought through which what counts as knowledge is filtered.

Thus the cultural work of the artist is not to exemplify a holistic imagination that counters economic and scientific atomism. In fact, Ruskin's definition of the artist in *Fors Clavigera* is very much like his 1872 definition of the scientist. The artist, he claims in letter 59, is "a person who has submitted to a law which it was painful to obey" (28 : 441). "True and vital" art was the product of "stringency, or constraint" of personality (28 : 442, 441). Like the future householders of the Guild of St. George, the true artist only nominally owns part of what is in fact a common "treasury": the "complete code" that is "the knowledge of the life and death of the recorded generations of mankind" (28 : 445, 451).

The letters of *Fors Clavigera* aim in part to transmit that code as it can be recovered in art, myth, and literature. As one reader has expressed it, they can often seem like a "University Extension Course," a textbook in western civilization.[33] Ruskin offers, in the manner of Cobbett, a political primer for the culturally illiterate. Both writers propose to make public the often unspoken or unrecognized codes by which our social life is regulated. While Cobbett's ultimate aim is to instruct rational actors in an unfolding political drama, Ruskin's view of constrained individuality seems to leave his readers no role at all. If Cobbett's confessional displays illustrate the self-mastery necessary to learn the codes and use them, Ruskin's dissolution leaves him wandering "listlessly, about the room," going nowhere (27 : 515).

Ruskin openly mocks the sort of heroic individualism of an account like Cobbett's. Mimicking popular self-help manuals that perpetuated such tales of the self-made man, Ruskin suggests that the title of his letters might be translated as "How you may make your fortune, or mar it" (28 : 107). Unlike conventional *Bildung* narratives, which traced a path of spiritual and material progress, Ruskin's scattered confessions lead to no definite destination. The constant disruptions of his narrative by the "Third Fors"—chance or Fate—show how little control individuals have over the course of their lives. "By the adoption of the title of 'Fors,'" he writes, "I meant . . . to indicate the desultory and accidental character of the work" (29 : 315). This "accidental character" describes both the unplotted course of his arguments and the seemingly plotless autobiography that drives them.

Cobbett's incidental tales of self in the *Political Register* evoke the conventions of the eighteenth-century picaresque novel, where accidentality shifts the emphasis from conscious artistic representation to faithful mimesis. His confessional spontaneity, that is, mimics the apparent plotlessness of everyday life. His tales of self are prompted in the *Register* by passing political events; like his journalistic commentary, they are presented as straightforward reportage. That there comes in the end to be a logical progression of Cobbett's confessions—we can see the consequent steps leading from plough-boy to public personality—clinches the case for his political theory. Polity is a kind of collective, rational *Bildung*, a progression from uncivilized man to consensual citizen. His seemingly undirected discourse falls naturally into a causal narrative not because he plans it but because it simply records the natural history of political life.

Ruskin's plotless letters also purport to reveal a kind of natural law. But that law is not hidden under the surface play of his text: it resembles the surface play of the text. There is no progressive narrative because for Ruskin we do not make our own way in the world. Our "fortune" is controlled by an "irresistible power" that, as the image of the title implies, "driv[es] the iron home with hammer-stroke, so that nothing shall be moved" (27:230, 231). Despite what we would like to believe about the consequence of our actions, there is, Ruskin explains, a "startlingly separate or counter ordinance of good and evil—one to this man, and the other to that,—ordinance which is entirely beyond our control." We think of ourselves as actors when, in fact, we are more like spectators to a political drama largely beyond our control.

In letter 39 Ruskin illustrates this point in a way that challenges a number of contemporary constructions of authority. The letter begins in the familiar mode of autobiographical narration: "On a foggy forenoon, two or three days ago, I wanted to make my way" (28:48). What we have here, he seems to indicate, is a short tale of self-development. What we quickly learn, however, is the difficulty, if not impossibility of "making one's way." By the end of this inaugural sentence Ruskin warns us that he may not even clear the first hurdle. He gets caught up in—as the next few paragraphs get caught up in—the problem of "how . . . to get past whatever is in front of him."

What follows is an apparent digression—"by the way," Ruskin in-serts—about how to figure the shortest route to the destination Ruskin heads for at the outset of the story. He makes mathematical calcula-tions, draws an illustrative diagram of the route, and talks of making the students of the future St. George's school trace the "actual" road with "actual" carts. Once the story resumes, however, we learn that, unlike conventional heroes of *Bildung* narratives, Ruskin has "gained no material advantage" from his careful effort to "move on . . . an economically drawn line" (28:49). His journey ends, at least momentarily, in a "dead pause" (28:50).

This brief "by way," in fact, broaches the epistemological problem that provides the one link in what is a particularly fragmented letter. Like the coachman with whom he supposedly argues about the shortest route, Ruskin constructs his own version of the "hypothenuse" of the area he means to traverse (28:48). This misspelling (not uncommon in the pe-riod) brings into play both the geometrical figure and the logical ruse. We tend to construct our experience, Ruskin implies, as if it were a mathematical straight line. We proceed, as he does at the beginning of his journey, on the hypothesis that we move from the point A to the point C represented on his sketch. But this "self-abstraction" (28:49), this habit of construing ourselves *as* purposive selves apart from the contingencies of our journeys, leads us to the dead end Ruskin finds himself in on this particular foggy afternoon. There, signs hawking boots replace the vital presence of a shoemaker (28:50). Seeing ourselves as self-contained units of value turns us from human laborers into something resembling John Stuart Mill's definition of the product of labor, which Ruskin dismissively quotes: a "utility fixed and embodied in a material object" (27:399).[34]

In the same paragraph Ruskin also allies this view of self with the materialism of post-Darwinian science. Near the shoeshop is an empty building marked "by the sign of the 'Hôtel de l'Union des Peuples'" (28:50). The French designation links this letter to Ruskin's arguments earlier in *Fors* that the rhetoric of the French Commune and of related English republican movements simply incorporates the atomistic assump-tions of contemporary capitalism (see, e.g., letter 7). In place of a scene of human exchange, which the sign would suggest, a note on the shop-front indicates that the only thing to be exchanged here is "bœuf." This is the first of a series of substitutions in the letter of animal for human imagery. As Ruskin notes a few pages later, what seems a metaphorical slight of hand had been widely accepted as a literal correspondence in late Victorian scientific discourse. This was the logical conclusion of the enlightenment effort to construe individuals as empirical objects. There was no difference between humans and beasts in the biological determinism of writers like Huxley: both were represented as "carnivorous" creatures driven by evolutionary self-interest, fighting to consume before being consumed (28:53).[35]

Ruskin touches on this analogy throughout the letter, ultimately reinterpreting it in light of the constitutive self sketched out elsewhere in the series. In the translation of one of Gotthelf's tales with which he ends letter 39, he comes back to the substitution of cow for people in the shopfront advertisement. In this case, the beast stands for the woman who will become the wife of Hansli, the broom-maker, whom he chooses to marry precisely because she proves she can help him draw his cart like the cow his widowed mother prays God will send him. This, Ruskin says in the deliberately provocative last line of the letter, is "a final definition of proper wifely quality" (28:61). The surprising truth of the materialist view of human nature as Ruskin reveals it here is that we are determined, but not in the sense that the progressive evolutionary narrative has led us to expect. As the story of Hansli's perpetual journeys to and from the market town demonstrates, the pattern of our lives is to move not forward but merely back and forth in the same track. In this sense, Hansli and his wife *are* beasts of burden, fated to pull their cart, to accept their place without complaint.

What does distinguish them from such beasts is not a superior rationality. All of the characters in this story are portrayed as remarkably simple creatures. Hansli's superior quality, at least in Ruskin's translation, is that he "saw himself" (28:56). Ruskin renders "se revit" from the original French as "reviewed himself," instead of what would have seemed the more appropriate choice in context, "found himself at his cart again."[36] As he explains in a footnote, the latter would have brought into play an element of "surprise, or discovery," which is absent "in the doing once again what is done every week." Like Ruskin's artist and scientist, what Hansli does is not to discover something new or original but to represent anew what is already familiar: he "reviewed himself, literally." Like Ruskin the narrator of this letter, he "contemplates himself" in the course of his journey.

The result is not the kind of self-abstraction Ruskin mocks at the opening of the letter. What triggers this moment of self-representation in a character who is shown in earlier parts of the tale to be markedly un- aware of himself and his situation is not an illusion of independence. It is precisely Hansli's recognition of his dependence on the girl who helps him pull his cart that makes him see himself in human terms, as a potential husband, as more than a creature who pulls a load. Hansli suddenly real- izes that (in the words of Ruskin's title for this letter), "The cart goes better so." He does not get ahead by means of this realization: the cart simply goes "better," not "farther." He learns to construct a relational narrative of his situation (which he tells to his mother), to see himself in terms of a larger network of meanings and values.

Hansli's ability to see himself illustrates the difference between Cobbett's and Ruskin's instructional pamphlets. Where Cobbett's readers are put in the position of rational actors in the political drama, Ruskin's are more like spectators. We have little individual control over the course of events, Ruskin illustrates in his version of the tale, but we do have control over the way that we see them. We can make our actions matter, that is, not in the illusory sense of cause and effect, but in the sense that they signify within a recognizable framework of value. Even conven- tional Christianity, Ruskin argues in this letter, succumbs to the false logic of cause and effect: one does good in this world in order to get ahead in the next.

If Cobbett's disjointed method in the *Register* attempts to disguise representation as mimesis, the fragmentation in *Fors* reverses this effect. As in letter 39, the constantly shifting perspective of his pamphlets em- phasizes the ongoing process of representation. Letter 39 starts with past- tense narration of an event, moves to a present-tense aside, resumes the narrative, shifts to impersonal argument, and ends in translation. These abortive efforts at consequential narrative suggest the impossibility of cre- ating a finished abstraction, of constructing self-enclosed representations. The seamless story, as Ruskin shows in the central section of the letter, works only in the theater. The "cheerful state of things which the spectators . . . entirely applaud" in the afternoon pantomime "must nec- essarily be interrupted always by the woeful interlude of the outside world" (28:51).

At issue is not the difference between life on the stage and the life of the streets. "It appears to me not of much moment which we choose to call Reality," Ruskin writes. "Both are equally real." In either case, we are operating on the level of conventions of representation. But if, as in the conventions of the pantomimes Ruskin watches, we believe our destiny is the "happily ever after" of fairy tales, we simply write out of the picture what does not conform to our individual desires. As he leaves the theater, Ruskin remarks that "nobody cares to look at" the street children who do not figure in their self-centered narratives. To proceed as if we really were individual actors in a drama that revolved around us is to behave in practice like "carnivorous" beasts (28:53).

Giving up the center stage—abandoning the myth of the "punctual" self around which the world revolves—does not entail giving up our aspiration to lead meaningful lives. Rather, it involves closer attention to how we make meaning. Morality is not a matter of works, as in the evangelical Christianity Ruskin dismisses in this letter. Rightly understood it is a matter of words. To be moral—that is, to act in relation to human community rather than in accordance with biological drives— is to recognize our fundamental interdependence, to learn to orient ourselves within meaningful communities of discourse. What holds us together both as individuals and as a society is not that there really is a coherent center, but that we constantly engage in the effort to imagine such a center. The merely formal closure of Ruskin's letters with the convention of personal signature does not function as an ironic gesture, as it might first appear. It is in fact a sign of our continuing optimism, of our ability to proceed in good faith that our message will make meaning, that it will signify a space that comes to stand for a self.

Ruskin's staging of personality in *Fors Clavigera* ultimately conforms, then, neither to the indulgent egoism of the aesthete nor to the insistent empiricism of contemporary scientific and academic discourse. He attempts to exhibit instead an alternative position in the critical debates of the period. In the terms of those debates, it might be described as a kind of disinterested interest. Ruskin envisions, in the manner of Arnold, a critical perch from which one might view particular, parochial opinions. We *can* learn to recognize the codes that make us, but we cannot fly free of them. Actual disinterested would be blindness, not insight: one cannot see outside "figurative perceptions."

Acknowledging our participation in a community of representations helps us to recognize what Ruskin terms in a seemingly paradoxical note in his own copy of letter 39, the difference between "Theatric true life" and the "practical false" world of Victorian science and political economy (28:48n). There is, he emphasizes, no neutral spectator in the drama of representation. As Michael Fried has put it, one cannot represent the perspective of a "beholder *tout court*," of "spectatorship as such": one can only work "within the primary material of his own spectatorhood." In *Fors Clavigera* Ruskin can represent only through a perspective constructed by the conventions of autobiography, of political reportage, of historical narrative. "No quality of *Fors* is more remarkable than its disregard of the conventional boundaries separating the public from the private," John Rosenberg has remarked.[37] But such a transgression should not be mistaken for unchecked confessional impulse. Ruskin's letters recast romantic individuality as it had been formulated in the *Political Register* and *The Friend*. The individual voice here, as in Coleridge, is fundamentally social, but for a rather different reason than the one the earlier writer had posited. *Fors Clavigera* exactly reverses Coleridge's argument in *The Friend* that the individual is at the foundation of the public sphere. Instead, Ruskin suggests that the public sphere underwrites even our most private experience.

If there is no disinterested individual observer, there is by the same token no enlightened, rational society deracinated from its traditions. In subsequent chapters, I trace this analogy through Ruskin's organic nationalism and allegorical historicism in *Fors Clavigera*. Of interest here is the way Ruskin implicates social knowledge in conventions of artistic and linguistic representation. To argue with his scientifically minded contemporaries that "modern politics resolve themselves into the struggle between knowledge and tradition" was to generate bad social theory from flawed epistemology.[38] Ruskin's counterpoint to this Lockean proposition is not simply to insist on the vitality of an existing tradition, although he certainly does that. Rather, his larger concern is to pose a corollary to his theory of the inherently moral and political nature of art. In other words, not only is the aesthetic always already ideological: ideology is always already aesthetic. A social system is not an effort of consensual will, but a sort of communal pathetic fallacy: it is an affective projection, not an objective entity. It has power only insofar as the image of it can, as Ruskin says in his discussion of the pathetic fallacy in *Modern Painters*, "throw [a man] off his balance," that is, decenter him, destabilize the imperial cogito through an emotional impulse "by which his poor human capacity of thought should be conquered" (5 : 209).

In *Fors Clavigera* Ruskin collapses the distinction between public and private, a move he made as well in his first letters to working men, *Time and Tide*. In the earlier work the insulated speaker had stood as the type of the self-sufficient, model citizen in Ruskin's new world order. The public sphere was simply the aggregate of private, domesticated individuals. In *Fors* this relationship is turned inside out. The result is not only to reveal that the individual is always contingent on the social. More importantly, Ruskin points out that both self and society are powerful acts of imagination, not of ratiocination. The decentered, shifting perspective of his letters should be read not as a lapse into pathetic fallacy but as a deliberate foregrounding of that condition. Perspective and understanding are made contingent in a way that the critic in *Modern Painters* had not considered. Making representations in the manner of the epistolary writer of *Fors* is more than an indulgent pastime. It is the defining activity of personal and political life.

III

Motherhood of the Dust: Figuring National Affiliation

IN *FORS CLAVIGERA* Ruskin dramatizes our participation in a community of representations. The letter writer continually diverted by fate illustrates the futility of rational self-control in a world governed and constrained by inherited conventions. Such a view of the self challenges easy oppositions between clearheaded reason and timeworn custom, scientific discovery and inherited myth. Knowledge, Ruskin demonstrates, is always implicated in social traditions. The urgent task of political education is not to enlighten individuals. It is rather, in the terms of Ruskin's metaphor elaborated in the last chapter, to spin a web of representation that encompasses contradictory interpretations of modern experience.

Casting the individual citizen as a spectator rather than an actor in the political arena, Ruskin attempts to stage in *Fors Clavigera* a compelling drama of national *Bildung*. As Elizabeth Helsinger has noted in her discussion of his "politics of viewing," Ruskin's spectator had been figured in distinctively nationalist terms as early as *Modern Painters*. Ruskinian nationalism, in Helsinger's account, is a loose association of solitary male viewers for whom aesthetic experience would be a form of "physical and mental self-control." A cohesive English society might be forged through a kind of aestheticized Protestantism. Helsinger characterizes Ruskin's ideal citizen as "a student who comes to books or pictures for solitary self-improvement." She thus locates Ruskin's nationalist program within a recognizable Burkean tradition in which aesthetic appreciation serves as a way of internalizing social constraints. A "national subjectivity constructed in the viewing of art" would produce orderly, self-regulating citizens, whose experience of "readerly viewing"—"silent, serious, and essentially solitary"—should forestall the sort of unruly communal behavior occasionally exhibited by the working class.[1]

Many of Ruskin's "Letters to the Workmen and Labourers of Great Britain," with their detailed exercises in viewing photographs, paintings, and architectural detail, might seem to continue this brand of civic aesthetics. Yet as I have argued in chapter 2, *Fors Clavigera* challenges discourses of radical individualism that transform spectatorship into pure subjectivity. Ruskin critiques in his letters the kind of self-help mentality Helsinger describes. He mocks the spectator/reader who believes in the efficacy of rational self-control. An "enlightened" citizen, paradoxically, would be one who had rejected as illusory the enlightenment faith in national progress and self-improvement. One might speak of national subjects, but not as articulated in the terms of conventional bourgeois rhetoric. Helsinger contends that Ruskin, worried over the threat the irrational female poses to such rhetoric, constrains her participation in "national subjectivity."[2] In *Fors* political participation by any group or individual is similarly constrained. Ruskin overtly rejects social models dependent on privatized value in favor of a communal vision that equates subjectivity with subjection of individual will. His view of polity as a powerful act of imagination, not a product of rational consensus, had significant repercussions for late Victorian theories of nationality.

The authoritarian implications of Ruskin's nationalist ideals are spelled out explicitly in his aphorisms on education. "Moral education," he explains in *Fors*, "begins in making the creature to be educated, clean, and obedient. This must be done thoroughly, and at any cost, and with any kind of compulsion rendered necessary by the nature of the animal, be it dog, child, or man" (28:655). The results of this compulsory morality will be in "making the creature . . . serviceable to other creatures"; the "creature" must be "made to do its work with delight, and thoroughly" (28:655−56). The purpose of the ideal community sketched out in *Fors Clavigera*, the Guild of St. George, is in part to exercise these educational strictures on a new generation of citizens. The children in the Guild will be inculcated in "the habit of instant, finely accurate, and totally unreasoning obedience" to their parents and teachers (28:20). Ruskin purges the language of individual rights and rational choice from his utopia.

He excludes as well the discourses of "science, . . . economic arrangements, or commercial enterprise" that had made the talk of reason and rights common Victorian coin (33:47). The ideal education that

Ruskin outlines for his potential pupils is remarkable less for what it includes than for what it rejects. St. George's schools will be marked by "the total exclusion of the stimulus of competition in any form or disguise" (29:496). Arithmetic will never be taught, as the "importance at present attached to it"—the belief that individuals can self-realize through commercial success—"is a mere filthy folly." There will be no "merely descriptive" scientific books in the library, nor any maps detailing the path of railways and "the fungus growths of modern commercial towns" (29:503, 505). In an atmosphere of "shepherded peace" (29:528), children would soon learn to forget about the evils of society outside the home and the classroom, where the values of the home would be reinforced.

The domesticated morality that defines the Guild does more than reinforce the importance of home values for national health. It melds public and private virtue into a new kind of nationalistic rhetoric. Public value is not privatized, as it is in most contemporary conservative and liberal theory. The traditional realm of the private—irrational, imaginative, emotional—becomes the province of the state. Ruskin's rejection of the new Victorian landscape motivates his creation of a social topos not contained by or within existing boundaries. His utopian community figures the nation as a state of mind.

The modern idea of the nation-state as a notional entity, a communal fiction rather than an actual condition, had been memorably played out in the American and French Revolutions. On the one hand, these imagined communities configured the citizen as an autonomous actor liberated from local circumstances.[3] On the other, this deracinated everyman was in truth no man. The citizen's *Bildung* was a pattern book ideal unaffected by lived experience. This troubled legacy of enlightenment nationalism, which simultaneously constructs and deconstructs citizens as individual subjects, has preoccupied modern political theorists. In the nineteenth century John Stuart Mill performed a memorable and influential balancing act between nation as nomocracy and teleocracy—as legal contract among equal individuals, and as instrumental authority in which citizens were a means to achieving communal ends. Despite his early admiration for Mill's committed individualism (see, e.g., 7:229), Ruskin had by the 1870s revived authoritarian features of enlightenment thought, features that offered an inside critique of Millite liberalism. If

Mill only hesitantly outlines a "perfectionist teleology of progress" that might outweigh individual interests, Ruskin embraces the utopian potential of communal narratives defined apart from existing interests.[4] A newly fabricated rhetoric of Englishness, like the imagined revolutionary communities of American and French experience, could redeem the errors of Victorian life.

Refiguring national geography as topoi—that is, moving from definitions of Englishness that depend on locality to those that derive from the "figurative perceptions" described in chapter 2—marks a subtle shift in Ruskin's social theorizing. Statements in other of his works about the associations between nature and national sentiment are clearly derived from romantic ideals of social cohesiveness. In *Modern Painters* volume 3, Ruskin articulated an unmistakably Wordsworthian vision of organic community.[5] Man and nature, he explained in an essay on "The Moral of Landscape," are a part of one creation: "the simplest forms of nature are strangely animated by the sense of the Divine presence; the trees and flowers seem all, in a sort, children of God; and we ourselves, their fellows, made out of the same dust, and greater than they only in having a greater portion of the Divine power exerted on our frame, and all the common uses and palpably visible forms of things, become subordinate in our minds to their inner glory,—to the mysterious voices in which they talk to us about God, and the changeful and typical aspects by which they witness to us of holy truth, and fill us with obedient, joyful, and thankful emotion" (5:386). Through "clear and calm beholding" of visible natural forms, individual perception is transformed into spiritual communion. Careful observation of a particular scene yields a general understanding of vital human relations.

Spiritual naturalism informs Ruskin's account of social relations in *The Bible of Amiens* as well. But locality is no longer just a springboard for an ideal of community. If in the passage from *Modern Painters* the "changeful and typical aspects" of a specific place lead us to unchanging, universal emotions, here particularity in landscape shapes particularity in feeling. Nature breeds a specifically national spirit: "No matter who rules a country, no matter what it is officially called, or how it is formally divided. . . . The people that are born on it are *its* people, be they a thousand times again and again conquered, exiled, or captive . . . and, although just laws, maintained whether by the people or their conquerors, have always the appointed good and strength of justice, nothing is permanently helpful to any race or condition of men but the spirit that is in their own hearts, kindled by the love of their native land" (33:93–94). The cohesiveness of a nation is shown to be organic not merely in its internal relations, but in a much more literal sense: it comes from the soil. Ruskin's "love of their native land" has a close equivalent in the writings of early nineteenth-century German *volkisch* nationalists, whose work had again become current in the 1870s and 1880s: *Vaterlandslieber.*[6]

A version of organic nationalism is also apparent, as Helsinger notes, in the memorialized landscapes of Ruskin's 1870 inaugural Slade lecture.[7] Yet Ruskin refigures national affiliation through a new metaphor of ideal community: "Motherhood of the dust" (20:36). This striking image does connect with conventional strains of English agrarian nationalism, in which national identity is grounded in a pastoral landscape. Elaborating his maternal community by reference to the goddess Demeter, Ruskin gestures toward such an idea, but only to lay it to rest. His is the goddess not only of bountiful harvests and beneficent nature but of decay and destruction.[8] Nationality does not spring organically from healthy soil; rather, it is built on the "waste ground" of existing communities (20:42). Its "ghostly inscription" marks out a landscape that "none may remove" and "none may pollute" precisely because it does not literally exist, except as a landscape of the mind (20:36). Unlike the "mysterious voices" of nature in the passage it recalls from *Modern Painters*, this floating signifier is not animated by a living scene. Anyplace, Ruskin tells his audience of young imperialists, can be reconfigured as England because England cannot be equated with an actual location or race.

Ruskin echoes here important late nineteenth-century formulations of nationality. Europe and America in the 1870s saw the beginnings of an intellectual reaction against classical liberalism.[9] Emerging ideas of the modern state, formulated in response to economic depression and increasing political participation by new social groups, moved away from notions of rights and rational association. The nation was not a consensual contract or a physical location, one influential theory ran, but a matter of "the spirit . . . a spiritual principle . . . a spiritual family" that resisted demystification.[10] Nation as embodied in myth, symbol and rite—rather than as represented in a narrative of progress and civilization—offered the possibility of communities cemented "beyond the confines of rational consciousness."[11] This portable topography was auspiciously inaugurated on the continent in the nationalist rhetoric surrounding the Franco-Prussian War.

Ruskin's Guild of St. George was fashioned against this dramatic backdrop. It fleshes out his image of the "Motherhood of the dust," identifying nationality as irrational, community not as association, but as nonindividuation. His childlike citizen, a descendent of Rousseau's, stubbornly opposes developing theories of race and civilization that supported a very different national ideal. While the new discipline of sociology provided a terminology for understanding the state as a merely bureaucratic instrument smoothing over essentially private transactions, Ruskin insisted on an authoritarian rhetoric that made the private an inherently public concern. Moreover, it was a rhetoric with unmistakable contemporary resonances. Germany's rise as an imperial power gave new force to his paternalistic vision of molding citizens in "the interests of England" (29:128).

Ruskin consolidated his nationalist musings through an extended framework of commentary on current events. Both in *Fors* and in the 1873 reissue of *The Crown of Wild Olive*, he put forward his version of the contemporary European "struggle . . . between the newly-risen power of democracy and the apparently departing power of feudalism" (18:494). The lecture added to the new edition of *The Crown of Wild Olive*, "The Future of England," might have been dismissed as a merely nostalgic paean to feudalism when it was first delivered in 1869. The new appendix on *Frederick the Great* might have been similarly discounted, in other circumstances, as a belated endorsement of Carlyle's laborious biography. But Ruskin gives both essays critical edge by engaging feudal history in the effort to explain "the necessities of the time" (18:515). Germany's victories in the Franco-Prussian War made Carlyle's feudal tale urgently interesting. In *Fors* Ruskin cited *Frederick* at length to give historical perspective to recent skirmishes (27:46–47). Writing to C. E. Norton, he remarked on the sudden political currency of Carlyle's work. Carlyle "did his Friedrich exactly at the right time," he insisted, in a challenge to Norton's support of France in 1870. With reference to *Frederick*, the war clearly could be read as another chapter in the contest between the Prussians' "Personal Hereditary Feudal government as stern as Barbarossas [sic]" as chronicled by Carlyle, and the "purest and intensest republicanism" of the French (*CRN* 207). France's defeat, and the abortive republican experiment of the Paris Commune, stood as salient

examples of the potential weakness of a divided democracy. As Ruskin
wrote another correspondent a few months after the failure of the Commune, a resurrection of the principles of a German-style "Feudal System" was "at this crisis, the only chance . . . of saving England from
revolution." [12]

Ruskin announced his support of the Prussians at the outset of the
war. In letters to the *Daily Telegraph* on 7 and 8 October 1870, he declared
his admiration for "one of the truest Monarchies and schools of honour
and obedience yet organized under heaven" (34:501). If Prussia would
offer France "unconditional armistice" under "terms that France can accept with honour," it would "bear such rank among the nations as never
yet shone on Christian history" (34:502).[13] The qualification is crucial.
Written a month earlier, Ruskin's praise for Prussia would have echoed
public sentiment in England. It was precisely King Wilhelm's refusal to
accept the French offer of peace without significant reparations that had
turned the tide of English opinion. As one popular account of the war
put it, what had seemed at first "the legitimate purpose of self-protection"
was now revealed as "a settled resolve to humble France and extend the
boundaries of Germany." [14] A local territorial struggle in which the British government remained resolutely neutral was quickly elevated in the
press to a battle between empires. Germany, warned one newspaper correspondent who had traveled with its armies and had formerly admired
their "valour," was at this juncture driven "solely from a passion for nationality": advancing the cause of the "Teutons" had become "a religious
duty." [15]

The British press reacted sharply to what was now seen as a war that
would decide, as the French Revolution had done nearly a century earlier, the prevailing definition of the modern European nation state. "The
system of European policy has been destroyed," the *Edinburgh Review* lamented. Regulation by law, by mutual consent, and by historical alliance
were swept aside by the compelling example of government by well-
drilled force. "The boasted unification" of Germany, the *Pall Mall Gazette* declared, "is not, it seems, to be union, but subordination." The
new empire displayed the power of the Teutonic insistence on feudal
obedience. The "probable consequences in the future" for other European polities "now imperiously demand attention," one writer warned.[16]

Ruskin's defense of German feudalism places his own communal vision at the center of this growing anxiety about new formulations of nationality. Although he condemned in *Fors Clavigera* the conduct of Bismarck and his armies, his adherence to the German nationalist style never faltered.[17] Juxtaposing passages from Carlyle's *Frederick the Great* with accounts of the European crisis, Ruskin constructs in *Fors* an alternative modern European history, one rejecting the centrality of the French Revolution, following instead the gradual development of what he calls "the root of modern German power" (27:47). He carefully grafts discussions of his Guild of St. George onto this larger narrative. Through the organization of his guild, which follows closely the principles of nationalism outlined in his 1873 appendix on *Frederick*, he reconstructs in miniature what he called there the "Dawn of Order in Christian Germany" (18:517). As Ruskin wrote a Liverpool journalist in 1870, the outcome of the Franco-Prussian War might "render it possible to do what otherwise it would have been vain to think of yet—take up the sixth volume of Carlyle's *Frederick*, sift out of it the great principles of government, which have made Prussia what she is, and ally a few of our workmen . . . into a nucleus to be gradually enlarged for simple obedience to these laws among themselves" (37:15).[18] Ruskin's vision of an orderly community of workers gathered on Prussian principles takes shape in the early pages of *Fors Clavigera*. "Happy the nation," he says, quoting Carlyle's biography, which is schooled in strict obedience; "it advances steadily, with consciousness or not, in the way of well-doing; and, after long times, the harvest of this diligent sowing becomes manifest to the Nation, and to all Nations" (27:47; *WTC* 12:342). This agricultural metaphor stands behind the reclamation work of the first Guild communities. Their harvest would be both literal and figurative. Not only would they produce crops from waste or fallow land, they would show the fruits of cooperative effort under strict routine. Their simple manual labor would be transformed into the "thoughtful labour of true education" through a public display of the "sweet order and obedience of life." Such communities would provide a counterexample to the "now widely and openly proclaimed design, of making the words 'obedience' and 'loyalty' to cease from the English tongue" (27:297).

Ruskin's organic, integrated model of English society superficially resembles the patriotic pictures of both Conservatives and Liberals, who in the 1870s appealed to "an unchanging England in the countryside to set against rising social unrest and foreign threats."[19] He certainly plays on a familiar English rhetoric of the rural in his discussions of the Guild of St. George, but his project is not simply to resurrect a "Merrie England" of self-sufficient peasants. Describing the ideal plot of land for his first experimental community, he says, "I would rather it should be poor": the object of the community is "to work for the redemption of any desert land" (28:19), not to inhabit an already peopled landscape. This England, like the ghostly landscapes evoked in the inaugural Slade lecture, is utterly changed, denatured, reduced to a wasteland. The members of the Guild are to be like "settlers" who will relandscape according to the now alien principles of "servitude to the will of another" (28:21). The "commandments" of this new community, he proposes in the charged military language of the moment, are to be "veteran soldiers." In Ruskin's feudal vision, rural England does not act as a comforting image of order against the foreign threat of German nationalist ideas. Such ideas come to occupy the new English landscape.

In characterizing Ruskin's authoritarianism in this way I do not mean to propose a facile equation between his utopian ideals and the fascism of the coming century. Ruskin draws significantly on British utopian traditions of a very different cast of mind. Thus Francis Bacon's Calvinist vision of a community united in stewardship of the land, which Ruskin acknowledges in *Fors Clavigera* (see esp. 28:520), provides a ready "religious idiom" of *laborare est orare*.[20] The romantic feudalism of Walter Scott is also a frequent point of reference in discussions of the Guild: one of its principal objects, Ruskin wrote in a "Master's Report" to Guild members, was "the restoration, to such extent as might be possible . . . of . . . the feeling of a Scottish clansman to his chief, or of an old Saxon servant to his Lord" (30:94).[21] To read these remarks in the context of British reaction to the Franco-Prussian War, is, however, to suggest that feudalism would have been read very differently in the 1870s than earlier in the century when, for example, Carlyle wrote *Past and Present* or Disraeli sketched the outlines of Young England. The defeat of France in 1870 and the installation of Wilhelm I as Emperor of Germany in January 1871 instigated in England what Cecil Eby has called a "proliferating literature of invasion." Ruskin's military rhetoric astutely exploits this "epidemic of martial feeling" to which "nearly all young Englishmen were exposed."[22] His social ideal clearly addresses this transitional moment when the roots of nationalism were being reconsidered. Assimilating his position prematurely to the outcomes of the German imperial model would replicate the ahistorical leap that makes of his feudalism a simply nostalgic echo.

In their biographical readings of *Fors*, both Rosenberg and Sawyer have too quickly dismissed Ruskin's Guild as eccentrically nostalgic. My quarrel is not with the contention that Ruskin's feudalism conjoined public with private mythos: as Sawyer elegantly argues, "Ruskin had instinctively come to organize his experience around a few basic symbols," symbols that organized his social theories as well. The confrontation between Saint George and his dragon, for example, comes to stand for the perils of private as well as public life: "my mind so paralysed with disgust, sorrow, indignation, and weary sense of my own faults and miseries," Ruskin complains in an 1874 diary entry, "unfitting me sorely to cope with my dragon." But to read Ruskin's rhetoric primarily in terms of personal events occludes its engagement with vital public debates. Spear, who carefully historicizes Ruskin's practical experiments in the period, argues that "the Guild for all its medieval trappings did not look as absurd in its own time as it does today."[23] My argument here takes on Spear's qualifying phrase by suggesting that the "medieval trappings" should not, in contemporary context, be seen as mere costuming disguising the relevance of Ruskin's social theory.

To associate authoritarian notions like Ruskin's with a dead past was, in fact, a deliberate strategy of those who tried to shore up individualist theories of association in the period. This is strikingly evident in the first volume of Herbert Spencer's influential *Principles of Sociology* (1876). In spite of the force of the modern German example, Spencer places militant societies—that is, those held together by a strong state promoting compulsory cooperation—at the lowest stage in his progressive hierarchy of social development. At the other extreme is the deregulated industrialism of the classical liberal state. As the power of the state decays, Spencer argues, individual freedom flourishes. At the same time, the unity of the body politic (Spencer's metaphor) increases. Just as in a complex organism, so in a complex society the constituent parts become both increasingly discrete and interdependent: "The change from *homogeneity* to *heterogeneity* is multitudinously exemplified; up from the simple tribe, alike in all its parts, to the civilized nation . . . consolidated enough to hold together for a thousand years or more." The reference to tribal forms of society certainly would have been associated with modern Germany, as well as with the primitive societies described in British anthropological theory; the connection was current in European nationalist writing after the Franco-Prussian War.[24]

Spencer's treatise neatly polarizes what some British observers saw as a potent combination of military organization and industrialism in Bismarck's Germany. Public debate in the 1870s about compulsory national education, for example, was driven in part by a feeling that only a well-drilled workforce, "more orderly, more amenable to discipline, and much more intelligent," could ensure England's industrial competitiveness. As a leading industrialist put it in a lecture to the Birmingham and Midland Institute, compulsory education must be designed with constant reference to the question, "Whence the success which crowned the Prussian arms?"[25] Spencer opposed any such state interference in personal development, as he had made clear in *Social Statics* (1851), and, more strenuously, in *The Man versus the State* (1884). At a time when the liberal idea of the state looked particularly vulnerable, his evolutionary sociology gave it new theoretical ballast.

In *Fors Clavigera* Ruskin condemns social theorists who, with Spencer, would claim to provide scientific support for what he felt was failed ideology. In an open letter to Frederic Harrison printed as part of his June 1876 pamphlet, he lashes out against writers who promulgated notions about the "collected evolution" of the human race, as well as those who, following John Stuart Mill, charted its progress through the mechanisms of political economy (28:619).[26] Harrison's Comtean sociology, elaborated in *Order and Progress* (1875), enforced a hierarchy much like Spencer's. On a developmental scale beginning with irrational, childlike communities ruled necessarily by harsh discipline, industrial societies— in which rational citizens operated like "free shareholders"—represented the most evolved form of human association. In Harrison as in Spencer, industrialism and individualism were inextricably linked. Industry could only flourish as a "free co-operation of intelligent masses."[27] An authoritarian industrial society would be a horrible developmental freak that certainly could not survive.

Ruskin refracts this correspondence between individualism and industrialism in his counterimage of the state as corporation. His "company"—the name he originally proposed for the Guild—would be like the medieval knights of Sir John Hawkwood's "White Company": an organized military unit (27:16). Its members would be considered "free" not in the "present singular use of it respecting trade": "Only those soldiers and merchants are truly free," he says, "who fight and sell as their country needs, and bids them" (27:266–7). When for legal reasons Ruskin substituted "Guild" for "Company" in the name of his model society, he was careful to distinguish his project from existing forms of cooperative association.[28] In a brief nod to the history of trade guilds, he judged that "the real ground of their decay" as vital communities lay in their vestigial individualism. Separate guilds encouraged "selfishness and isolation," the mainsprings of competitive capitalism (29:147). What Ruskin envisioned was not a series of guilds in which "a body of tradesmen gathered for the promotion even of the honestest and usefullest trade." Rather, he hoped that the principle of "unity of effort" would permeate society, so that all citizens would feel themselves absorbed in the "interests of England." In this new nation-state, feudal "loyalty and obedience" would not be considered a thing of the past, but "virtues . . . capable of development" in modern industrial settings (29:148).

It was not the first time Ruskin had argued that martial virtues were the engine of social development. "The notion of Discipline and Interference" that "has hitherto knit the sinews of battle," he claimed in an 1857 lecture, "lies at the very root of all human progress and power" (16:26). His Manchester audience would not have missed this direct assault on the laissez-faire philosophy associated with their city. But Ruskin aims here at more than an economic policy. He targets those who would make the language of political economy not prescriptive but descriptive, turning a specific government policy into an objective account of natural law. Herbert Spencer memorably performs this move in *Social Statics* (1851), where he purports to describe the action of "a felicity-pursuing law, which never swerves for the avoidance of partial or temporary suffering. The poverty of the incapable, the distresses that come on the improvident, the starvation of the idle, and those shoulderings aside of the weak by the strong, which leave so many 'in shallows and in miseries' are the decrees of a large, far-seeing benevolence." The "conditions of human happiness" specified in Spencer's title depend on a strict observance of such decrees. Sympathy—an emotion based on a superficial understanding of social process—breeds philanthropy, defeating the natural selection that ensures species survival. In Spencer's evolutionary utopia, government, an increasingly useless appendage, will eventually wither away. Individuals in the new benevolent social order will "be quite self-sufficing . . . hav[ing] powers exactly commensurate with what ought to be done": they will "be organically moral."[29]

Spencer's stark picture of social process is reproduced in more nuanced tones in both Samuel Smiles's *Self-Help* (1859) and John Stuart Mill's *On Liberty* (1859). In each of these progressive tales, national redemption is achieved through the efforts of individuals. Like Spencer, Mill optimistically anticipates a society of self-sufficiently moral citizens with little need of external restraint. Ruskin, on the other hand, did not share their progressive Victorian faith in "character."[30] "Restraint (or the action of superior law)," he argued, promoted healthy society. Too great an emphasis on "character (or the action of inherent law)" reduced social relations to the level of animal instinct (8:250). Absolute liberty is "an attribute of the lower creatures"; what sets man apart from the animals "is his Restraint" (16:407). Unlike Mill and Spencer, Ruskin did not believe that encouraging an individual "to be that which he naturally is—to do just what he would spontaneously do" would produce social equilibrium.[31] Strong government was necessary to continually chastise and redirect raw instinct. "Wise laws and just restraints are to a noble nation," Ruskin asserted in 1858, "not chains, but chain mail—strength and defence" (16:407).

Liberals at midcentury saw government interference as a threat to individual development; Ruskin worried about the decay of national culture as a result of unlicensed individualism. This might not have been a popular argument in the days of prosperity and security. In the 1870s, as Britain stepped up its armaments in response to a possible German threat, Ruskin's martial images played on public preoccupations. A nation driven by dogged individualism was like a ship in a state of mutiny, he warned. "You are called into a Christian ship of war," prospective members of his Guild were advised; only "loyalty and obedience" to their common mission would keep the operation afloat (29:148). The atomistic language of classical political economy was inadequate for formulating a coherent national ideal. As Eric Hobsbawm has pointed out, Adam Smith intentionally forestalled the notion that markets could be conceived in national terms.[32] Only by abandoning "Economical Theology," Ruskin urged, would it be possible to elaborate a creed that put national interest ahead of personal gain (28:516).

Ruskin's paternalistic state, headed by a father/master to whom citizens gave "obedience . . . absolute, and without question" and to whom they would be "faithful to the uttermost" (28:649) derives in part from the metaphorical structure of the early church.[33] But his vision of a highly unified and collective polity eschews the Evangelical rhetoric that contributed to the Victorian notion of character. Individual will should not be at issue in educating future citizens, he argued, rejecting conventional religious and secular curricula. For the sake of the state a child should be made to "live a life which, whether it will or no, shall enforce honourable hope of continuing long in the land—whether of men or God" (28:255). The nobility of a nation, he contends in an extended discussion of the figure of Britannia, like the "nobility of Education" consists "in the rule over our Thoughts" (27:459). Strong polity is not the result of rational agreement, but of a national spirit, a communal pathetic fallacy by which the citizen's "poor human capacity of thought should be conquered" (5:209). The "breeding" of a vital race, Ruskin asserts, depends on "the habits *enforced* in youth: entirely excluding intellectual conclusion" (27:468). In a unified state, what matters is not that citizens rationally determine to do "a right thing," but rather that everyone is doing "a thing we entirely *suppose* to be right" according to the prevailing moral framework.

For a language adequate to describe this enforced morality of the common good, Ruskin turns to the ancients. He seizes the political moment to revive the "moral idiom" of classical polity, "in which extreme socialization was natural," and in which individual will simply does not exist apart from the larger interests of the state.[34] A comparison of his translation of a passage from Plato's *Laws* with Jowett's 1871 translation highlights Ruskin's insistence on the difference between modern and classical ideas of citizenship. Plato's definition of the citizen's education reads, in Jowett's version: "that training which is given by suitable habits to the first instincts of virtue in children;—when pleasure, and friendship, and pain, and hatred, are rightly implanted in souls not yet capable of understanding the nature of them, and who find them, after they have attained reason, to be in harmony with her. This harmony of the soul, when perfected, is virtue; but the particular training in respect of pleasure and pain . . . may be separated off; and in my view, will be rightly called education."[35] Children's naturally virtuous instincts are carefully cultivated until they are old enough to understand why these instincts are important to the maintenance of the community as a whole. Jowett's rendition of Plato fits comfortably with Victorian social theories, like those of Spencer and Mill, that stress the importance for social harmony of self-regulating individuals.

Ruskin's emphasis falls elsewhere, as he is quick to point out in his retranslation of the passage in *Fors Clavigera*. Jowett misunderstands Plato's "discipline of childhood," Ruskin asserts: the point at which he begins his process of "training" should in fact be regarded as the end "result of education" (29:237). In other words, children do not already possess, *in potentia*, proper instincts that need to be controlled and guided. Those instincts are the *product* of education: the point of the disciplinary process is to instill them in the first place.

Ruskin renders Plato's definition of education as "that first virtue which can be attained by children, when pleasure and liking, and pain and disliking, are properly implanted in their souls while yet they cannot understand why; but so that when they get the power of reasoning, its perfect symphony may assure them that they have been rightly moralled into their existing morals" (29:237). In this translation nature is not perfected by nurture. Virtue is implanted in souls that are not merely immature, as in Jowett's translation—the children are "not yet capable of understanding the nature" of their instincts—but stripped of rational agency—"while yet they cannot understand why." In Ruskin's version, what children cannot grasp is not the importance of their natural propensities but rather the process by which they are made virtuous in the first instance: the point of "the discipline of childhood" is to forestall critical dissent. At the age of reason, in Jowett's Plato, children find that the instincts cultivated in them are "in harmony with" their rational powers because the process of education has led them to behave in the way they would naturally have behaved had they understood their early actions. Reason, therefore, confirms their upbringing. In Ruskin's interpretation of the passage, "the power of reasoning" itself is dependent on that early discipline. Ruskin retranslates harmony, which implies a joining together of distinct elements, that is, reason and passion, as "symphony" (in fact,

Jowett had changed Plato's meaning: the original word is *symphonia*). Reason works well, is pleasing, *appears* harmonious, because children have been disciplined correctly. For Ruskin reason is not a faculty separate from inculcated morals: children have been "moralled" so that there can be no contrast between thought and feeling.

The change from education as training of natural virtues in Jowett to education as the process of inculcating virtue in Ruskin signals a shift from a morality that originates with individuals to one that originates with social authority. Following the early Greek writers, Ruskin emphasizes not the rights of the individual citizen in the *polis* but the community's willing recognition of and submission to legitimate authority.[36] "We Communists of the old school," he declares in *Fors*, unlike the "baby Communists" of the Paris Commune, "know, and have known, what Communism is—for our fathers knew it, and told us, three thousand years ago" (27:117). The reference is never fully explained in subsequent letters; however, an outline in his 1869–71 diary locates the "moral idea" of ancient Greek communities in the "*Pride* of Fatherhood with Citizenship making state our family."[37] The "chief concern" of these "thorough-going Communists" was to discover those "wiser and of better make than the rest, and to get them . . . to rule over us, and teach us how to behave, and make the most of what little good is in us" (27:119–20). This simple code of conduct sounds more like a prescription for the nursery than for the nation; it is the voice of the man of the old guard giving the "baby Communists" a political lesson. "Learn to obey good laws," he concludes his diatribe on communism, "and in a little while you will reach the better learning—how to obey good Men, who are living, breathing, unblinded law" (27:131).

This maxim, too, is a bit of paternalistic wisdom, which would be echoed in Ruskin's recalling his obedience to his parents as to a "helpful law" that was followed "without idea of resistance." For Ruskin, the child was truly the father of the political man: its self-abnegation in the face of a stronger and more developed will was a model for the citizen's submission to vested authority. He exemplifies this correspondence through autobiographical anecdote, metaphorically linked to the military rhetoric of his utopian society. "I obeyed word, or lifted finger, of father or mother," he remembers in the June 1875 number of *Fors Clavigera*, "simply as a ship her helm; not only without idea of resistance, but receiving the direction as a part of my own life and force, and helpful law, as necessary to me in every moral action as the law of gravity in leaping" (28:350). At a time when he complained to C. E. Norton that he had "been an infinite ass to let myself drift as I have," and to Carlyle that he was feeling "more than usually helpless," the absolute authority in his early life seemed an oasis of security (*CRN* 352, *CCR* 224). When England looked to Ruskin to be adrift as well, the strong patriarchal structure of ancient polity seemed equally appealing. For him the modern English temper could be summed up in the phrase "I must do what *I* think right" (28:342). Just as in his letter to Norton he doubted his own judgment, so in *Fors* he expressed his misgivings about a democratic nation swayed by those with "the conscience of an ass" (28:342). "Obey *something*," he offers as both a public and a personal maxim in the number in *Fors* in which he considers his upbringing, "and you will have a chance some day of finding out what is best to obey" (28:343).

Shifting seamlessly in this letter between descriptions of private experience and of political life, Ruskin subtly translates the assumptions of ancient polity into a modern idiom. Contemporary sociologists used the terminology of developmental psychology to chart the history of social organization from childlike dependence to complex, individualistic communities.[38] Ruskin, however, makes the psychological dependency of childhood the defining experience of social life in any age. Just as a child can exist only in relation to "some creature larger than himself" (28:343), so the citizen exists only in reference to some larger community. Like his parents' strict discipline, a rigid social structure acts as a gravitational law orienting "every moral action." An ethical idiom in which individual will is not suppressed because it never develops should not, as progressive theorists suggested, be consigned to a remote social past. As Ruskin dramatizes through the meandering, confessional style of *Fors*, individuals left to their own devices have no moorings outside the nuclear family. In the terms of his extended metaphor in *Fors* for effective community—a disciplined ship of war—they are simply "cast out . . . into the world" and left to "drift with its elements" (28:352).

The importance of the German militarist model as Ruskin elaborates it in *Fors* is that it demonstrates the power of a national ideal articulated in reference to the individual's fundamental psychological dependence. The success of the German armies should not be attributed to Bismarck, he argues in letter 40. Rather, it was the result of institutionalizing "sacred domestic life" through public policy (28:68). The phrase is illustrated by a little domestic idyll from a correspondent's letter—a hearth-side scene of a German mother and daughter peacefully spinning (28:66–67). Such a scene might seem no different from the sentimentalized private sphere familiar to his Victorian readers, but Ruskin quickly distinguishes the foreign significance of this example. Behind the sentimental veneer stands the harsh social discipline initiated by the father of Frederick the Great, who would "like to have shot" his own son "as a disobedient and dissipated character" (28:68). Carlyle's "great Drill-sergeant of the Prussian nation" made strong authority the leading principle of national life. The orderly obedience of German citizens produced an empire which "in peace, is entirely happy . . . and, in war, irresistible" (28:68).[39]

In a passage juxtaposed with his correspondent's account of German home life, Ruskin reveals by contrast a British empire "corrupted by the dismal science" of laissez-faire individualism, where starving citizens are left to their own resources (28:67). To bring this point home, Ruskin ends letter 40 with a description of the wretched conditions of a family in Edinburgh. Society could not, as Victorian convention would have it (and as Ruskin himself had propounded in *Sesame and Lilies*), be redeemed through the private sphere, through the sanctifying efforts of "angels in the house." In fact, national regeneration worked in precisely the opposite direction: the sentimental domestic ideal could be realized, as the German experience showed, only by means of paternalistic public policy.

Ruskin's utopian family/nation explores a political terrain where the boundary between public and private is reconfigured. Classical liberals recognized in such a model a potent challenge to their philosophy. "The salvation of every society," Herbert Spencer stressed in *The Principles of Sociology*, "as of every species, depends on the maintenance of an absolute opposition between the regime of the family and the regime of the State." A nation in which "family-policy and state-policy become confused"— in which citizens did not see themselves as engaged in a competitive struggle for survival—would quickly decline.[40] Spencer couches here in sociological terminology what he reveals elsewhere to be an ideological complaint. Two opposing views "have become confused," he writes in 1881. The "coercive power of the state" had been linked in recent arguments with "the freedom of the individual." The recognized "line between" public and private "has to be drawn afresh," he contends.[41] Spencer feared that Millite liberalism, with its strict separation of individual rights and state authority, would pass out of political currency.

Spencer's remarks show up the loaded significance of Ruskin's nationalist rhetoric. His adoption of the language of family values for national purposes domesticates European politics, challenging a distinctively British tradition. Domestic ideology, which had served since Burke to support classical liberal theory, was seen in the context of a changing Europe as a potential threat to the crucial distinction in that theory between public and private. In an 1873 *Contemporary Review* essay provocatively entitled "Home and Its Economies," Ruskin took issue with Spencer's rejection of the classical idea of "corporate conscience" (17:556n). Spencer's definition of patriotism amounted to little more than "reflex egoism" on the part of individuals. But in a nation governed by true corporate sentiment, in which citizenship were understood in terms of familial relations, patriotism would be valued as a noble "sacrifice of . . . egoism" to public principles. Self-interest, that natural virtue central to capitalist economics, would be eradicated in a society whose citizens habitually "defer their own interests to those of their country" (17:557).

As it turned out, Spencer's fears about the effect of such communal schemes on contemporary political theory were justified. In an ironic turn on tradition, Ruskin's deliberately antiliberal rhetoric was incorporated into British liberalism at the end of the century. His nationalist ideals helped shape a new generation's rejection of the liberal discourse of the 1870s. One critic has characterized the emerging platform as "idealist liberalism."[42] The proponents of New Liberalism, who sought "to establish an ethical framework to prescribe and evaluate human behaviour," turned in part to Ruskin for interpretive tools.[43] J. A. Hobson, for example, who acknowledged in *Confessions of an Economic Heretic* (1938) his intellectual debt to Ruskin, declared in terms recalling Ruskin's guild that society "as an organism must be animated by a common moral and intellectual life, vested in individuals who are working in conscious cooperation for a common end." In a similar vein, D. G. Ritchie formulated a rejection of classical liberalism that echoes Ruskin's views of constitutive national morality: "the individual, apart from all relations to a community, is a negation. . . . the citizen is a member of the body politic . . . [not] merely . . . a unit in a political aggregate."[44] Ruskin's strong communitarianism offered a striking alternative to Spencer's ruthless individualism.

The increasingly nationalist strain of European politics in late century reflected the changing tide remarked by Spencer. The individual and the state were no longer seen as necessarily at odds. They could be fused in an organic ideal of national life. The scientific optimism of Spencer's *The Man versus the State* (1884), which reveals a society neatly ordered by natural rights, was in fact more parochial than the sentimental vision of community sketched out in Ruskin's series of letters that ended that year. Ruskin's utopian rhetoric, far from being a "negation of politics," connects to a wider discourse of nationalism rapidly gaining force in the period. In that discourse, democratic citizenship was frequently characterized as "participation in the drama" of national self-realization, a characterization reminiscent of Ruskin's citizen/spectator.[45]

Reading the liberal critics who reviewed *Fors Clavigera*, it is easy to miss the currency of Ruskin's nationalism. In the struggle over definitions of liberalism in the 1870s and 1880s, communal schemes such as Ruskin's had to be roundly dismissed. The terms through which his contemporaries repudiated his social program are of particular interest. In the battle over the relationship between individual and community, Ruskin's authoritarian utopia was lumped with the work of another writer whose political theories were characterized as outmoded: Jean-Jacques Rousseau. Despite the fact that Gosse would claim in 1911 that Rousseau's presence in Ruskin's work was "subterraneous, and, in a sense, secret," several contemporary readers of *Fors* tried hard to make it public.[46] For them, Ruskin's attempt to fashion a community around domestic ideology represented a rejection not only of a particular political program, but more generally, of a whole mode of historical representation rooted in a vigorous faith in progress and rationality. The version of nationalism Ruskin works out in *Fors Clavigera* taps into an alternate strain of enlightenment thinking about the nation-state, a strain rejected in the first instance by Burke. In his reaction to the French Revolutionary fervor of the 1790s, Burke had warned against the radical potential of the kind of utopian nationalism represented in certain of Rousseau's works. That Ruskin's imagined community has its roots in Rousseau explains in part his attraction to the German national style. Herder, whose political ideals set the stage for Prussian imperialism, had translated Rousseau's collectivist theories into a German romantic idiom.[47] Ruskin's Rousseauan grounding also explains the curious resemblance between his rhetoric and the battle cries of the French Communists, whose schemes he resoundingly opposed. Quietly co-opting a Rousseauan idiom, Ruskin makes his own nationalism conspicuously current.

In his reading of the German example in *Fors* and in other writings of the 1870s, Ruskin weds a harsh paternalistic language of obedience and subjection with a sentimentalized vocabulary of the domestic. Through what seems at times a peculiarly inharmonious coupling, Ruskin generates a distinctively hybrid version of nationalism, one that marks a departure from his earlier writings on community. The new England he envisions, like the ideal school he describes in *Fors*, exemplifies "shepherded peace." In his inaugural Slade lecture, Ruskin characterizes the attractions of his "Motherhood of the dust" in terms that signal the move from actual terrain liable to be "trampled by contending and miserable crowds" to an unsullied image of nationality. This new nation is "so happy, so secluded, and so pure . . . her sky—polluted by no unholy clouds . . . under the green avenues of her enchanted garden . . . she must guide the human arts, and gather the divine knowledge, of distant nations, transformed from savageness to manhood, and redeemed from despairing into Peace" (20:43). This passage forcefully evokes Ruskin's much anthologized description of the domestic ideal in *Sesame and Lilies*. There the ideal English home is described as "a sacred place," a garden world unpolluted by industrial values, "the place of Peace" where crude instincts are transformed into manly virtue (18:122). If the hearth is emphatically separate from the public domain in his earlier lecture, here Ruskin uses the familiar tags of domestic ideology to supersede such distinctions. Cultural regeneration is no longer seen as a matter of private effort tended by the queenly mothers of *Sesame and Lilies*. It is not that the nation is like a home, in Ruskin's metaphorical shuttle between these sites. Rather, the nation assumes the sanctifying power of the home. In an open play in *Fors Clavigera* on Coventry Patmore's familiar title, Ruskin figures cultural redemption as the work not of queenly individuals, but of the "Angel of England" (29:316).

This feminized vision of community with its appeal to sentiment rather than reason had been a central component of British political thought since Burke.[48] Burke rejected a revolutionary rationality that offered "nothing . . . which engages the affections on the part of the commonwealth." He cloaked the state in an image calculated to inspire reverence and devotion: the sanctity of the family bond. Retaining an ancient constitution was not an act of superstition, as the French *philosophes* had argued, but a "choice of inheritance," giving "to our frame of polity the image of a relation in blood; adopting our fundamental laws into the bosom of our family affections; keeping inseparable and cherishing with the warmth of all their combined and mutually reflected charities, our state, our hearths, our sepulchres, and our actions."[49] Burke's image was meant to provide more than a sentimental diversion from the revolutionary challenge to authority. The family served as an important mediating figure in his theory of civil society. The "relation between parents and children is the first amongst the elements of vulgar, natural morality," Burke argued. In the family setting, naturally willful individuals were subjected to a restraint that shaped them into self-restraining citizens, for "this vulgar relation . . . is not, of course, the result of *free election*." What began as forced obedience turned into ingrained instincts of "domestic trust and fidelity, which form the discipline of social life."[50]

Just as natural morality would model national morality, so the reverse would also be true, as Burke suggests in his metaphor of "adopting our fundamental laws into the bosom of our family affections." Social rules inculcated through the family circle would be naturalized more effectively than when imposed by an oppressive regime. On that basis, Burke argues for an alternative to rationalist reactions to tyranny. Absolute individual freedom was not a practicable option. "Society cannot exist unless a controlling power upon will and appetite be placed somewhere," he stated, "and the less of it there is within, the more there must be without."[51] Self-regulating individuals could be trusted to maintain social order. Burke preserves at the center of his argument the enlightenment emphasis on individual *Bildung* as the progressive engine of modern society.

Posing hearth as the site of exchange between public and private value became a convention of nineteenth-century writing.[52] *Sesame and Lilies* succinctly articulates this familiar formula. Ruskin's admiration in

Fors Clavigera for the "sacred domestic life" of Wilhelmine Germany is less formulaic (28:68). What Ruskin sees there is not a nation of self-restraining individuals united by a sentiment transferred from family to state. Rather, he admires a national style that institutionalizes the paternal role, that recognizes citizens as though the "vulgar relation" of parents and children were not a step toward national morality but its defining principle. It is not enough, he argues, to raise "well-disposed persons" who act "according to their own conscience" (28:342). As his own abortive attempts at autobiography in *Fors* dramatize, individuals never develop as progressive thinkers propose. Like Rousseau before him, Ruskin believes in the "Wild Man . . . within us" who cannot be civilized but must instead be subdued, as he was in his own childhood, by continual "submissions to external Force" (28:343).[53] In *Fors Clavigera*, *Bildung* is strictly a national affair. Ruskin's letters tell the tale not of heroic individualism but of heroic nations overcoming recalcitrant individuals to realize their full potential.

Already a charged ideological figure in nineteenth-century discourse, the domestic ideal took on added political urgency in the early 1870s. A contrary idea of political and social organization had been at work in the Paris Commune of 1871. Domestic hierarchies were disrupted by a communitarian ideal in which all individuals were considered *citoyens*. A French Positivist who was for a time a member of the Commune reported that it set out to oppose "mother institutions" such as "property, family and government" so carefully guarded by those who favored "order" over "progress." In the Commune, social patterns of dominance and subjection were subverted by an emphasis on lateral relations within a circle of equals. Paternalistic rhetoric was displaced in English reports of the Commune by a quite different figure. The new revolutionaries were a "brotherhood" of workers for whom English working men "entertained a warm and decided sympathy." This "greatest of all class struggles" in Paris threatened to erase national loyalties, cementing "the fraternal spirit growing up between the working classes of all countries" in a "cosmopolitan" society after the model of the International Working Men's Association. The Communists attempted, as one contemporary observed, to achieve "what no revolutionists, no rioters, had ever dreamt of . . . to do away with the very notion of a fatherland."[54]

To Ruskin, such a cross-cultural brotherhood of the working classes posed a clear threat to the patriarchal state he advocated in *Fors Clavigera*. It was against the cosmopolitan example of the Commune that Ruskin defined his paternalistic nationalism. Unlike the "baby Communists" in Paris, Ruskin's model citizens would practice communalism as "our fathers knew it, and told us, three thousand years ago" (27:117). In opposition to what he called the "Kakotopia" of the Paris Commune, Ruskin proposed his nationalist "Utopia" that would replicate the Greek ideal of strong civic identity (27:144). "The main curse of modern society," he complained, was that it encouraged a new generation in "rejecting whatever is noble and honourable in their fathers' houses" (28:545). By contrast, the Companions of the Guild would be schooled in a patriotism that would make them respect their fatherland. Unlike the cosmopolitan Communists, they would seek only to implement what they knew to be "absolutely right, and, so far as it may be kindly and inoffensively practised, to fulfil it, at home."

Ruskin's authoritarian community took its contemporary bearings from Prussian imperialist rhetoric. This alliance clearly set his Guild of St. George at odds with French republicanism. His language of paternal inheritance has surprising affinities, however, with the antiestablishment slogans of the Communards. For the details of his community he relies, as did the French Communists who declared their allegiance to the 1789 Revolution, on the ideals of Jean-Jacques Rousseau. This common intellectual lineage firmly situates Ruskin's nationalism in the cultural moment. Like the advocates of the French Commune, Ruskin admired the utopian spirit of Rousseau's work. Against the rational progressivism of British political theory, Rousseau offered an approach to writing national history *de nouveau*. Although ideologically opposed to the republican ethic of the Communists, Ruskin mimicked their tactics in constructing his guild. His descriptions of ideal community exploit domestic metaphors to radical purpose. Conflating public and private morality in his image of the nation as home, Ruskin introduced a revolutionary turn on British political narratives. The connection by way of Rousseau between the Communards' discussions of community and Ruskin's was not lost on his contemporaries.

In Rousseau's work Ruskin found a compelling model of the kind of public sentimental education represented in the Guild of St. George. The literary antecedent for his paternalist utopia can be found in a novel that had stood in the British imagination for, in Burke's influential words, the subversion of "those principles of domestic trust and fidelity, which form the discipline of social life": *Julie, ou La Nouvelle Héloïse.*[55] This work, which had seemed to violate the Victorian domestic ideal, paves the way for refiguring that ideal in nationalist terms. Whereas in more overtly political writings Rousseau often wavered between contractual and authoritarian social theory, in *La Nouvelle Héloïse* he created an unambiguous picture of strictly ordered communal life. Frequent references to the novel in letters of the 1860s show Ruskin reading his own experiences in light of Rousseau's sentimental civics.[56] When he came to consider the conduct of national morality, this work in particular offered him a ready means of linking obedience to affection, subjection to sentiment.

Although Rousseau is never referred to by name in *Fors Clavigera,* he is an unmistakable presence. Recounting his own moral education, Ruskin speaks of the influence of "a Savoyard guide" who recalls the Savoyard vicar of *Émile.* "As we walked up some quiet valley," Ruskin narrates, "he would generally," like Émile's tutor, "give me a little lecture on philosophy" (27:61). In a Rousseauan lament Ruskin's tutor regrets that with all of his fine English upbringing, the young Ruskin "ne sait pas vivre." Ruskin's literal translation of the phrase—"he doesn't know how to live"—contrasts with the colloquial French meaning of knowing one's manners and serves to distinguish true moral education from superficial self-betterment. Similarly, in *La Nouvelle Héloïse* Saint-Preux, explaining the key to the domestic order he finds at Clarens (the country estate around which the second half of the novel hinges) writes that "*On y sait vivre,*" not, he continues, "in the meaning which in France we give to this phrase, which is to act around others according to the manners prescribed by fashion," but rather in the sense of knowing how to "bring into play" the elements of a communal morality (*NH* 9:202; all translations mine).

This view of morality as foundationally social—rather than, for example, a result of rational consideration or of natural instinct—is central to the model of political life sketched in *Fors Clavigera.* Rousseau provides a blueprint for this type of carefully controlled sociality. In Wolmar's efficient and simple household at Clarens, the disordered Saint-Preux finds "about everything a fine order that shows the harmony of the whole household and the uniformity of purpose of the manager" (*NH* 9:228).

Wolmar's community, like Ruskin's ideal one, is self-contained, with a self-sufficient economy. Neither involves middlemen (Ruskin declared he abhorred them and vowed they would be abolished in the Guild, 29:21, 28:30−31); both are based on a close and constant interaction between a patriarchal master and loyal servants. Under Wolmar's management, Saint-Preux observes: "There is so much restraint on the part of those who command and so much zeal on the part of those who obey" that "no one is envious of anyone else; no one believes he could better his lot except by bettering the common good" (*NH* 9:231). Ruskin's community is also free from self-interest and envy: Master and citizen act in "continual reference to the cause for which [they] are contending,— not to the advantage [they] hope to reap" (29:148). As in Ruskin's well-run ship of state, where "loyalty and obedience" forestall "mutiny" (29: 147−48), at Clarens "There is never either bad will or mutiny in their obedience [obéissance]" (*NH* 9:113).

At the head of both communities is the stern but benevolent pater-familias. The Master of St. George "concerns himself only with the life of the workman,—refers all to that,—measures all by that"; his "entire sharing and understanding of the hardship of that,—and his fellowship with it" are "the only foundation of his authority over it" (29:172). So, too, the master of the Rousseauan estate judges his "success" only "by the measure of folk" who work for him, to the extent that he brings a "rustic" home for dinner and "inquires about his family, about his personal concerns" (*NH* 9:231, 242). Saint-Preux is quick to see the benefits of such fatherly interest: "Everyone blesses with one accord this illustrious and generous family" (*NH* 9:243−44). In this harmonious world, as in Ruskin's stratified utopia where citizens know their place, each domestic and agricultural worker finds "in his condition all that he requires to be content and does not at all desire to leave it; he sticks to it as though he would remain there all his life, and the only ambition he retains is to perform his duty well" (*NH* 9:231). Each is determined only, as Ruskin hopes the members of his ideal community will be, "to do good work whether you live or die" (27:129).

The outlines of both Ruskin's and Rousseau's paternalistic utopias can be traced back to Plato's civic ideals. What makes Rousseau's mediation of those ideals so important for Ruskin's later project is the way in which he domesticates them. The strong authority of the ancient polity

is wedded to eighteenth-century sentimentality. As one critic has remarked, in *La Nouvelle Héloïse* Rousseau "transposed" the martial ethic of
the ancients "to a different register": the "ideals of courage, patriotism,
integrity, selflessness" become the foundation of "domestic and civic virtues."[57] In his late Victorian reassessment of Rousseau's writings, John
Morley suggests the influence of this example for subsequent domestic
narratives. And yet, as Morley also recognizes, the household at Clarens
is not so easily assimilated to the Victorian private sphere, where sentiment sanctifies political and economic vice.[58] In fact, it is sentiment—
the passionate attraction between Julie and Saint-Preux—that must be
institutionally controlled at Clarens. Families are broken up; men and
women are kept strictly apart. The nuclear family does not figure as a
center of social virtue. Workers and domestics regard themselves, and are
regarded as, children of the estate: "They must see it as their paternal
house where all are as one family" (*NH* 9:102). If in the conventional
nineteenth-century domestic narrative "political conflict was . . . thoroughly transformed by middle-class love," here sentimental love is transformed by a carefully controlled political order.[59] Underlying Rousseau's
fictional household, Morley points out, is the classical idea of "moulding
a social state" after the legislator's ethical imperatives.[60] Unlike the unre-
gulated household of Julie's father where her scandalous attachment to
her tutor was first formed, at Clarens all personal relations are carried out
and monitored in a public space.

While Clarens may be removed from the center of power at Paris, it
is not quite accurate to describe it as "anti-political."[61] The provincial
estate does not function as the idealized opposite of an existing order, as
does the domestic hearth in conventional Victorian narrative. If the
household came to be seen in the period as "an apolitical realm of culture" in which individual gratification was defined within a "private
framework," the household in *La Nouvelle Héloïse* might be described, by
contrast, as a realm in which the political framework defines individual
gratification.[62] Happiness and morality are not private affairs. Clarens
thus figures in this novel as more than a rural retreat, a secluded haven
from the evils of the London and Parisian scenes against which it is con-
trasted. Like Julie's garden, the order of Clarens appears to be natural, but
it is in fact carefully engineered. As Saint-Preux comments in a remark
cited at length above, the domestic harmony is a result of "uniformity of

purpose of the manager [ordonnateur]." It is not the case, as it is in the work of many romantic writers influenced by Rousseau's social theories, that the rustic household exemplifies virtue uncorrupted by the vices of civilization. This distinction must have been apparent to Ruskin, as he moved away from the Wordsworthian ideal of community summarized in *Modern Painters*, in which nature prompts the expression of inherent virtue. Virtuous citizens, like honest servants, as Saint-Preux says, must be made, not discovered: "it is necessary for them to be created" by "an upright man who understands the art of forming others in his likeness" (*NH* 9:110). H. Gaston Hall points out that in this novel, like *Émile*, "Conscience is innate, virtue is not."[63] As in Ruskin's account of Platonic education, so in Rousseau's utopia individuals are harmoniously "moralled into their existing morals" (29:237).

Ruskin's domestic utopia works to similar ends. What he defines is not a sentimental sphere apart from political questions. To the contrary, in a discussion of the relations between Britain and its colonies he contends that all political issues are indistinguishable from "sentimental questions" (27:627). For sentiment, rightly understood, is not a matter of private emotion, the merely "bestial" instincts that rule the first half of Rousseau's novel—"lust, covetousness, and vanity" which are "naturally grasped at." Instead, it resembles the kind of public virtue displayed at Clarens, a "fellow-feeling" Ruskin assimilates in *Fors* to a classical notion of civic imagination. This virtue must be taught, instilled: it is not innate, but the product of "mental government" (27:630). Sentimental education of the kind described in *La Nouvelle Héloïse* or *Émile* or *Fors Clavigera* consists in subordinating natural instinct to the civic good. Its goal is to transform natural man into moral citizen.

In the strict order of Ruskin's utopian guild, the companions would learn to recognize that personal independence is a delusion. Committed to the common goal of "the health, wealth, and long life of the British nation," they would find that they had little scope for "much independent action of any kind" (28:638, 545). The hierarchical structure of the Guild reinforces the lesson that we are "bound" to the society around us "as to the immediate members of our own households" (29:193). In this scenario, personal development is as constrained by our social framework as by biological ties. The nation should not, according to Ruskin, be understood as merely "an aggregate of individual conditions," in the terms of Samuel Smiles's popular formula.[64] Nor is it exactly, as in Carlyle's organic social vision, "the vital articulation of many individuals into a collective individual" (*WTC* 28:12). In *Fors Clavigera* the nation is portrayed as itself an agent who, like Rousseau's "ordonnateur," embodies a "uniformity of purpose." Just as Wolmar practices "the art of forming others in his likeness," Ruskin's nation sets the patterns in which individual citizens will be molded.

Rousseau provided a particular instance of effectively renegotiating individual and civil interests. His strong vision of community offered one means of breaking through the public/private impasse in British liberal theory, an impasse starkly apparent in the decade inaugurated by Prussian nationalism and Parisian Communism. Ruskin was not the only writer who saw in Rousseau the potential for revitalizing national life in this context. In his influential recasting of liberal theory in the 1870s and 1880s, T. H. Green used the enlightenment philosopher to develop a vision of national life very close in some respects to Ruskin's.[65] Green finds in Rousseau's "bien commun" a way of contextualizing the atomistic rights theory that dominated Victorian liberalism. Purely contractual ideas of society, in Green's view as in Ruskin's, ignored the fact that morality was rooted in "political subjection." Constraint was morality; radical independence was simply unchecked animal instinct. The "fallacy" of classical liberalism "lies in the implication that the individuals could be what they are, could have their moral and spiritual qualities, independently of their existence in a nation." The "confinement" of social life "is the condition of the only personality . . . we know," he argued. "Social life is to personality what language is to thought." In Green's theory of political obligation, there is no natural morality or transcendent "rights of humanity." "It is only as members of a society," he claimed, with "common interests and objects, that individuals come to have these attributes and rights; and the power, which in a political society they have to obey, is derived from the development and systematisation of those institutions for the regulation of a common life without which they would have no rights at all." Green translates Rousseau's contractual theory in a way that sounds very like Ruskin's translation of Plato's process of education. Natural man must be "moralised"; he must learn to "express a conception of a common good" that has a "constraining power over him." Public life must be reoriented around a strong conception of the "patria," Green argues in a political metaphor that exploits domestic ideology in the manner of Rousseau and Ruskin: an individual should feel "himself bound by ties analogous to those which bind him to his family." [66]

In *Fors Clavigera* Ruskin distinguishes this kind of nationalist vision from prevailing definitions of a "'civilized nation'" (28:639): a loosely administered association of "mob" and "capitalist" (28:639–40). In most Victorian social theories, citizens were considered as distinct subjects related only by their mutual recognition of certain codes of conduct or civility. For Ruskin this notion of civil association amounted to little more than *savoir-vivre* in the conventional sense. It promoted manners over morality, surface representation over praxis. One could go about "saying anything" or "saying nothing at all" as long as it corresponded to proper codes (28:639–40). But such a conversation had the effect of "disguising . . . action," of providing a superficial veneer of commonality over very real battles of self-interest. It made possible what Ruskin calls in *Fors* "Occult Theft,—Theft which hides itself even from itself" through good breeding (27:127).

What Ruskin expresses here is more than his familiar distaste for capitalist ideology. He rejects one important strand of thought about the modern European state, a strand which Michael Oakeshott has summed up in the term *societas*: a civil association of individuals joined by a recognition of certain codes, not "of a common substantive purpose." [67] For Ruskin, construing society in this way involved a profound misunderstanding of civil morality. Social codes and institutions were not simply arrangements of convenience, artificial conventions to be altered at will. They were constitutive of individual thought and behavior. To posit a moral private sphere that functioned independently from and offered a check to an amoral public sphere—or, more narrowly, to pose domestic sentiment against competitive capitalism—was to misrepresent the necessary connection between public and private morality.

In the *Contrat social* Rousseau had struggled to balance this notion of society as civil association with a notion of a common morality. The structure of the ideal society in *La Nouvelle Héloïse* makes such a balancing act unnecessary. Clarens is a perfect model of the social theory Oakeshott poses as the direct antithesis to *societas*: *universitas*, a "notion of a state in which there are managers, not rulers; role-performers related to a common purpose, not *cives* or subjects."[68] Rousseau's rural utopia does not require a *deus ex machina* (like the great legislator of the *Contrat*) to reconcile private and public good. Individual morality is articulated from the start in terms of the common good. To attempt to function outside that common moral idiom—to articulate an "absolute of personal well-being"—results not in agency but annihilation, as Julie's death in *La Nouvelle Héloïse* reveals.[69]

Seen in this light, Rousseau's novel transgresses nineteenth-century conventions of domesticity in precisely the manner of Ruskin's sentimentalized image of "Motherhood of the dust." The domestic is no longer regarded as a sanctuary from corrupting social mores. In Rousseau's world the border between public and private is completely permeable. The picture of family life early in the work—the scene of Julie's early attachment to Saint-Preux—exposes conventional domestic values not as an antidote to corrupted social mores but as their mirror image. This distinction is precisely the one Ruskin draws in *Fors Clavigera* when he compares the home life of an Edinburgh family corroded by capitalism to the orderly domesticity of a German family under an authoritarian state. Only a clearly defined public ethic could produce the kind of domestic harmony achieved at Clarens or in contemporary Prussia.

Ruskin begins *Fors Clavigera* with the rhetoric of social contract. A strong government, he says in the opening letter, has its foundation in "the considerate acceptance of a code of laws" (27:16). When Ruskin turns to sketching out an ideal society, however, his terms, like Rousseau's, shift toward a rhetoric of *universitas*. Citizens will forsake efforts at individual improvement, operating instead in "effective and constant unison" to ensure the "long life of the British nation" (28:638). Like members of a family who commit themselves to the good of the whole, the members of St. George's Company will seek not personal "gain," but the gain of "the Nation only" (28:641). Each functions as a part of "the entire body of the British nation" (28:642). The nation, in return, will provide physical nurture and moral education for its citizens. They will be taught to be "obedient" to the national purpose and "serviceable to other creatures" (28:655): in other words, their education will be instrumental to the larger purpose of ensuring that the British nation will not "perish, as a power, from the face of the earth" (28:638).

At the center of this education Ruskin places his proposed "grammars"—books on botany, geology, and zoology (28:647). As the context in which he describes them makes clear, these are more than whimsical treatises on pet subjects. They exemplify the need for a common social idiom. Unlike the artificial conversations of a society in which public representation has little to do with private practice, the discourse in Ruskin's ideal state will emphasize the vital connection between public and private. In society conceived as *universitas*, Oakeshott remarks, citizens "are agreed, not merely to speak the same language [the conventions of *societas*], but to say the same thing and are equipped with the means of committing themselves to or acknowledging such common utterances as their own." Because Ruskin's citizens must articulate their own interests in terms of a common good, there would be, he explains, no question of misrepresentation. Whereas in contemporary society individuals could "say anything," in his unified nation "anything gravely said . . . may be, without investigation believed; and anything sold by one, without scrutiny, bought for what it is said to be" (28:639, 643). This literal correspondence between signifier and signified is not the product of an inherent faith that "material reality is trustworthy."[70] Rather, it is the result of Ruskin's insistence that systems of meaning shape our perceptions of material reality.

In his pragmatic critique of such a nationalist project, Raymond Williams faults Ruskin for adhering "to an idea of 'inherent design' as a model for society—a commitment which led him into a familiar type of general replanning of society on paper." This kind of wholescale replanning is precisely the point for Ruskin. If institutions and conventions are constitutive of morality, then change cannot come about through "existing forces and institutions."[71] Ruskin deliberately breaks rank with the line of cultural critique to which Williams tries unsuccessfully to relegate him. Beginning from the Burkean sentimental ideal, Williams, not surprisingly, cannot quite accommodate Ruskin's Rousseauan turn. In his late writings, Ruskin rejects the British progressive tradition in which Williams writes, adopting instead the revolutionary rhetoric of radical origination. Like Rousseau before him, he lays out an alternative means of defining national association. Through their domestic utopias both writers offer a way of realigning individual and society, of reconfiguring the space of national life as a "domestic treasury" common to all (28:445).

For Ruskin's contemporaries this break with the British political mainstream resembled the utopian gestures of the Paris Communards. In 1871 the *Republican*, a newspaper that championed the Commune in the face of criticism from other British papers, also came to Ruskin's support when his guild was ridiculed by the *Daily News*. It endorsed Ruskin's community as a noble effort in reimagining civic life.[72] The *Atlantic Monthly* remarked in 1878 that while Ruskin "has been crying passionately that the axe is laid at the root of the tree" in social movements like the Commune, he simultaneously "take[s] up the axe himself" in his utopian nationalism. In Ruskin's guild, as in other nationalist movements of the decade, the language of rational association was replaced by a strong familial rhetoric. His sentimental education of citizens was based on revolutionary ideals, not actual historical process: "growth must constantly 'put out' the well-ordered schemes."[73]

Frederic Harrison argued that Ruskin's familial metaphors of the state aggravated rather than assuaged the political "chaos" of the moment. Ruskin's appeal to emotion instead of to "a reasonable use of tradition" made of any rational "bond of society" a "more worthless old rag than it is to the wildest communist." Harrison, who elsewhere had declared his sympathy with the spirit of the Paris Commune, had also expressed his reservations about "its principles" and "its method." Even the usual opponents of change seemed to the republican Harrison to be on better footing than the Master of St. George's Guild. At least the staunch protectors of tradition—the "modern Conservatives and men in authority" in church and state—had a rationale behind their "cling[ing] to political and social systems." "But I cannot find the same good motives," he argued, "for those who repudiate tradition while they still defy progress, for those who with Rousseau make a clean sweep of human things, to build an Utopia with eloquent phrases."[74]

For Ruskin's critics, the danger of his Rousseauan project was, as Homi Bhabha puts it in his discussion of nationalism, that "the nation as symbolic denominator" threatens to "eras[e] the rationalist and progressivist logics" of conventional historical narration. Ruskin and contemporary liberal historians were engaged in a turf battle over "the site of *writing the nation.*" The political theories of both camps required radically different accounts of English history. As I will suggest in chapter 4, the contrast between "the continuist, accumulative temporality" of liberal historians and the "repetitious, recursive strategy" of Ruskin's letters reveals the contradictions inherent in any attempt to narrate national history.[75]

Moreover, it points to a fundamental contradiction in Ruskin's own nationalism. If the citizen/spectator is the product of national tradition—if existing institutions are constitutive of public morality—how does one refigure communal life? Can one address, as Ruskin claims to do in *Fors*, both an existing audience and readers of "a day [that] will come," a day when "we shall have men resolute to do good work" for national gain (27:669)? Ruskin's new landscape of national life imagined apart from existing interests must, by his own account of "figurative perception," be derivative. The tension between a community both deracinated and firmly rooted in tradition places Ruskin's thinking back in the central enlightenment dilemma he hoped to elude. Through sometimes conflicting accounts of figuration, Ruskin will attempt an allegorical reading of history that negotiates between the cumulative and prefigurative impulses of enlightenment nationalism.

IV

Conjuring the Necromantic Evidence of History

IN HIS EARLY APOLOGIA for Ruskin's career, J. A. Hobson wondered about a conservative impulse underlying the sage's utopian rhetoric. On the one hand, Ruskin's discursive method in *Fors*—detailed reportage of current events—would seem to lead to a logical analysis of "general law[s] . . . operative through history." At the same time Ruskin repeatedly eschewed analytic method in favor of apparently romantic, anachronistic explanations of contemporary problems. In the end, Hobson concluded, Ruskin's "survey of history and his theory of human nature oblige him . . . to turn his back upon the trend of recent history, which he so vividly describes . . . and to stake everything upon the miraculous reversal of modern movements." [1]

The contradiction Hobson observes between progressive argument and nostalgic narrative in Ruskin's work particularly plagues *Fors Clavigera*. His journalistic format combines documentary (reprints from contemporary newspapers, eyewitness accounts) with myth (stories of Greek, Egyptian and Christian figures) in an idiosyncratic mix that has continued to puzzle readers. Contemporary attempts to categorize the work suggest, however, that what Hobson and critics after him have interpreted as merely personal ambivalence about the condition of modern England is rather a reflection of heated public debates in the 1870s about methods of historical interpretation. Provoked by the challenge of a powerful Prussia and by the brief glory of the French Commune, prominent writers reassessed the bearings of Victorian society. A new generation of liberal thinkers, concerned to legitimize Millite doctrines, held up Enlightenment rationalism as the muse of national progress. Such works as John Morley's studies of the French *philosophes* and Leslie Stephen's *English*

Thought in the Eighteenth Century traced a succession from the skeptical inquiry of Enlightenment thinkers to the modern liberal enterprise. Their histories were meant to provide a credible context for laissez-faire policies. Only liberalism, such studies suggested, would ensure that the nation continued to follow "the true line of human progress."[2]

Fors Clavigera encapsulates competing modes of historical narrative in a decade marked by zealous efforts to tell the story of modern England. In his letters Ruskin replicates his critics' positivist methods only to subvert them, illustrating a divergent means of historical reconstruction. Like his contemporaries' orderly historical accounts, the letters of *Fors* are presented chronologically, yet individual letters are deliberately anachronistic, moving back in time from the current circumstances of the writer to his childhood, from the lives of contemporary working men to the lives of ancient mythical figures. Conjuring the "necromantic . . . evidence" of history (28:488), Ruskin resists positivist reconstructions of the past, while pursuing an allegorical approach that looks forward to versions of postmodern historicism.

The title of Ruskin's series of letters makes a strong statement of his position on reading the records of the past. He found the image of Fors Clavigera, as he explains, in Horace's Odes, and confirmed its truth by a "steady effort to read history with impartiality" (28:106–7). In *Fors* he determines to lay out for his readers "so much of the past history of the world, in an intelligible manner, as may enable you to see the laws of Fortune or Destiny, 'Clavigera,' Nail bearing; or, in the full idea, nail-and-hammer bearing; driving the iron home with hammer-stroke, so that nothing shall be moved" (27:230–31). In other words, reading history is a matter of learning to trace the hand of Destiny not in order to assess the evolution of modern life, but in order to discern its conformity to predictable patterns of experience. Like reading novels, interpreting the historical record is an exercise in following the plot. By breaking the chronological sequence of current events, juxtaposing them with past facts and fictions, Ruskin exposes all history as a repetition and fulfillment of fixed narrative devices. He deliberately recurs, as Carlyle did in his histories, to an early eighteenth-century understanding of history as literature.[3] "The very gist and essence of everything St. George orders," unlike the "absurd endeavours of modern . . . republicans," Ruskin asserts in a rejection of the scientific language of positivist history, is that "it shall *not* be new, and not an 'experiment'" (29:133). For Ruskin's scientifically minded contemporaries, looking critically at the past was an effort of factual documentation. For Ruskin it was a hermeneutic exercise in re-covering the elementary structures of human society.

Liberal historians objected to this kind of juggling of chronological evidence in an attempt to legitimate an *a priori* political position. In his *History of English Thought in the Eighteenth Century* Leslie Stephen argued that such a reading of history was not properly historical at all: "Its for-mulae are deducible by rigorous logic from a fundamental axiom abso-lutely independent of time and place." To subscribe to such methods, as did Rousseau, for example, would be to "annihilate history." In his re-view of *Fors Clavigera*, Stephen judges Ruskin's method in terms that an-ticipate his sustained critique of certain strains of eighteenth-century his-toricism. If Ruskin, Stephen asserted, "does not talk about an ideal 'state of nature'" as Rousseau did, "he is equally anxious to meet corruption by returning to a simpler order of society." Ruskin's epistolary periodical sidestepped serious political argument by way of "fanciful etymologies, strained allegories, questionable interpretations of history." Instead of pursuing causes and effects, "Mr. Ruskin, to speak logically, is a little too fond of the induction by simple enumeration in dealing with historical problems"; he was misled by "an excessive sensibility which bursts all restraints of logic and common sense."[4] Ruskin, like Rousseau before him, was shown to be sadly out of step with the rational modern age.

Stephen bypasses contemporary analogies to Ruskin's political proj-ect, exposing instead the Rousseauan affinities never overtly mentioned by Ruskin. This move had special significance in a decade in which Rous-seau became a frequent reference point in discussions about historical narrative. Linking Ruskin's style with Rousseau's, Stephen strategically sites his work in the context of an already compromised position. Since Edmund Burke's attack on Rousseau in the 1790s, the Genevan's writings had been made to stand for the sentimental excesses of the eighteenth century. More recently, he had been characterized as the high priest of a fanatical revolutionary spirit at odds with the new liberals' portrait of a rational Enlightenment.[5] In the first major Victorian reconsideration of Rousseau, John Morley in effect excommunicates him from the liberal canon by showing him to be unable or unwilling to subscribe whole-heartedly to the faith in progress preached by Diderot and the other

Encyclopaedists. "His narrow, symmetrical, impatient humour unfitted him to deal with the complex tangle of the history of social growths," Morley argued. His works were "inevitably fraught with confusion"; for "not to be scientific, not to be careful in tracing effects to their true causes, is to be without any security that the causes with which we try to deal will lead to the effects that we desire." While his contemporaries analyzed the growth of traditions in order to test their validity, Rousseau dismissed tradition, positing an original state of perfection, displaying "an ignorance alike of the ends and means of history, which, considering that he was living in the midst of a singular revival of historical study, is not easy to pardon." Reviving old myths and social arrangements, Rousseau was shown to have betrayed the insistence of the *philosophes* on a "historic method which traces the present along a line of ascertained circumstances, and seeks an improved future in an unbroken continuation of that line."[6]

In the rationalist revival of the 1870s, Rousseau became a cipher for reason gone wrong, for clear-headed inquiry clouded by romantic reflection. British liberals anxious to claim their allegiance to enlightenment skepticism repeatedly defined their own positions by contrast with Rousseau's. His inside critique of the ideology of progress posed problems for writers arguing that they were the continuers of a vital intellectual tradition devolving from the *philosophes*. Ruskin presented a contemporary version of Rousseau's early challenge, and it was urgent that he be discredited in similar terms. His Rousseauan nationalism offered an alternative cultural genealogy for modern England, one that threatened the enlightenment project from its birth. Associating Ruskin with what had been defined as an abortive intellectual theory consigned him to a past that had little relation to Victorian social problems. In his review of *Fors*, Stephen "ticket[s] Mr. Ruskin as an oddity" in a political landscape that encompasses John Stuart Mill and Auguste Comte.[7] Aligning Rousseau and Ruskin—and passing silently over the affinities between Ruskin's historicism and contemporary European accounts of national tradition—Stephen safely concludes that Ruskin's historical analysis belongs to another age.

Frederic Harrison dismissed Ruskin's method in *Fors* through a similar strategy. Like Rousseau, he argued, Ruskin rejected the natural progress of history and investigated contemporary problems through literary, not scientific strategies. In his biography of Ruskin for John Morley's *English Men of Letters* series, Harrison described the sage's allegorical history as "a form of graceful trifling." Under the guise of defending *Fors*, he discredits both man and message in terms remarkably like those Morley had used to question Rousseau's intellectual soundness in *his* biography. "Reasonable judges" of Ruskin's letters would see "self-unveiled, a noble nature and beautiful aspirations . . . debarred from bearing fruit by . . . a sort of mental and moral incontinence."[8] *Fors* was a moving work of literature, but its political vision should not be taken too seriously.

Harrison's remarks about *Fors Clavigera* were motivated in part by his own investment in the positivist historicism Ruskin mocked. "Let this be our test of what is history and what is not," Harrison had said in 1862, as though establishing objective criteria by which to try scientific data, "that it teaches us something of the advance of human progress . . . or is lit up with those great ideas and those great purposes which have kindled the conscience of mankind." "Progress" he defined in good Comtean terminology as "enlightened" public opinion: "All other progress than this . . . is transitory and delusive." In 1871 he had no trouble identifying the true historical "fact" that emerged from the new decade. The triumphs of Prussia he dismissed as "but part of the dismal annals of war." With the birth of the Commune, "Paris had again become, in spite of all the soldiery and discipline of Germany, the true centre of political progress." This resurrection of the revolutionary ideal in France proved the period of authoritarian regimes and Napoleonic empire to be "transitory and delusive," a mere digression in the historical master narrative. While the English press generally denounced the Commune as a violent and spurious uprising, Harrison sympathetically interpreted the popular rebellion through Comte's laws of social change. At the same time, by using it as "evidence" for his historical theory, Harrison validated Comte's system. He validated as well his own political writings, with their vision of "the final or republican type of society" based on "the free and continual expression of Opinion by the great labouring masses."[9]

Interpreting current events according to his own ideological agenda, Harrison challenged Ruskin's use of the Prussian example. Ruskin's utopian nationalism had to be rejected out of hand as merely anachronistic, just as Harrison had to reject Prussian imperialism as a temporary survival of outdated authoritarian regimes. What made Ruskin's reading of modern history so provoking for readers like Harrison and Stephen was not that it was hopelessly nostalgic, but that it demonstrated the currency of political alternatives that were unacceptable in the new liberal program. His critics were right to charge that Ruskin's arguments, in the manner of Rousseau's, were not systematic. He never meant for them to be. One of the uses of utopian rhetoric is to call into question cause and effect as the only accepted terms of political analysis: "it subverts, or renders unnecessary, reasoned argument and replaces it by symbols, inversions and the all-powerful *reductio ad absurdum*."[10] At a moment when his critics were making a claim both for their own kind of historical investigation and for their own political programs, Ruskin's utopian writings had to be rejected as a serious alternative. Like Rousseau, he pushed the logical arguments of his contemporaries to their limits. He, too, constructed an ideal by playing with, in Morley's words, "verbal definitions," employing an argumentative style of seeming "certitude and precision" that held many of his readers "captive." He built a utopia not around historical evidence, but around powerful symbols of family and of mythological virtues. Writing against positivist reconstructions of history, Ruskin, in the mode of Rousseau, fashioned history as sentimental allegory. European nationalists had discovered the power of such a narrative.

With its seemingly contradictory prospective and retrospective gazes, *Fors Clavigera* plays out the tensions inherent in any account of national heritage. Ruskin's allegorical history tries to negotiate the gap between the present performance of national identity and the construction of that identity through symbols from the past. For Ruskin's critics, who openly rejected his version of history, that gap was especially problematic. Liberal writers argued for the claims of rational experience against tradition. And yet the credibility of their political program was underwritten by a version of national tradition. Casting the intellectual genealogy of Victorian England involved an inevitable appeal to an "atavistic national past" that "marginalizes the present of the 'modernity' of the national culture."[11] The selective rewriting of current events that so concerned Ruskin's readers is implicit in all narratives of political origins. Both Ruskin and his critics filtered modern experience through their particular histories of national life. Legitimizing their agendas required turning backward: to be judged "authentic," modern life had to be presented as the coda to an inevitable historical movement.

The new liberals were involved in precisely the kind of imaginative recasting of history of which they accused Ruskin. Mark Pattison, for example, boldly excised Rousseauan social theory from the historical record. The political writings of the first half of the nineteenth century, he declared, amounted to "fifty years lost." In reaction to the excesses of the Enlightenment, the progressive faith of the *philosophes* had been temporarily abandoned. But it was undeniable now that "the rights of the legitimate monarch—the sovereign reason—have only been in abeyance the while; they are inalienable." The eighteenth century could no longer be portrayed, as it had been in Carlyle's histories, as an age that collapsed into anarchy and ruin. Its "vices . . . were indeed many," Mark Pattison conceded, "but it was withal on the true line of human progress." [12] Anything that did not carry on the spirit of inquiry and skepticism initiated in that century should be seen as a hindrance to the development of a better society.

John Morley provided a detailed account of this foreshortened nineteenth century. In the same decades that Ruskin revived Rousseauan ideas, Morley resurrected the progressive and revolutionary thinkers of the Enlightenment. Through his series of studies of French *philosophes*, he tried to underwrite the social schemes of the new liberals. [13] In reaffirming the principles of the Enlightenment, he, like Pattison, rejected one strain of modern political thought, carving out a tradition that supported his liberal views. "Forty years ago," Morley proclaimed in 1878, "when Carlyle wrote [his 1833 essay on Diderot], it might really seem to a prejudiced observer as if the encyclopaedic tree had borne no fruit. . . . But now that the last vapours of the transcendental reaction are clearing away, we see that the movement initiated by the Encyclopaedia is again in full progress. Materialistic solutions in the science of man, humanitarian ends in legislation . . . active faith in the improvableness of institutions—all these are once more the marks of speculation and the guiding ideals of practical energy." [14] Ruskin's outcries against scientific thinking, his dismissal of legislative solutions to what he saw as essentially moral, not political problems, are swept away in Morley's division of the century. Ruskin and Carlyle belonged to the brief historical digression away from progress, away from the movement toward "conceptions . . . more conformable to the facts."

The premises elaborated in Morley's French studies can be read in a kind of running dialogue with Ruskin's positions in *Fors*. While Ruskin insisted that the "absolute and perpetual truth" as preached by Carlyle was "the eternity of good law, and the need of obedience to it" (27:170, 180), Morley reemphasized the French philosophers' rational scrutiny of all law and challenge to authority. Ruskin predicted that "Enlightenment, and Freedom . . . and Science of the superbest and trustworthiest character" were the way to "Ruin—inevitable and terrible" (28:263), whereas Morley heralded them as the sure ingredients of progress. For the march of history was not, as Ruskin or Carlyle would have it, the playing out of eternal laws in various circumstances. "The history of civilisation," Morley wrote in terms echoed by other contemporaries, "is the history of the displacement of old conceptions by new ones more conformable to the facts."[15]

Contemporary readers were well aware of Morley's aim in reviving Condorcet, Vauvenargues, Turgot, and later Voltaire, Robespierre, and Diderot. Reevaluating the thinking of the *philosophes* according to the Liberal agenda of the 1870s, Morley revealed, according to one contemporary reviewer, that though the revolutionary spirit "failed historically it did not fail ultimately, for the wave of thought and action to which it gave birth has not yet subsided, and is not likely to subside till the world gets some sort of a glimpse of a true social polity." This declaration of the intellectual legacy of the century in the *Contemporary Review* was made more emphatic by its juxtaposition with an article in praise of the revolutionary spirit of the French Commune. The "Spiritual Revolution" sketched out in Morley's portraits of the last century seemed indeed to be at full swell.[16]

Ruskin took such offense at this reading of Morley's French studies in the *Contemporary* that he publicly attacked it in *Fors*. He strenuously objected to the elevation of Morley's view of the eighteenth century at the expense of Carlyle's. Although Ruskin's immediate complaint was about "an incidental page" of the review that assailed Carlyle's character (27:180), the vehemence of his reaction suggests there was much more at stake than the defense of a friend.[17] "Now, I tell you once for all," he insisted, "Carlyle is the only living writer who has spoken the absolute and perpetual truth . . . and exactly in proportion to the inherent weakness of brain in your lying guides, will be their animosity against Carlyle" (27:179). The enemy here, labeled simply the "modern Liberal," is not only Morley's reviewer. Morley had himself recently published a skeptical account of Carlyle's career.

In the context of this letter of *Fors Clavigera*, reasserting the primacy of Carlyle's example over Morley's has a special significance. Beginning from a liberal newspaper's "rational" solution to the land question (mechanize farming and retain merely "a few well-paid labourers," 27: 166), Ruskin illustrates an alternate approach to associated social problems. He traces the history of landlords through a literary tradition from Homer to Scott to Carlyle. This march through fiction seems at first a digression from the issue at hand, but Ruskin eventually asserts a connection. Like his own idiosyncratic politics as he describes them here, all political behavior is revealed to be the product of imaginary conceptions. For all of Morley's talk about rational scrutiny as the motive of historical change, the Republican revolutionaries in Paris were driven by their own invented "shadow of a King," not by the behavior of "the extant and visible King" (27:172). Just as the young Ruskin was enchanted by mythical gods, so the most radical reformers were held in thrall by a symbolic role, not an actual person. Liberal critics, with their skeptical "squinting" (27:180), ignored the political truth that Carlyle had long recognized: a rational law having no roots in public imagination "cannot hold, however much you ordain and pronounce it" (27:179). Effective social policies, according to Ruskin, must be "rational *as well as* romantic" (27:171, emphasis added).

Ruskin tries to reintegrate these two terms, which had been so decisively separated in both Morley's and Pattison's political histories. Moreover, he addresses in *Fors Clavigera* an element of social behavior completely ignored in such accounts. Like Rousseau, he insists on inserting a third term into the Enlightenment opposition between reason and passion. The great truth of the St. George myth was in its characterization of the tension not between the sentimental and the rational, but, he says in an unexpected conjunction, between the sentimental and the "bestial" (27:627). His choice of words seems a deliberate challenge to the kinds of historical analysis he confronts in *Fors*, a definite refusal to buy into the notion either that human society had progressed from the savage to the civilized, or that thinking man had learned to suppress those instincts which dominated the life of a ruder age. Ruskin's examples are all to the contrary. The Greek Minotaur, which he saw as the pagan counterpart to St. George's dragon, represented "the more terrible and mysterious relations between the lower creatures and man" (27:387). It had, he explained, "a man's body, a bull's head (which is precisely the general type of the English nation to-day)": this figure signified the mingling of "a brutal instinct with the human mind" where "the brute rules, the humanity is subordinate" (27:428). The future of society was determined by which instinct was allowed to gain the upper hand.

By Ruskin's lights, nineteenth-century English history was not, as others were claiming, a story of progress. His Evangelical mistrust of human nature permeated his historical understanding: material progress and rational reforms had little relation to the essential evil of the human heart. In one of the few diary sketches for *Fors* that was never used, Ruskin reveals how this belief shapes his process of reading history. Like a vituperative preacher he castigates his "Divinely minded modern Reader," who will make of a brief passage in Venetian history "what dirty thoughts you can—Worms all . . . in the hearts of these [Venetian] men no doubt—as in yours and mine—much dirt. . . . Any quantity indeed—you may find to eat, if you like the Dish—Frantic ambition—mere cock of the game—Pugnacity—Pure Robber's lust of gold—not a little of women—And Sneaking treachery . . . you wretched nineteenth century born rogue."[18] This remarkable double projection—Ruskin transferring to his imagined reader a displaced reaction to past history—displays the fluidity with which he moves between historical time frames. Interpreting history becomes a complicated process of revelation and transference: bringing to light the Venetian "rogue" serves as a means of ousting the Victorian villain. The modern reader's reaction, ironically, is both projection and reflection. He does not merely construct the historical subject out of his own obsessions: his encounter with the records of Venetian life force him to reexamine his perception of himself as superior Victorian subject. The disgust he feels for the Venetians allows him to recognize the truth about himself. Learning history, we learn to recognize the true patterns of human behavior and to discount the temporary trappings of contemporary life.

Ruskin's outburst against the modern reader is prompted by his own obsessive rereading of the records of the past. During the summer and autumn of 1876, he enters in his diary observations based on an ongoing study of Venetian history. It becomes apparent that the fortunes of Venice are interpreted not in terms of politics, economics, or geographical limitations, but rather in terms of religious allegory. Ruskin reads in that city the lesson of the Fall. A page after his diatribe on modern readers, he notes excitedly of his day's historical reading: "Seed of Evil growing! Result beginning to show." Looking at Venetian history through biblical paradigms was certainly not new to Ruskin. It had formed the kernel of his aesthetic analysis in the second volume of *The Stones of Venice*.[19] What is interesting about his examination in the diaries is that it becomes an integral part of its context. His commentaries on the fate of Venice, recorded on the backs of his more personal diary entries, read like a parallel commentary on his own experience. As in the proposed passage for *Fors* cited above, the diary in its format weaves together modern and medieval history in a way that makes historical interpretation a multilayered process. Interpretation in the present moment is guided by contemporary concerns (Ruskin's preoccupation with the process of the Fall); at the same time, events from the past, juxtaposed with modern experience, serve as guides to interpreting current behavior.

Ruskin replicates the construction of his diaries in letter 42 of *Fors Clavigera*. Explaining why this letter, unlike most of the others in the series, does not begin with the date of composition, Ruskin explains in a prefatory paragraph: "I must construct my letters . . . for a while, of swept-up fragments; every day provokes me to write new matter; but I must not lose the fruit of the old days" (28:90). The initial effect of the letter does indeed seem to be that of a haphazard arrangement of scattered scraps of material: it includes old passages not before included in *Fors*, an extract from Lady Montagu's letters, a recent letter published in the Venetian paper *Rinnovamento*, an eyewitness account of thirteenth-century Venice published in a sixteenth-century French history of the city, a quotation from a recent number of *Punch*, a citation of a paper read at an 1860 Social Science meeting in Glasgow. In fact, Ruskin's prefatory apologia becomes an important statement about the process of reading and writing history exemplified in this letter. The older material mixes with and provides commentary on the "new matter": the "fruit of the old days" can be seen in modern times. In what on the surface appears to be an unfolding argument about modern political economy, the various texts of which the letter is composed move chronologically backward and forward with little warning. After the opening paragraph, the only date given to the text appears at the head of an apparently disused fragment from an 1873 number of *Fors*. Lady Montagu's letter in Venice is printed immediately afterward, as though it originates from and addresses the circumstances of the same date. The 1872 letter from a Venetian paper, which on the one hand clinches Ruskin's case about the downfall of that state, is made a "pregnant" critique of modern British habits (28:93). This "swept-up" material is suddenly brought up to date by the end of the letter, where Ruskin's mention of his age puts his text closer to the date of its issue, June 1874.

What is ingenuously presented as an assorted scrapbook, ending with a contemporary account of "the English notion of civilizing" others in the "Notes and Correspondence" appendix, becomes an apocalyptic warning about the machinery of empire. The fall of Venice, progressively revealed in the letter in historical snippets that at first glance seem to apply to Victorian England, foretells the fate of "falling London" (28:488). It is not just that Ruskin posits a link between the destinies of Venice and of the present age, as he does in *The Stones of Venice*. Landow explains how that work is permeated with Ruskin's early belief that "God structured time so that the events of the scriptural narrative would prefigure contemporary history."[20] In letter 42 he develops a mode of historical narrative that enacts this understanding and complicates it. Past and present are brought sharply together in a way that both implies a typological connection and erases historical distance. The historicity of actual events is blurred in the present tense of the letter (itself depicted in the prefatory paragraph as already belated). Reading history is both synchronic— everything is consumed as part of the contemporary moment—and diachronic—his audience's understanding, Ruskin argues, is the product of Venetian imperial assumptions. And the writing of history becomes a part of the process of history; it is "swept up" in the movement of events. There is no clear vantage point, no fixed prospect from which to decipher the final effect of an originary cause. Allegorical narrative, which moves easily across time, becomes the only possible "true" version of history, because history properly understood is always in process, and always in the process of being reinterpreted for the present. Thus Ruskin's

"Utopian" explanations, he contends, quoting his detractors, and his seemingly illogical historical method marked by "effeminate sentimentality" (28:92, 102), provide a more accurate account of social development than the strictly chronological, progressive narratives of his critics.

The figure of St. George plays an integral part in Ruskin's argument that true historical narrative proceeds allegorically. The Christian saint represented what for Ruskin was the only "true" law of social existence: the eternal battle between love or charity and the bestial elements in human nature, embodied in St. George's legendary foe, the dragon. Ruskin's view of history as the continual reenactment of the Fall is played out in *Fors* in terms of the dragon; each age he considers is judged according to its treatment of this "visible symbol of the everlasting Disobedience" (27: 483). Previous centuries had taken to heart St. George as "the leader of a sacred soldiership, which conquers more than its mortal enemies, and prevails against the poison, and the shadow, of Pride, and Death" (27: 481). The modern age had taken the demonic image as the "Rod of their lawgiver" (27:483), turning "rational" disobedience into its godhead. Ruskin carefully weaves an old story, as Paul Sawyer puts it, into "a redemptive plot" for secular society.[21] "Modern extremely wise and liberal historians" would scoff at such a myth (27:399). But it embodied a law of human nature "for ever unchangeable" and "long since . . . known . . . by wise nations" (28:30).

At certain moments, Ruskin's rejection of the liberals' scientific notion of history sounds somewhat like Nietzsche's in the same period. Nietzsche, too, had begun to criticize materialist and positivist accounts of the past in his 1874 essay, "The Use and Abuse of History." He, like Ruskin, insists on the importance of the irrational in comprehending the course of human behavior. For both writers, the past was a record not of developing reason but of passion and illogicality. Moreover, neither saw in scientific ideas of history a means of addressing the needs of, in Nietzsche's words, the present "health of a man, a people, or a culture."[22] Ruskin charged that no matter how rational the arrangement of public affairs, the real cultural dilemma was how to address and channel that part of human nature which could not be quantified and explained. All action, he claimed in his antirationalist terminology, fell ultimately into the pattern of either the sentimental or the bestial: "Into one or the other . . . of these two forms of sentiment, conjugal and family love, or compassion, all human happiness, properly so called, resolves itself; but the spurious or counter-happiness of lust, covetousness, and vanity being easily obtained, and naturally grasped at, instead, may altogether occupy the lives of men, without ever allowing them to know what happiness means" (27: 627). In this struggle for resolution, Ruskin's domestic ideal of the nation (outlined at length in chapter 3) sets the conditions for psychological stability. The bestial has no place in the well-ordered household; the sentimental is strengthened and sanctified. The irrational was most strongly at work in childhood: children were not little, rational adults, but rather untamed, driven by desire. Those desires that were healthy—what Ruskin called the sentimental—were encouraged in their affectionate relations with their parents; those which were unhealthy—Ruskin's bestial—were checked by the discipline of the father. It is a small step from this stern paternal theory of child-rearing to Ruskin's theory of a nation, in which the citizen's virtues are encouraged in their investment in one another and in the feminized "Angel of England," and their vices discouraged by a strong fatherly authority.

In letter 74, entitled "Father-Law," Ruskin demonstrates the connection between such a social theory and his version of historical narrative. The letter begins with a fifteen-line sentence, with three distinctive time-frames, each representing one possible version of historical "data." It opens with a mythological symbol: St. Ursula's dianthus, sent as a mysterious "sign" to the sleeping Ruskin. A reading of the sign is interrupted by an excursus in hyphens. This seeming digression sets up alternative ways of describing the moment at which Ruskin writes his letter. References to chronological time are introduced parenthetically (the clock "has just struck eight," 29:30) and immediately displaced by a description of a much more expansive chronological time-frame—the diurnal sunrise over sixteenth-century domed churches. This in turn is replaced by Ruskin's thoughts about current affairs (the Eastern question). As the excursus comes to a close, Ruskin admits that he has nearly "lost sight" (as his reader now has) of what turns out to be the key in the rest of the letter to interpreting contemporary events, medieval Venetian laws, and progressive views of history: the mysterious mythological sign with which the sentence began.

The syncretic argument of letter 74—which juxtaposes sixteenth-century Venetian markets with modern markets in Sheffield, recent

political speeches with eighteenth-century Venetian decrees—shows
how such signs can function as *figurae*, figures by which we interpret history. Ursula's dianthus is both a figure grounded in a particular historical
moment (Ruskin explains its origins and its representation in Carpaccio's
painting of the saint) and one that points beyond that moment to its fulfillment at another point in history. Although it does not conform to
positivist notions of history, this kind of typological reading is foundationally historical, as Erich Auerbach has pointed out in his discussion of
figura: "Real historical figures are to be interpreted spiritually, but the
interpretation points to a carnal, hence historical fulfillment."[23] The difference between Ruskin's typological historicism and rationalist historicism is exemplified in the letter's structure. The general direction of the
argument seems to be a roughly chronological treatment of trade policy,
culminating in "all the glorious liberties of British trade" (29:41), but the
letter ends with a rather different fulfillment of the "Father-Law" pointed
to by Ursula's dianthus (the name of which, as Ruskin translates it, means
"'Flower of God,' or especially of the Greek Father of the Gods," 29:31).
"Modern liberties" (29:37) are characterized as a falling away from the
strong regulatory policies of sixteenth-century Venice (derivative from
Greek laws, 29:38, and operative when Carpaccio painted Ursula's "bal-
cony window-flower," 29:33). Ruskin's paternalistic St. George's Guild,
invoked at the very end of the letter in a set of cryptic aphorisms that
finally refer the reader back to the Eastern question broached in the first
sentence, represents the historical fulfillment of the opening *figura*. It
stands for a "father-law" addressing "the Evil Spirit [that] indeed exists"
in contemporary society (29:44). The letter displaces with figural interpretation a chronological, "progressive" tale of history, briefly invoked
in Ruskin's first sentence. Through an argument organized around a symbol rather than around logical cause and effect, he attempts to illustrate
"the use of myths, when they are living" (29:31). Past events are not a
dead letter but a living scripture to be used in the ongoing struggle to
establish political order against irrational instinct.

Ruskin's typological histories in *Fors Clavigera* dramatize this continuing battle. He reinterprets familiar contemporary narratives of economic and political development as, at bottom, moral allegories of progress *and* decline. The event that so inspired many liberal historians, the
rule of the French Commune, serves as a topical example of his revisionist

method. Beginning with factual accounts culled from the newspapers, Ruskin's description of the recent massacres in France evolves into a biblical vision. The blood was as much on English as on French hands, Ruskin warned: "This cruelty has been done by the kindest of us, and the most honourable; by the delicate women, by the nobly-nurtured men, who through their happy and, as they thought, holy lives, have sought, and still seek, only 'the entertainment of the hour.' And this robbery has been taught to the hands,—this blasphemy to the lips,—of the lost poor, by the False Prophets who have taken the name of Christ in vain, and leagued themselves with His chief enemy, 'Covetousness, which is idolatry'" (27:111). The vice of Covetousness or Envy, the Giotto fresco of which was reproduced as the frontispiece to the original issue of this letter, becomes a symbol for the state of modern society (fig. 1). Its effect is diminished in the Library Edition, where it faces the page close to the end of the letter in which it is mentioned. Like the rest of the plates of Giotto's virtues and vices published in the first year of *Fors*, it should stand as the allegorical figurehead for the entire letter, determining the significance of the contemporary issues which follow. Thus, the French Commune, in its acts of destruction and vengeance, is seen as a fallen community, bereft of the virtue of Charity. In letters 8 and 9, the theorems of political economy are judged by the standards of Justice and Injustice. More than exercises in art appreciation, the plates serve as graphic markers, as illustrations of the key symbols by which any "notable sign of the times" is to be deciphered (28:766).

With its Giotto plates and series of Lesson Photographs, *Fors Clavigera* offers a kind of pictorial history of national life, one that attempts to rival "all the illustrations in your *Illustrated News* or *Illustrated Times* from one year's end to another" (27:512). Ruskin's letters provide common reference points for interpreting experience, much like the paintings and carvings in Gothic cathedrals. This means of proceeding recalls Ruskin's earlier works, particularly *The Stones of Venice* and *Seven Lamps*. What is striking in *Fors Clavigera* is the task that this kind of allegorical scene-painting performs in Ruskin's developing theories of nationality. His pictographs, as a closer comparison between his use of St. Ursula's dianthus and the Giotto frescoes suggests, play a complicated role in mediating between Ruskin's historical scheme and his nationalist vision.

His reading of the first of these images is both broadly allegorical

Fig. 1. Envy. Photogravure from the fresco by Giotto in the Arena Chapel, Padua. *Works of John Ruskin*, vol. 27.

(the dianthus is associated with a range of moral values, which have no essential connection to the image itself) and more narrowly typological (the image is read as a *figura* with a particular historical meaning). The allegorical reading corresponds to what Ruskin defines in an 1870 lecture (later printed in *Aratra Pentelici*) as the "imaginative" use of myth, "that is to say, the invention of material symbols which may lead us to contemplate the character and nature of gods, spirits, or abstract virtues and powers, without in the least implying the actual presence of such Beings among us, or even their possession, in reality, of the forms we attribute to them" (20:242). Ruskin talks at length in that lecture about the vital importance of such symbols for national culture. These images of "spiritual power" function as a "safe basis of some of the happiest impulses of [a noble people's] moral nature" (20:259). They become, like the myth of St. George as Ruskin uses it in his letters, public icons of national moral values. These purely imaginary symbols cannot be dismissed by the rational explanations of material historians and scientists, he explains, in the same manner that they can dismiss myths as used in literalist interpretations of the Bible. The power of such figures is that they come to form a part of the collective imagination, and thus part of the way in which individuals perceive themselves as national subjects. Their force does not depend on the veracity of a literal referent.

Ruskin's interpretation of St. Ursula's dianthus as a concrete, historical *figura*, on the other hand, challenges such a distinction between imaginative, allegorical signs and those that are read literally. This latter construction comes perilously close, in Ruskin's own terms from the 1870 lectures, to "idolatry": "the attribution of a spiritual power to a material thing" (20:242). Although both imaginative and literal interpretations are operative in Ruskin's earlier works, as he employs alternately highchurch and evangelical methods of typology, he tries here to insist on the priority of the former hermeneutic mode.[24] As Gary Wihl has cogently argued in his look at *Aratra Pentelici*, Ruskin has difficulty sustaining the difference between imagination and idolatry in the very lectures that are devoted to distinguishing them. In his discussion of the Greek figure *Charis*, Wihl contends, Ruskin "confuses the distinction between literal and figurative meanings."[25] What begins as a defense of the allegorical power of *Charis* turns, in Ruskin's own language, into an idolatrous description of *Charis*'s literal force.

He seems close to this kind of confusion in *Fors Clavigera* as well in his discussion of St. Ursula's flower. When readers apparently wrote to inquire whether they were to take his remarks about the dianthus allegorically or literally, Ruskin deliberately conflates the two kinds of interpretation in his reply: "whatever spiritual powers are in true personality appointed to go to and fro in the earth . . . can only be revealed, in their reality, by the gradual confirmation in the matured soul of what at first were only its instinctive desires, and figurative perceptions" (29:54). Here it seems that an imaginative use of myth is important because it enables idolatry: the "reality" of a symbol like St. Ursula can be recognized by those whose perceptions were figured according to the virtues she is made to represent. Does Ruskin imply here that she already exists, or that she is revealed *as* real to those whose way of seeing the world prompts them to idolatrously attribute spiritual power to her? Is she the product of a noble pathetic fallacy—the projection of strengthening "instinctive desires" and "figurative perceptions," which then reveal themselves "in their reality" as a "true personality" apparently outside subjective experience—or a true incarnation of spiritual power (29:54)? The question is crucial to Ruskin's narration of national history. How are his readers to take his allegorical method? Is he an anguished preacher urging his readers to redeem national behavior by learning literally to "believe in guardian angels" (29:54)? If so, *Fors* would seem to have little to say to its skeptical, late Victorian audience. Does his allegory of the ages address general moral issues, or does it purport to affect actual civic behavior? Should it be regarded, as his critics insisted, as a stirring literary creation with no practical effect?

Ruskin attempts to negotiate these issues through elaborate instructions on how to read his pictographs. Early on in *Fors Clavigera* the distinction between imaginative and idolatrous interpretation is brought into play. Ruskin deliberately confounds the difference between these terms in his treatment of the Giotto frescoes, which at first appears to conform more closely to his discussion of the imagination. In the letter entitled "Charitas" Giotto's figure of that virtue functions first as a way of spinning out a moral allegory (fig. 2). The French Commune, Ruskin argues, can be seen as antiprogressive because its violence betrays Christian ideals. But at the end of the letter he insists that Giotto's representation is not merely imaginative: "Giotto is quite literal in his meaning, as

Fig. 2. Charitas. Photogravure from the fresco by Giotto in the Arena Chapel, Padua. *Works of John Ruskin*, vol. 27.

well as figurative" (27:130).[26] His readers are exhorted to carry out literally the action Giotto portrays: "Your love is to give food and flowers, and to labour for them only." This image is not "allegorical": it does not function as the imaginative image does in Ruskin's lectures, where "the visible stands for the invisible; the literal sign has a purely figurative value."[27] To ensure that readers cannot miss the collapse of literal and figurative value here, Ruskin emphatically repeats the former term. We should "be sure of" the truth of Giotto's representation "literally": "You are to be *literally* employed in cultivating the ground," laboring only, as Giotto's Charitas does, for food and flowers (27:129).

The point of this conjunction between imagination and idolatry can be grasped through an earlier passage in the same letter. "The *Real* war in Europe," Ruskin explains in reference to the French Commune and the Franco-Prussian War, "of which this fighting in Paris is the Inauguration," is not the one between French Communists and the French government, nor the one between France and Prussia. Rather, it is a contest between "the Capitalists" and "the workman, such as these have made him" (27:127). Such an assertion elsewhere in Ruskin's work might lead to one of his familiar discussions of public idolatry, of evil behavior based on a too-literal worship of the idols of the marketplace. Here, however, the problem is tagged as the elevation of imagination over idolatry. Too great a separation between symbol and material referent, between signifier and signified, meant a radical disjunction between public rhetoric and individual behavior. Such a disjunction made it possible to celebrate laissez-faire trade and personal liberty as ideals, while constraining others' actions through a kind of economic practice that "hides itself even from itself" (27:127). Symbolic virtues were not being literally translated into practice, in the manner of Ruskin's reading of Charitas. There was too little correspondence, in the words of his description of the imagination, between "abstract virtues and powers" and the actual "forms we attribute to them" (20:242).

Ruskin puts the problem in a different context earlier in the letter. The French Communists had raised the battle cry, "Vive la République!" (27:122). This personification of national life had remained at the level of abstract rhetoric. The French, Ruskin charges, had not taken their credo literally enough. He dramatizes this both with a lesson in etymology and with a definition of the nature of national culture. The "Re" in "République" "is not like the mischievous Re in Reform and

Refaire . . . but it is short for *res*, which means 'thing.'" When the French shouted "Vive la République" they should consider "what thing it is [they] wish to be publicly alive." Public symbols must be made to have a literal referent in social practice. In the absence of such a referent, the nation remained at the level of vague personification, "without in the least implying the actual presence of such [a] Being" (20:242). The actual "commonalty or publicity" of a group of people depended "on the nature of the *thing* that is common" (27:122). Merely imaginative symbols of nationality were not adequate for creating and maintaining a distinctive national identity. A coherent nation, in the terms of Ruskin's definition of idolatry, "begins . . . in the idea or belief of a real presence . . . in a thing in which there is no such presence" (20:230). In this scenario strong belief *creates* public reality; faith in the exitence of a distinctive national *res* will in time shape a people into an identifiable national *race*.

Ruskin rings a change here on his familiar formulation that the art of a nation is an index of the people's morality: "The art of any country *is the exponent of its social and political virtues*" (20:39). This statement is turned around in his nationalist program in *Fors Clavigera*. The images represented in the plates accompanying the letters, like Giotto's image of Charitas, are meant to figure, not merely reflect, national behavior. As I argued in chapter 3, Ruskin in his late works sees national life in terms of a communal morality to be instilled in its citizens, not in terms of rational association or instinctive racial behavior. The gallery of pictures in *Fors* functions as a way of joining Ruskin's allegorical vision of history with his nationalist theory. Each image acts as *figura*, a representation grounded in a particular moment; we can learn to appreciate it as a concrete cultural artifact. At the same time it acts as a means of realizing the *figura*. When Ruskin's readers internalize the image, at the moment at which it enters into their "figurative perceptions," it influences their conception of Victorian life. It becomes both a part of the reader's cultural history and a vital influence on historical experience. Through this negotiation between two historical moments, Ruskin hopes to effect a reconfiguration of the "waste ground" of modern English life (20:42). In a striking reversal of his early statements about the pathetic fallacy in *Modern Painters*, he declares in *Fors* that material reality *can* be forcefully changed by our imaginative conceptions: "the facts of the universe are NOT steadfast . . . they ARE changed by human fancies . . . the laws of the universe are no more relentless than the God who wrote them . . .

[they] DO give way under the pressure of human passion and force" (29: 371). Communal fancies could, in this telling, literally change the landscape of Victorian life.

The dual extension of Ruskin's historicism, pointing both to prefiguration and fulfillment, openly embodies what Timothy Bahti describes as the duality of any historical narrative. The term history, Bahti contends, "names two notions, ontologically opposed as origin and representation." History as origin, as an account of the past, must reduce one particular moment into a "what happened," an event whose significance is both explained by and fulfilled in its narrative representation. The past is made into a "literal sign for an allegorical meaning."[28] Part of the problem entailed in such an allegory is that the *figura* must have a fixed meaning that is simultaneously embedded in its originary moment and relevant to the larger narrative in which it is represented. The figure operates, in effect, in two separate historical registers: its "truth" supposedly derives from its existence as a material event, and yet that event has meaning only as it can be detached from its initial circumstances and translated into the present tense. If the value of an historical fact or image is its portability, not its concrete historicity, the *figura* becomes eminently unstable. Ruskin encounters this difficulty in his description of the "literal and figurative meaning" of Giotto's Charitas. His explication of the present day fulfillment of Giotto's literal figure is compromised, at least in the Library Edition of the letter, by a personal note appended by his editors. "I do not doubt I read the action wrong," he admits, in a comment written while he was compiling an index to *Fors* (27: 130n). If there is a possibility of such a misreading, if an interpretation is not fixed by particular historical circumstances but rather can be adjusted according to the needs of the narrative of the moment, how can it be said to be prefigurative? Ruskin insists on the literal force of Giotto's figure in an effort to firmly fix social practice to political symbols. But when Charitas can be said to represent two radically different actions (is she giving her heart to God or receiving it? does she signify a division of our personal investments— our soul should be given to God, material gifts to our neighbors? or does she stand for the inadequacy of human efforts—we can do our material duty to our neighbors, but God gives the only meaningful gift?), Ruskin finds himself back in the predicament he hoped to solve. Charitas functions, at best, as a precarious icon.

This potential slippage in figurative narrative threatens both Ruskin's historicism and his nationalist rhetoric. For the ontological ambivalence of the historical referent is also inherent in any attempt to narrate the nation. On the one hand, claims for the coherence of a culture must be anchored in a specific moment, an inaugural historical event. All national stories, in other words, depend on an originary *figura*. Just as Ruskin referred back to myth or religious types, Victorian liberal historians figured their origins through the Enlightenment. Using the past to validate the cultural present, however, creates a frame that subtly reverses a conventional narrative movement from cause to effect. That is, the ostensible authority of the argument lies in the seemingly sequential unfolding of national history: the culture is the logical outcome of its moment of inception. Even Ruskin's loosely allegorical history proceeds through the logic of rise and fall. And yet the narrative procedure takes the form of a quest, instigated in the present: the narrative "cause" is a particular interpretation of the *Zeitgeist*, the "effect" a mapping of history. Moreover, the ideological motivations for telling national history make this paradox particularly pressing. Constructing a "people" is an attempt to influence actual behavior. Is the life of a country a vital force, capable of regeneration and reproduction, or a belated expression of an earlier time? Does it carry the seeds of a national future, or merely the vestiges of a once potent past? Not only is national history troubled by a narrative tension between past and present, then, but also by the question of whether it can be performative. To use Homi Bhabha's summary of this problem, the idea of a national culture "must be thought in a double-time." [29] Nationalist discourse must successfully project a cultural future, as well as demonstrate the ways in which national life can be said to complete a narrative of origins.

Positivist histories, committed, in Bhabha's words, to a kind of "discourse of historicism where narrative is only the agency of the event, or the medium of a naturalistic continuity of Community or Tradition," eschew from the start this crucial present and future tense. Their accounts are plagued, as is Ruskin's, by the potentially weak link between political rhetoric and public behavior. When Victorian liberals argued for a connection between tradition and present policy, they undermined their own political theory, whose starting premise was the rational rejection of any form of tradition. Their orderly narratives could claim to reflect natural political process. But their assumption that historical progress followed natural laws of cause and effect left little ground for actual intervention in public life. John Morley recognized this problem, as he concluded his most active period as a literary historian and embarked on the political career that would lead to his entry into Parliament. Although he once had rejected a priori historical arguments, he reconsidered the question when he speculated how best "to hold [public opinion] steadfastly against wayward gusts of passion." Announcing a "thorough unity of conviction which comes from sincerely accepting a common set of principles to start from," rather than purporting to trace a logical analysis of historical cause and effect, might, he felt, be the most efficacious means of presenting national narrative.[30]

Ruskin's typological readings can more effectively address the "double-time" of cultural life than the sequential presentation of positivist historians, but his letters still must find a way to fix a specific interpretation of tradition to living cultural practice. He tries first to make this connection by linking his nationalist vision to symbols already current in contemporary rhetoric. For example, although he draws heavily on Carpaccio's Venetian canvasses to flesh out the significance of the myth of St. George, it already had a familiar gloss. St. George was, of course, the patron saint of England. Since the Tudors he had been associated with the Order of the Garter and with all the pomp and ceremony attending on monarchy. At the same time, he had remained a saint of the people, the subject of eighteenth-century chapbooks and of the most popular mumming play in the middle ages, *Saint George and the Dragon*, versions of which were still performed into the 1860s.[31] As Mark Girouard has noted, St. George was also current in imperialist rhetoric of the period.[32] Ruskin's discussions of the Guild of St. George tapped into an existing rhetoric of chauvinism, heroism and nationalism.

Through emphasizing dramatic performance, Ruskin tries yet another means of directly connecting his allegorical figures with actual practice. In his lecture on idolatry, he had argued that such performances helped to close the gap between imaginative conceptions and daily life. "The energy of growth in any people," he claimed, "may be almost directly measured by their passion for imitative art," for acting brought together the process of "*making*" with "*making believe*" (20:221). In *Fors Clavigera* Ruskin translates a passage from Plato to illustrate the potency of acting out public symbols: "the kind of play customary with the children [of a state] is the principal of the forces that maintain the established laws. For when the kind of play is determined, and so regulated that the children always play and use their fancies in the same way . . . this quietness allows the laws which are established in earnest to remain quiet also" (29:239–40).[33] Fanciful play becomes a way of linking imagination to civic action: making believe, when rightly regulated, makes for political order. Laws "remain quiet" because there is no cause to enforce them; they are enacted by a people who "use their fancies in the same way." Just as German nationalists early in the nineteenth century sought social regeneration in a revival of Greek gymnastics and choral singing, Ruskin advocated such a revival as well in *Fors Clavigera*, calling dancing and music the "two primal instruments of education" and linking them with the establishment of civil harmony (28:405).[34] Ruskin's May Queen festivals are reminiscent of the popular German festivals that mixed pagan and Christian symbolism to draw together a disparate nation. "Ruskin wanted singing and movement, the means of rejoicing, to be once more the accepted expression of secure mores," Catherine Morley observes.[35] He was also quite aware, it seems, of their usefulness in promoting and instilling such mores. Like the popular St. George, they could turn national symbols into dramatic national practice.

Collectively dramatizing national tradition did not, however, guarantee against potential misreadings of that tradition, misreadings of the kind that Ruskin himself committed in his interpretation of Giotto's figure of Charitas. His awareness of such a possibility is suggested in a subtle shift in his historical method in *Fors Clavigera*. The legibility of the syncretic style of the letters depends on Ruskin's willingness to at least offer hints that might help the reader negotiate between figurative and literal interpretations. But particularly in the letters of the last few years of the series, those hints are much harder to find. Jeffrey Spear accounts for the change by suggesting that Ruskin's "social purpose was increasingly enveloped in private myth and personal obsession."[36] A somewhat different account can be suggested through remarking a change in Ruskin's allegorical use of history. If the letters of the 1870s rely on a pattern of prefiguration and fulfillment, the letters of the following decade stop at the moment of the *figura*. That is, Ruskin still proposes mythological types for national experience, but he resists offering a narrative for their contemporary relevance. For example, instead of "The Two Clavigerae" of his August 1877 letter—two real female nail-makers who literally act out

Fig. 3. "Fors Infantiae." Engraving from a drawing by Kate Greenaway. *Works of John Ruskin*, vol. 29.

in the nineteenth century part of the symbolic significance of the title of Ruskin's series—two "Fors Infantiae" from a Kate Greenaway drawing serve as the allegorical figurehead to letter 95 (fig. 3). As Ruskin said in one of his Oxford lectures, Greenaway's illustrations are notable for excluding all traces of Victorian life: "none of [the] things which the English mind now rages after, possess any attraction whatever for this unimpressionable person" (33:347). The importance in his eyes of her child portraits is that they symbolize girls who might one day exist given different cultural values. The quizzical pair in the plate to letter 95 are neither entirely contemporary—their toy windmill either recalls or looks forward to days when all "vestige . . . of science, civilization, economic arrangements, or commercial enterprise" is absent from the landscape (33:347)—nor, in their fashionable outfits, merely nostalgic. They seem to exemplify, literally, the childhood issue of *Fors Clavigera*, the likely product of the compulsory moral education Ruskin outlines in the letter, the inhabitants of his "true Utopia" (29:499). The future significance of Ruskin's letters is implied in these figures that are never fully explained. They do not operate as fulfillment of *figura* in the present moment; they are *figura* for some later audience that will have different interpretive skills.

In the same way, Ruskin asserts that his own letters will be meaningful signs for readers of "a day [that] will come" (27:669). If contemporary readers cannot understand his series, he states, it is because he has written not for "men who have been produced by the instructions of Mr. John Stuart Mill" but for readers who one day will be practiced in allegorical understanding. At the end of the run of *Fors Clavigera* he seems to imply that he cannot, from the vantage point of 1884, decode his own narrative. The last letter of the series provides almost no extended interpretations of the symbols and stories presented in it. It consists largely of the kind of long excerpts from other texts with which it begins. Ruskin the explanatory guide to modern history is hardly present. Indeed, this number ends with a prediction that Ruskin's letters are themselves the origin of a new narrative yet to be written: "The story of Rosy Vale is not ended;—surely out of its silence the mountains and the hills shall break forth into singing" (29:528). Ruskin's story does not speak for itself; it awaits its proper historian. In this cryptic ending, Ruskin moves from one kind of allegory of history to another, from typological history to what Bahti has called "the allegory of the *eschatology* of historical meaning." In such a model "the meaning of historiography" would be "the presentation of reality itself, as history, in its very ongoing deferral of fulfillment—reality preserved, that is, as signs to be read, preserved as literature to be read."[37] Ruskin is no longer the critical analyst of history but a chronicler whose impressions of Victorian life are important because they point to a fulfillment they cannot provide. Their meaning lies beyond the immediate story, in a future England that will recognize in these letters the kind of typological significance Ruskin unfolds in his interpretations of Venetian life.

There is no chance of misreading in this allegory of history. Signs contain their own meaning that need not—indeed cannot—be translated into narrative. Such a radical and radically ahistorical solution to problems inherent in writing national tradition had been implicit in *Fors*

Clavigera at the start. After all, Ruskin's nationalism was premised on the possibility of inscribing cultural life from a position outside of existing circumstances. At the same time, he promulgated this ideal in a work committed to exploring the historically contingent construction of identity. His epistemology was, from the first, in tension with his political theory. In the final letter of *Fors* Ruskin tries to circumvent the problem by reducing his own voice to footnotes. What he offers us here, he hints at the end, is not the process of making representations, a process deeply embedded in conventions. His epistolary project, Ruskin now says regretfully, was too imbricated in "this outer world," too committed to exploring ways of translating images into "visible utility" (29:527). This attempt to link *"making"* with *"making believe,"* as he had called it in *Aratra*, could too easily be corrupted by the vagaries of interpretation. Despite his former insistence that individual action could not be understood apart from communal "figurative perceptions," he claims in the last letter that actions supersede representations. In the course of thirteen years he had failed to explain his project clearly; now he realizes that it could be succinctly "sum[med] and illumine[d]" by the "history, of a life" of a particular woman in Italy. The Giotto figures had been important because they could be said to embody a typological narrative. The closing figure of Signora Maria matters because she resists allegorical significance: the meaning of her actions is limited to a specific moment in time. Ruskin does not reinterpret or explicate her life; rather, he indicates, her life should be seen as an interpretation of his text. In the same way, the Kate Greenaway illustration for this letter—three girls surrounded by roses— is not explained in Ruskin's text (fig. 4). Presumably, it contains, without need for discursive narrative, the real significance of the mysterious "Rosy Vale." It is a literal translation of Ruskin's own figure. And yet, with no referent in past or present reality—it is a realis*tic* image of Ruskin's metaphorical gesture to a coming utopia—it is incorruptible. It is not susceptible to the slippery slope of allegorical narrative because, like the figure of Signora Maria, it is made to appear self-sufficient. Its meaning is on the surface; it is just what it appears to be. To explain it would be to suggest that it is not complete, that it must be fulfilled to be meaningful. And that simply reintroduces the possibility of attributing to actions or images a meaning which is not already immanent.

Ruskin was anxiously alert to the challenge of making interpretations

Fig. 4. "Rosy Vale." Engraving from a drawing by Kate Greenaway. *Works of John Ruskin*, vol. 29.

stick, as I elaborate in a rather different context in chapter 5. In his discussions of the process of reading he tries to sketch out a way of distinguishing true and false interpretations. He attempts to link the act of reading with practical behavior in much the same way that he tries to link figurative and literal interpretation in his nationalist narrative. His effort to elaborate a theory of reading and a canon that would embody it falls prey to many of the difficulties he encountered in outlining national tradition. Just as his allegorical explanation of history becomes, in the end, a cryptic sign, so his literary history is made finally to stand as part of the tradition it purportedly explains. In an attempt to strengthen the political authority of his letters, Ruskin will only strengthen his opponents' characterization of *Fors Clavigera* as a moving literary curiosity.

That Ruskin's methods of literary history resemble his efforts at national history is hardly surprising. The two efforts are interrelated. Particularly in the public stir over German imperialism, literary history was seen as a forceful means of telling national history. Both Ruskin and the liberal critics who dismissed his historicism were committed to producing canons that would validate their politics. In fact, the very writers who rejected Ruskin's ahistorical procedures replicated those procedures when it came to literary criticism. They, too, had discovered the difficulty of making even the most logical interpretations stick. While they denounced Ruskin for neglecting scientific method, they were themselves berated by the new school of academic historians at Cambridge and Oxford. J. B. Bury, claiming the tradition of the Enlightenment for rather different purposes, voiced the objections of a new generation to the liberal histories of writers such as Morley, Stephen, and Harrison: "It is one of the remarkable ideas which first emerged explicitly into consciousness in the last century that the unique series of phenomena of human development is worthy to be studied for itself, without any ulterior purpose, without any obligation to serve ethical or theological, or any practical ends." [38] The past should be studied for the intrinsic interest of the enterprise; it should not be made a handmaiden to political theory. In the end, neither Ruskin nor his detractors won the war of historical interpretation in the 1870s, a war increasingly waged in the universities. Their skirmishes were reconstituted, with some interesting narrative twists, as a battle over books.

V

The Guidance of Household Gods: Power, Politics, and Nineteenth-Century Canons

ETHICS OF THE DUST (1866) stands out as perhaps the most fanciful and experimental of Ruskin's mature works. Like *Sesame and Lilies* (1865) and *The Crown of Wild Olive* (1866) it is a collection of lectures; unlike them, it reproduces the process of lecturing, including the audience as well as the speaker in the printed text. It resembles the later *Proserpina* (1875–86) in its effort to make scientific investigation into a playground for the imagination. In *Ethics* this move is graphically tried out, as principles of crystallization are turned into the rules of a game at a girls' school: the children translate the formations of minerals into a kind of playground dance.[1] Taking the form of a play, the work refers repeatedly to the idea of production, whether of minerals, metaphors, or morals.

What distinguishes *Ethics of the Dust* from Ruskin's other works of the 1860s—and what makes it more like *Fors Clavigera* than like the earlier political writings—is its representation of narrative self-consciousness. The text incorporates a reflection on the process of storytelling in the course of the tale itself. The Old Lecturer announces the theme in his opening lines: "Come here, Isabel, and tell me what the make-believe was, this afternoon" (18:209). The first lecture becomes less a discussion of "The Valley of Diamonds"—both the title of the chapter and the make-believe that Isabel recounts and the Old Lecturer later expands—than of the fictive status of the story. "But there's no real Valley of Diamonds, is there?" Isabel queries at the end of her tale. "Yes . . . very real indeed," the Lecturer answers, as he begins to spin out an allegory (18:210). "Now you're just playing, you know," interrupts another of the girls. "So are you, you know," he replies, "why mustn't I, if you may?"

(18:211). The bantering turns into an exchange on the difference between play and fact, between story and reality.

One of the first lessons the girls learn in this primer of mineralogy is that fantasy and fact cannot easily be distinguished. Empirical evidence, the Lecturer shows Isabel, is not always reliable. The girls are disappointed when they discover that one of the Lecturer's stories is "only a dream": "Some dreams are truer than some wakings," he admonishes them (18:224). Confused and frustrated, the older girls tell the Lecturer that he is "quite spoiling the children; the poor little things' heads are turning round like kaleidoscopes; and they don't know in the least what you mean." They demand, like little Gradgrinds, "nothing but facts" (18:233). In response, the Lecturer begins by reciting the principles of crystallization; he ends in explaining the "true meaning" of myth. This time, however, there is no complaining about his digressions. In the final line of the scene, one of the girls, in a joking aside about looking for "little Pthahs in the kitchen cupboards," indicates their willingness to proceed on the Lecturer's whimsical terms (18:245). When the next scene begins, the girls are "disconsolate" at being prevented by rain from playing the Lecturer's crystallization game, which, he reminds them, they did not want to do before their last lesson (18:246).

From that point the Lecturer's audience is subdued. The stage directions reveal that the girls no longer speak in a "saucy" manner but "meekly" (18:260); instead of showing "symptoms of high displeasure" and shaking their heads "violently" (18:221), they are "pictures of resignation" who, when chastised, hide their faces behind curtains, under tablecloths, and in their hands (18:248, 260–61). When they question the Lecturer, it is now in a spirit of genuine inquiry, not challenge. They no longer declare that they do not believe in dreams or fantasies, but ask what they "*may* believe" (18:346; emphasis added). When they read scientific books, they are disappointed that the "facts" seem to reveal nothing about the things they really care for. Turning to the Lecturer, they ask that he "tell us where we may stand" on philosophical and moral issues (18:341). In the final scene, there is no more running about or popping out from behind chairs and doorways. The pupils have finally "crystallised" into a unified, orderly group of auditors who seat the Lecturer in the place of authority, offer to serve him his supper, and sit at his feet to receive his answers to their questions.

While ostensibly about the process of crystallization of minerals, Ruskin's text can thus be read as a parable of the formation of audiences. The Lecturer tells the girls early on that they are, as they "sit in [their] ranks, nothing . . . but a lovely group of rosy sugar-candy, arranged by atomic forces" (18:221). By the end of the work, they understand the force of the metaphor. Physically arranging themselves in "orderly rows, each in her proper place" is only the first step in becoming "crystalline." They must, as one of the girls says, "put our little minds, such as they are, in the best trim we can" before they are in the proper state to receive the final lecture (18:339).

Reading *Ethics* in this way would make it follow from Ruskin's publication of the previous year, *Sesame and Lilies*. "You must, in a word, love these people," Ruskin there had told those who would read great authors: "You must love them, and show your love . . . by a true desire to be taught by them, and to enter into their thoughts" (18:63). The statement from "Of Kings' Treasuries" aptly describes both the affectionate relationship the schoolgirls have with the Lecturer and their willingness in the end to quiet their objections and accept his teachings in good faith. It is only by "striving to enter into the faith of others, and to sympathise, in imagination, with the guiding principles of their lives," the Lecturer tells the girls in the final meeting, that one can "justly love them" (18:356). In *Sesame and Lilies* Ruskin had specified that the act of reading required "putting ourselves always in the author's place, annihilating our own personality, and seeking to enter into his" (18:75). In *Ethics* the girls begin to accept the Lecturer's teaching after he tells them the importance of forgetting one's self and focusing completely on another.[2] In the last scene of *Ethics*, the girls become less distinct personalities than part of a chorus which echoes the Lecturer's statements. Indeed, the last female voice we hear is that of one of the girls speaking in the Lecturer's own words, reading from one of his books. So in tune is she with his thoughts that she finds the passage he wants read without a specific reference: "You know the place I mean, do not you?" he asks, confident that she does (18:358).

The circumstances of Ruskin's republication of *Ethics of the Dust* in 1877 reinforce its significance as a parable of reading. Once again it came on the heels of a discussion of how to read, published the previous year as the preface to *The Economist of Xenophon*. Of the four orders of readers

Ruskin had described there, the first three were misled by their dismissal of the truth of "pure fiction," their insistence on "facts," and a belief in their "own superior knowledge" (31:19). These are precisely the attitudes adopted by the schoolgirls at the beginning of *Ethics*. Their final position is emblematic of the ideal audience of the fourth order whom Ruskin praises. He or she is, above all else, "teachable." The "centrally powerful reader," Ruskin explains, "discovers and acknowledges in his own mind the tendency to self-deception" (like the girls who come to see the Lecturer "to be made ashamed of [them]selves," 18:260).

Ruskin's use of the term "powerful" is, in this context, paradoxical, for his ideal reader is clearly characterized by docility. The adjective "teachable" reveals that the metaphorical meeting ground of author and reader as Ruskin envisions it in his preface is the boarding school of *Ethics*. The young girl sent away to be trained and formed depends, like Ruskin's imagined audience, on an external arbiter of meaning and value. The reader is powerful in imagination only: he or she can share vicariously in the creative force of great writers—indeed, must do so in order to understand them—but cannot pretend to possess an autonomous authority.

Sharing the artist's vision was, as G. Robert Stange and Elizabeth Helsinger have demonstrated, the guiding principle of much of Ruskin's work.[3] Helsinger points out that it was precisely on this principle that Ruskin built his own authority in *Modern Painters*. There, she argues, "the ability to see in a certain way, and hence to acquire knowledge" is not exclusive, but democratizing: Ruskin "tries to transfer [it] to his readers through description. The implication is that Ruskin's readers, by the time they finish *Modern Painters*, may have as much authority as Ruskin himself lays claim to."[4] The separation between the audience and the high Romantic critic, who spoke of art always from the artist's perspective, is effaced in Helsinger's reading of Ruskin's early work. Concerned to preserve aesthetic appreciation from the skepticism of empirical science, Ruskin intends to make the artist's vision inclusive and accessible. Disseminating an imaginative means of seeing meant ensuring the survival of art in an increasingly scientific culture.

To put on equal footing those who shared an interest in art was one thing; to give authority to the wide range of readers who might form a part of Ruskin's audience in the 1870s was another. Ruskin is explicit

about the political undertones of his metaphors of reading in the preface
to Xenophon's *Economist*. The works of the great writers form a "high-
storied temple" which is "established for ever" and cannot be "super-
seded" (31:8). At that temple "men of highest power and truest honour"
congregate to "frame the laws" of "the great system of universal truth"
(31:9, 7). The common reader, like the common peasant "withdrawn
. . . from the concerns of policy," is content to live in pastoral innocence,
"confident in the guidance of his household gods" (31:11). Inspiration is
not to be found everywhere, as modern theologians, "with proud sense
of enlightenment, declare" (31:10). It remains, like the God of the Old
Testament, in the temple where "the mightiest of the people" are "gathered always." The great city-states of history flourished when they re-
spected the wisdom of this "eternal senate" (31:8n); they fell when "the
multiplied swarms of [their] inhabitants disgrace[d] the monuments of . . .
majesty, like an ants' nest built in a skull" (31:10).

There is no question of a shared critical authority between author
and reader in this metaphor, as there had been in Ruskin's writings of
the 1840s. The "peasant" readers and the "senate" of writers are firmly
separated by class and even geographical location. Ruskin's reflection on
the proper relation between country and city turns, in context, into a general meditation on the place of "classic books"—those expressing " 'unchanging' or 'eternal' truth" (31:7)—in the nineteenth-century world of
mass audiences. Linda Austin argues that Ruskin increasingly "had to face
the city as an image of the collective form of response to literature."[5] In
the preface to *Xenophon* he addresses that problem by metaphorically sit-
ing the act of reading not in the modern English city, but in the city-
states of Greece and Venice, where the "Metropolis is properly the city
in which the chief temple of the nation's God is built" (31:9). Such cities
were the "heart and sanctifying force" of "the countries they rule": the
majority of the people, who lived outside their gates, looked to them
as the intellectual and moral center of national life. Like the ancient
city-states, the classics should serve as a source of moral authority, as
a model of culture and learning. Like those city-states, they should be
set apart, protected. The reader who lives in "undivided peace" with
their teachings is promised intellectual "milk and honey" (31:11). Those
who disregard their authority are transformed, in Ruskin's metaphor,

into insects who desecrate the literary monuments of their ancestors and hold their thoughts in as little regard as does an ant who nests in an empty skull.

As the preface to a translation of a work neglected since the Renaissance, Ruskin's political analogy of the relationship between readers and great writers might have gone unremarked.[6] The preface was, however, part of a larger project. It served as the introduction to Ruskin's *Bibliotheca Pastorum*, of which *The Economist of Xenophon* was the first volume. The series had been announced in the January 1874 letter of *Fors Clavigera*, where Ruskin spoke of his plan to issue, in a standard format, selected books by classical authors. These would form the core of a list of "permitted books" from which members of the Guild of St. George could choose in forming their home libraries (28:20). "Epicurism in books" and "gluttonous reading" would not be allowed in Ruskin's society (28:501); only a few volumes offering "moral . . . nourishment" would be included on the annual list.[7] These books would be as "holy bibles" to the Guild members. Reverently and regularly studied, they, like Xenophon's *Economist*, with its instructions for dutiful wives and industrious agricultural labourers, would serve as helps to a "natural, modest, and honest manner" (28:276). Like the lessons to little housewives in *Ethics of the Dust*, the books in Ruskin's library would model good behavior not only in content. Through the reader's reverent relationship to them and to the critical authority which they embodied, individuals would be crystallized into the compliant citizenry called for in Ruskin's paternalistic state.

Frederic Harrison, already a vocal critic of Ruskin's nationalist utopia, appears to have taken notice of the political purpose underlying his canonical library. The preface to *Bibliotheca Pastorum* seems, for example, to have informed Frederic Harrison's choice of words when he addressed the subject of canons in an 1879 *Fortnightly Review* essay. In place of Ruskin's isolated "eternal senate," Harrison fashions a "great republic of letters," remarkable for its "freedom of intercourse and . . . spirit of equality." The attitude of his reader is far removed from the humility of Ruskin's humble peasant, and as though to mark the distance, Harrison employs the image of the skull to a different end: "Every reader who holds a book in his hand is free of the inmost minds of men past and present . . . he needs no introduction to the greatest; he stands on no ceremony with them; he may if he be so minded, scribble 'doggerel' on his Shelley, or he may kick Lord Byron, if he please, into a corner. . . . In the republic of letters there are no privileged orders or places reserved. . . . your 'general reader,' like the gravedigger in Hamlet, is hail-fellow with all the mighty dead; he pats the skull of the court jester."[8] It may be no accident that Harrison's disrespectful audience vents its ill-humor on two writers who were particularly important to Ruskin.[9] Not only is the reader here on equal terms with authors of the past, but, unlike the members of the Guild of St. George whose books are preselected, he or she is free to pass judgment. As Harrison's metaphor of the republic implies, there is no reigning standard of literary taste. Each reader is his or her own critic. Harrison does modify this position somewhat in the rest of the essay; nevertheless, his central metaphor sets the prevailing tone. He displays no Ruskinian dogmatism; rather, he speaks to his readers as fellow critics who can be persuaded of his opinion only through rational argument.

What is most remarkable in these passages from Ruskin and Harrison is less the differences they reveal in their authors' positions than the way in which those differences are expressed. Both writers characterize the act of reading and the choice of what to read in political terms. Much of the criticism of our own time is devoted to examining the literary canon and to exposing the unconscious or hidden agendas of those who defined it. To think of the choice of books as a strategic move that isolates or marginalizes groups of readers is usually considered a postmodern turn, one that has been associated with a hermeneutics of suspicion.[10] The talk of a connection between politics and literature has been described as the product of a "School of Resentment," one that mistakenly suggests that the making of a canon—which should be "anything but political or moral"—is "an ideological act *in itself.*"[11] Yet it is clear that both Harrison and Ruskin saw the making of a canon as the conscious expression of such a connection. There is no need to transport current vocabularies of power and alienation into their discussion of literature. Such terms were already integral to the critical vocabulary of the late nineteenth century.

Simply to state that behind standard lists of books lies an implicit social agenda is thus to acknowledge what was already evident to these Victorian writers. The dialogue between Ruskin and his contemporaries about literary canons sounds remarkably current in its concern with the reader's relation to texts and with the connection between criticism and politics. At first glance their arguments read like the tale of domination and repression that some recent critics have tried to make of literary history. A closer look, however, shows that their battle of the books was the enunciation of a new faith in the progressive power of literature, the same faith that underlies the arguments of the very critics who would summarily dismiss their voices. In a period marked by the increasing democratization of culture, late Victorian intellectuals formulated a discourse of literature that would mediate between power and progress. The tensions in their writings between political metaphors and transhistorical aesthetic principles echo those in our current canonical debates.

Frederic Harrison gave early warning of the potential power of literary canons to reinforce existing political divisions. Throughout his writings of the 1870s, he tried to expose sources of support for what remained, even after two reform bills, an essentially aristocratic government. An advocate for the working classes, Harrison saw in the choice of books a means of silencing the voice of the popular reader. He censured those who would "insist dogmatically upon any single name, or two or three" as the "accepted masters of the world," blaming particularly "Mr. Ruskin . . . for the taste for this one-sided and spasmodic criticism." At the end of what appears to be his own dogmatic essay on reading great writers, Harrison explains in a postscript that his list is to be taken only as "a type," not as a definitive selection; it presents the "literary résumé of Positivist teaching; and as such alone can it be used." [12] Although Harrison was not entirely opposed to making a selection of great literature, he did object to doing so in a way that precluded argument and summarily dismissed alternatives. He recognized no objective aesthetic criterion by which such choices could be made. Acknowledging his own bias toward Positivism, he saw critical judgments as reflective of a political position.

As Harrison's essay on canons makes clear, his uneasiness about singling out certain literary voices stems from his fear that making canons might be little more than a means of importing old political games to the parlor. To set over individual readers an "eternal senate" of writers was to recall traditional structures of authority, as Ruskin's feudal metaphors of peasant readers and lordly writers implied. Moreover, the insertion of the intermediary figure of the critic between the canonical text and the reader replicates in a different setting a system of government that had existed before the Second Reform Act. In a critical scheme such as Ruskin's, the general public would have no voice in selecting its literary representatives. The selection of the St. George's library was, Ruskin wrote, to be made "by one man . . . not by a council" (28:407). Public libraries, too, were to be under limited control; those who ran them would be charged with "choosing, for the public, books authoritatively or essentially true" (33:282). "Truth" and "literary value" were not terms open to rational argument but were the products of a certain "instinct" (28:648). Critics were "appointed" by Fate to intervene on behalf of the reader in the bewildering task of sifting through texts. "The function of the critic," Ruskin declared, was "to recommend 'authors' . . . of merit to public attention, and to prevent authors of no merit from occupying it" (29:585). His was the responsibility to nominate as well as to censure.

Ruskin's exclusive view of critical authority echoes the vision of contemporaries who in the 1870s were shaping the future of literary study. John Nichol, chair of English Language and Literature at Glasgow from 1862, and Henry Morley, lecturer in English at University College from 1865 to 1882, insisted on the ethical force of properly directed reading. Nichol, for example, argued that critics could help to strengthen established political authority by identifying for the reader universal truths that would stamp out "'native individuality.'" Henry Morley, writing in a similar vein, emphasized the importance to a strong polity of literary advisors who could promulgate to the populace a tradition of noble literature. Like Ruskin, these early academic literary critics were clearly conscious of the potential link between canon making and the politics of nationalism. As Franklin Court has recently demonstrated, the shape of and increasing emphasis on English Studies as an academic discipline in the 1870s can be traced directly to the perceived threat of the newly unified German nation.[13]

Ruskin contributed to this larger effort at securing an influential critical enclave within British society. Just as his nationalism mystified civil association, portraying it as the product of irrational, sentimental instincts, so his descriptions of the process of reading incorporate mythical references that would deflect the conventional connections in Victorian discourse between literacy, rational knowledge, and political power.

Reading is not, Ruskin emphasized, a straightforward matter of logically decoding arguments, but a complicated process of spiritual transformation. He repeatedly insisted on the difficulty of deciphering cryptic meaning. The truth of a work, he had argued in the 1860s, was frequently "withheld on purpose, and close-locked, that you may not get it till you have forged the key of it in a furnace of your own heating" (19:308). Hoping to set in motion this rigorous self-reformation, authors often deliberately obfuscated their message. Reading thus entailed making oneself worthy to receive the literary word.

In the critical model outlined in *Fors Clavigera*, however, the meaning of a work is inaccessible to even the most diligent reader. Elucidation becomes the preserve of the critic who recognizes truth not through the hard task of reconstructing the master narrative but through an insight born of instinct. As Ruskin discovered through his own attempts in *Fors* to fix interpretations to cryptic images, exegesis was all too easily marred by the exigencies of the moment. In his description of the role of criticism in *Fors*, he addresses that problem by bypassing altogether the hermeneutic imperative. Critics simply know intuitively what is and what is not good literature; they have no need of a critical trial by fire. Transformation is unnecessary for those already chosen. Ruskin presents the selection of a canon of books not as an intellectual decision to be debated, but rather as a physical reflex on the part of those whose unerring judgment guides their actions. Critics, alerted by instinct to pick out texts that are "true," stock the shelves of the public library. There is no need to explain their selection to the members of Ruskin's ideal society. The presence of a book in their "permitted" library attests ipso facto to its worthiness.

Literary value thus becomes a material fait accompli; it is not the product of a mental judgment on the part of the general reader, but an inherent property of the aesthetic object. This transference of critical power from reader to critic to artwork is exemplified in the course of letter 30. In the previous letter, Ruskin had exposed the cultural poverty of the "'rising' middle classes" and faulted them both for their lax reading habits and for their ignorance "of all the standard literature belonging to their own country, or to any other" (27:530). In letter 30 he begins by way of contrast with a glimpse at the classic titles lined up on one of his own library shelves. Singling out Jeremias Gotthelf's *Mirror of Peasants*, Ruskin makes it the occasion of a brief homily on Evangelicalism, humility, and class mobility. The translated passage from one of Gotthelf's tales is made to stand as a witness of the "universally true" content of Ruskin's statements, and as a model for the type of humble behavior he advocates. Like the Bible or the Koran, to which it is compared, Gotthelf's work is presented as "beyond all question true, in its reference to practical life" (27:546–7). It is made to intervene in a debate about class politics and economic systems; and yet, by emphasizing its existence as a finished book, a solid "volume, bound in green" (27:545), Ruskin secures it from the flux of contemporary life. This is not a tendentious interpretation of a passage from Gotthelf, he insists, sidestepping the objections that might be raised by the fact that he is translating into English a French translation of Gotthelf's text. Gotthelf's words are a bit of wisdom incarnated in an immutable physical form. They speak objectively to social questions just as Ruskin the critic, as he describes himself at the end of the letter, speaks not out of political interest—he does not want to be either "a champion or a leader" (27:557)—but out of an obligation to utter what he knows to be true. Both his words and Gotthelf's text are to be approached not as if they were corruptible linguistic signs, but rather, in his words, as if they were firmly anchored "sign-post[s]" directing their readers. Linking his epistolary project to the canonical contents of his library, Ruskin revises, for the moment at least, his claim to demonstrate in *Fors* the historically contingent nature of any representation.

Ruskin's treatment of Gotthelf's text looks forward to his approach to Xenophon's *Economist* in the preface to his proposed selected library, *Bibliotheca Pastorum*, where critical authority is reconstituted as an "eternal senate" of great books. Gotthelf was, in fact, one of the authors whose works were to have been included in the Guild library (28:499). A comparison of the preliminary outline of the *Bibliotheca* given in letter 61 with Ruskin's index to *Fors* reveals that this is not an isolated exercise in canonical reading. The list of works in that letter is remarkable less as a document of one of Ruskin's incomplete projects (which is how the Library Edition editors treat it),[14] than as a partial catalog of the many myths and stories embedded in the narrative of *Fors*. It is hardly surprising that the *Bibliotheca* as a series never materialized, when so much of David's Psalms, 1 John, and the works of Dante, Chaucer, and Gotthelf are quoted in Ruskin's political epistles. By citation, translation, and discussion of these authors, Ruskin had already evoked through the shape of his narrative what he reveals through literal description in letter 30: a selectively stocked library shelf. Issuing the *Bibliotheca* in separate volumes would have required a more overt justification of each chosen work as it appeared. By writing his literary canon into his letters, Ruskin's text literally embodies literary value in a way that dispenses with critical explanation.

In *Fors Clavigera* Ruskin aims at one level to illustrate what a viable national canon might look like. More importantly, by quoting extensively from his exemplary library, he makes it foundational to the very definition of British nationality. Citing fiction and gospel side by side with Victorian dailies, he weaves his selected classics into his larger chronicles of British life. Literary and political history are conflated; canonical books both comment on and help to create the everyday "reality" of modern experience as recorded in Ruskin's letters. Ensconced on a library shelf, these works are preserved from the ravages of history. At the same time, through the medium of Ruskin's epistolary pamphlets they intervene in the making of Victorian history. With this demonstration of the cultural work of canons, Ruskin reanimates what was by then a conventional turn of phrase in Victorian criticism: the reference to classical books as "household gods."

If *Fors* is the medium for translating his canon into practice, Ruskin's canon increasingly becomes a means of suggesting the lasting importance of *Fors*. Comparing a fascicle of his work to one of Gotthelf's published volumes, juxtaposing quotes from early numbers with citations from the classics, he insinuates his letters into the history of national life. Brian Maidment argues that it was Cook and Wedderburn, the Library Edition editors, who made of *Fors* a kind of edifice, violating the freedom of the individual letters by compiling them in volume form. "Ruskin's work," he claims, "while he remained active, was too elusive to become a canon. . . . the exegesis of Ruskin's book" could only be completed "without the distraction of his presence." Ruskin was, however, very clear about wanting to contain the flux of his letters within a more stable order. "I have ended it," he wrote of *Fors Clavigera* to a disappointed correspondent in 1884, "because I thought it could become more useful properly indexed."[15] As early as June 1873, Ruskin announced his intention to keep an index of *Fors* (27:553). He completed indices for letters 1 to 48, then asked friends to finish indexing the whole work. He also published the separate fascicles of *Fors* in volume form at the end of each year, issued only in fancy binding until 1882. Ruskin attempted, as he did in his description of a bound volume of Gotthelf, to give his letters an appearance of stability and closure.

Linda Austin has suggested that Ruskin's insistence in the initial years of *Fors Clavigera* on the finished appearance of his volumes had threatened to limit his epistolary project to the status of a "commodity book." Interestingly, Ruskin started to reconsider his strict line on circulation value precisely as his focus began to shift from discourse as process to a reified model of authority. In 1872 he had written to a correspondent: "It is of infinitely more importance eventually that I should sell my books justly than that they should be at present read." This sentiment is echoed throughout the early series of *Fors*, where Ruskin persisted in maintaining the high price of the fascicles. By contrast ten years later he told George Allen that he was willing to reduce his own profits, if required, to promote his reissued works: "for I really want to push the books now as representing a system of Christian philosophy against Materialism." [16] Subsequently, volumes of *Fors* were issued in pedestrian paper boards instead of fancy bindings. Although he had disavowed any systematic purpose for *Fors Clavigera* when he started the series—asserting instead that it represented the humors of the moment—he claimed in 1882 that with its conclusion, "the code of all I had to teach will . . . be, in form, as it is at this hour, in substance, completed" (29:137). He began to suggest that *Fors Clavigera* might function as the master key to the whole of his corpus. In 1882 he declared his determination to put his "house in order" and to give "some guidance . . . to the readers of *Fors*" by giving "each monthly part its own name" (29:423). At the same time he assigned titles to previously published letters, using them to create a kind of subject index that not only would apply to *Fors* but would explain its connection to his earlier writings (29:423). In a passage suggestive of the biblical paradigm of the rejected Word and its rising up to eternal life, Ruskin announced to a correspondent in 1881: "*All* I write now is very seriously written as a last will and testament and with final hammering down of nails in the elm, and in what work I leave behind me" (37:371). Comparing himself in *Fors* to the "Shepherd" who takes on "the Ruler's unstained authority," he attempted to give the tales in *Fors* the lasting force of biblical parables (29:136).

Such an attempt at self-canonization seems radically at odds with Ruskin's early emphasis that the form of his letters embodied historical process. If his opening aim, as I argued in the introduction, was to foreground the materiality of his project against the apparently disinterested discourse of Victorian liberalism, in the later series of *Fors Clavigera* materiality functions in a rather different way. His letters are consolidated as an object autonomous of contemporary conditions. Their power is cast in terms of ahistorical aesthetic principles. Ruskin seems to emphasize exactly what his critics had suggested all along: that he is composing an admirable work of literature, but hardly a political treatise that engages the realities of Victorian life.

Ruskin does not solve such contradictions. That he was unable to do so says less, perhaps, about his personal difficulties than about the complexity of the critical project in which he engaged. In the changing political landscape of the late nineteenth century, literature was increasingly construed both as a powerful agent of social transformation and as an aesthetic enclave against such a transformation. Nor were these characterizations neatly split between two ideological groups. If this had been the case, Ruskin's paradoxical position in *Fors Clavigera* might be explained by reference to his idiosyncratic mix of conservative and liberal politics. A wider look at the contemporary debate about books, however, shows that Ruskin's contradictions are replicated in the work of writers addressing the issue from various political angles. Even Victorian liberals found themselves making precisely the kinds of conflicted critical moves displayed in *Fors Clavigera*.

Mark Pattison, for example, in "Books and Critics" (1879), echoes Ruskin's distinction between a mass audience and a more privileged—and more powerful—group. Modern readers, he argued, "must now be divided into two classes—the general public and the professional literary man: the author, or critic, let us call him. I am not proposing that the general public should read, or look at, all this mass of current literature. . . . You must be guided by selection; but for your selection you will be guided—you are so in fact—by the opinion of those whom I must now speak of as a class, by the name of critics."[17] The terms in which Pattison casts his vision of a kind of Coleridgean clerisy are remarkable in contemporary context. In a decade marked by open debate about national unity, the liberal Pattison reasserts the inevitability of class divisions. Although certain political distinctions had been effaced by an expanded franchise, others are reaffirmed in a cultural sphere in which qualitative differences could still be recognized. Pattison's earlier advocacy of democratic rule and laissez-faire in his influential essay "The Age of Reason" (1877) gives way here to an insistence on hierarchy and on the regulation of cultural consumption. The institutional power he had so carefully dismantled in his earlier work is reconstituted in the clerical power of the critic.

Pattison is just as unwilling as Ruskin to concede that aesthetic taste might be influenced by historical or political circumstance. Only those who had been brought up on the "literature of the past" were suited to sit in "the judgment-seat of letters." Readers not classically educated were unfit to decide the merits of contemporary literature. Pattison creates a hierarchy of readers crowned by a privileged class that by its very function is insulated from political questions. His critic finds "his whole time . . . consumed, and his powers of attention strained to the utmost, in the effort to keep abreast of that contemporary literature which he is to watch and report upon." Pattison's language of class is thus used to characterize a critical authority that rises above class politics, that is marked by its distance from issues of power and equality. Applauded by John Morley for adhering in biblical studies to arguments based on the process of historical, "dynamic movement" rather than on "dogmatic immobility," Pattison seems here more like those whom Morley dismisses as favoring a separate "science of literature" seen apart from its history.[18] Indeed, he seems to create a literary version of the kind of ahistorical, utopian order that he had ridiculed in works like *Fors Clavigera*.

It could be argued that it was precisely because Pattison had exposed the biblical canon to historical scrutiny in his contribution to *Essays and Reviews* that he seemed unwilling to do so to the literary canon. Institutionalized religion had been discredited; the institution of criticism might take its place. This reinvocation of an absolute authority drives the change from Pattison's progressive position in his 1877 essay, "The Age of Reason," to his more conservative posture in "Books and Critics," written two years later. In the former he asserted the priority of "the legitimate monarch—the sovereign reason" against entrenched political institutions, whose power derived from a medieval habit of deference. In "Books and Critics" he reinvokes the very type of mystified authority he had so peremptorily swept aside in his rationalist review of social development. The work of the critic is valuable because it exists apart from social process. Dogmatic immobility, in this instance, is justified by the critic's unique cultural position; his judgment cannot be swayed by the fluctuations of a world with which he has so little contact. Unlike the religious and political establishments he had formerly attacked, literature and criticism are portrayed as pure institutions, undeflected by interested motives or by historical change. The true critic is formed not by experience but by something outside experience: as Pierre Bourdieu puts it, "the pure gaze implies a break with the ordinary attitude towards the world which, as such, is a social break." [19] The new system of criticism naturalized social distinctions—reinforcing the division between acquired education and inherited taste—that would have been blurred by the growing emphasis on democratic participation in public affairs.

What Ruskin had termed the "eternal senate" of intuitive critics became a mainstay of literary discourse after the Second Reform Act (31:8n). It appears in the work of liberal critics such as Pattison, as well as in the work of more traditionally conservative writers, such as Edmund Gosse. In a related discussion of how to define a poetic canon, Edmund Gosse reiterates Ruskin's and Pattison's determination to establish a new site of institutional authority. His choice of words leaves no doubt about how the Second Reform Act and its consequences were felt to impinge on the world of letters. "One danger which I have long foreseen from the spread of the democratic sentiment," he wrote, "is that of the traditions of literary taste, the canons of literature, being reversed with success by a popular vote. Up to the present time . . . the masses of uneducated or semi-educated persons, who form the vast majority of readers . . . have been content to acknowledge their traditional supremacy. Of late there have seemed to me to be certain signs . . . of a revolt of the mob against our literary masters. . . . If literature is to be judged by a *plebiscite* and if the *plebs* recognize its power, it will certainly by degrees cease to support reputations which give it no pleasure and which it cannot comprehend." This lament for "traditional supremacy" is surprising from the pen of one who had declared that he "cared nothing about politics." [20] Like Pattison, Gosse separates the reading audience into two groups: the "mob" unable to judge correctly in matters of "literary taste," and its implied opposite, the well-educated, perceptive reader or critic to whom Gosse's rhetoric makes its appeal. To allow the general reader to choose his or her own literary masters would amount to a "revolution in taste" that would end in "irreparable chaos" and widespread social discontent.

Ruskin was not alone, then, in associating a hierarchy of readers and critics with political stability. Nor is such an attempt to privilege one group of readers at the expense of a larger reading public unfamiliar in modern criticism. Paul de Man, to take an exemplary instance, speaks of the difference between the "naive" reader and the critic who is alert to the force of figurative language. Unlike de Man, whose critical rhetoric has been charged with concealing an ideological subtext, Ruskin and his contemporaries were open about the social circumstances to which they wrote.[21] Paradoxically, their conspicuously political language seeks to establish the same apolitical, ahistorical authority for literature—and for the critic—as does de Man's talk of universal rhetorical "moments." Gosse, for instance, invokes the specter of democracy only to assert that literature must be exorcised from it. Willing to allow open discussion of *contemporary* literature, Gosse nevertheless holds that the traditional canon was not, as he says in the preface to the collection in which his essay was reissued, a "question at issue." In a passage that recalls Ruskin's metaphorical equation of canonical texts with the laws of ancient city-states, Gosse declares that the works of the "great" writers were like "ancient laws" whose precepts were "impeccable."[22]

These Victorian writers engaged in the culture wars of the 1870s and 1880s felt, as have some current literary critics, that "the pure authority of great literature may be the only image of pure authority we have." Such an idealization of literature has come to be associated in most accounts of canon-making with Matthew Arnold. Ruth apRoberts, for example, has described how Arnold's claims for the social function of literature were made at the moment when religion and political institutions seemed most under attack. "All dogma is vulnerable," she argues, "because presented as absolute. But what is blessedly *in*vulnerable is literature . . . because it acknowledges its fictionality." In other words, literature was safe from "the spread of skepticism" that had, as Arnold explained in *Literature and Dogma* (1873), broken the hold of the clergy over the masses. While not discomfited by the decline of the "fixed authority" of the church, Arnold nevertheless regretted the loss of an organized means of socialization, or, in his words, of culture. Culture, as he describes it in the preface to *Literature and Dogma*, is the true guide to conduct; here Arnold's often elusive notion of culture is defined specifically as a product of reading. It must, however, be "reading with a purpose to guide it, and with system." In other words, a plan of literature, a canon, was necessary to fill the gap left by the rules of conduct as outlined by the church. "He does a good work who does anything to help this" working out of a systematic reading plan, Arnold declared; "indeed, it is the one essential service now to be rendered education."[23]

What Arnold elucidates in his preface is a growing recognition that there had been a crucial shift in the location of cultural authority and in its methods. In Arnold's account, as in other accounts of the period, social norms are no longer defined and administered by an external body or institution; they are learned individually through the process of reading. In her Foucauldian reading of the history of the novel, Nancy Armstrong argues that this notion of the cultural power of texts was formulated as early as the late eighteenth century. The "moral hegemony" of the middle classes "triumphed in nineteenth century England," she claims, "largely through consent rather than coercion." This consent was gained through the "appropriation of the time during which the poor carried on traditional collective activities." Church activities and reading were promoted as substitutes for potentially subversive forms of socialization. Pattison's essay reflects and makes public this understanding of literary power. "The tendency of education through books," he remarks, "is to sharpen individuality."[24] The statement reflects Pattison's faith in the rational progress and perfection of the individual as expressed in "The Age of Reason," while the context makes clear that the individual's progress is deliberately directed by the critic. For Pattison, as for Arnold, the importance of literature is less that it is invulnerable to rational attack than that it both guides reason and models behavior. Constructing a canon seemed a means of uniting strong social authority with enlightenment ideals of individual development.

The difficulty of thus mediating between power and progress is evident in the language of the essays cited above. Political metaphors mix uneasily with supposedly pure aesthetic principles. Literature is described both as a force of social change and as a closed system of value. Individual development is encouraged, but within a critical context that relies on structures of class and dominance. In the politically charged atmosphere of the late nineteenth century, the balance between power and progress was subtly shifted, as writers moved from discussing the process of reading in general to the process of literary criticism. As in Arnold's discussion of literary academies, the issue at hand was now national, not individual development. Writers moved beyond posing a general connection between habits of reading and personal behavior to argue for literature's essential role in forging a national audience across class lines. They envisioned that the institution of criticism could mediate the citizens' relationships to books and encourage them to focus less on acquiring knowledge than on learning to replicate a distinctively British notion of taste.[25]

This same shift can be seen in the progression of Ruskin's ideas about the ways in which literature might operate as a powerful cultural vehicle. In a student essay on literature written in 1836, he already posits a connection between reading and individual development. Reading "cultivate[s] and polish[es] the mind," he wrote; through contact with the best authors "our opinions are sculptured into more accurate forms, our judgment is guided, our reason directed, our intellect made more keen" (1:366). In *The Elements of Drawing* (1857) the influence of literature goes beyond mental refinement: books are shown to have a strong moral effect as well. They have the potential, Ruskin claims, to "agitate" or to "confirm"; they can cause "helpless or hopeless indignation" in the reader, or instil the habits of "reverence," "quiet virtue" and contentment with one's "obscurity" (15:228). Though fiction does not and should not "wast[e] our hours in political discussion," he says more pointedly in *The Eagle's Nest* (1872), it does have a political purpose. Good literature can "breathe calm upon the sea of lawless passion" and help in the "communication of clear thoughts and faithful purposes, among distant nations" (22:263–64). In a manuscript passage of *Fors*, he declares that political difficulties are, in fact, best handled through "stories, sermons, and songs" (29:588). Debates about reform and national unity could best be settled through the calming influence of orderly narrative. Every story has a "moral purpose" that is deliberately "hidden" so "that it heals and saves like the medicinal power in a herb, which we gather only for its sweet scent and beauty." Unlike his discussion of cryptic meaning in *Sesame and Lilies*, the focus in this passage does not fall on the task of "deep mining" for underlying significance. The moral import of a story is absorbed imperceptibly in a reading experience defined by aesthetic pleasure. Literature, in other words, is an effective source of political and moral authority precisely because it presents a serious purpose in the form of a pleasurable tale.

Ruskin exploits this notion to create a semblance of narrative movement across his scattered series of letters. *Fors* is littered with unfinished business, with incomplete narrative lines, and with broken promises of future discussions. Not accidentally, nearly all of these fragments are connected with stories, either of his own childhood or of mythical figures; or they are promises of sequels to discussions of books or authors. Even when Ruskin does elaborate a subject such as the life of Walter Scott, he strings it out not only through several letters, but through several years. The myths of Theseus and of St. Ursula are fitfully spun out over the entire series. These continuing tales work in the manner of a Victorian serial novel: they capture the reader's interest and keep him or her searching for an ending. They act, in effect, like the plot and its echoing subplots in a Dickens novel, providing a dramatic framework over many installments for an extended social or moral exposé.[26] Ruskin suggests something of this strategy when he writes to a correspondent in 1884 that he is finishing *Fors* because he wants it to "be read without always expecting more." The stories in *Fors*, as a contemporary reviewer noted, "carry the reader over many doubtful stretches of logic, and make the entire scheme of St. George's Company assume an ideal perfectness of proportion and a grace of being which fill the eye as a poetic structure."[27]

Ruskin's tales are meant to be both pleasurable and profitable. They keep the audience reading; through the reading, the author's values are internalized. The format of *Fors Clavigera* can be read as a textual paradigm of the new construction of critical authority in the 1870s and early 1880s. Ruskin's monthly "Letters to the Workmen and Labourers of Great Britain," usually faulted for their alternation between polemic and story, work out an integral relationship between political life and literary discourse. Like his contemporaries, Ruskin recognized the potential power of literature for an increasingly educated populace. Circulated in a format resembling eighteenth-century chapbooks, his political pamphlets mixed theories of nationality with fairy tales and discussions of the ideal state with Christian mythology. Far from byways, the stories in *Fors* are an integral part of the main course of the letters. Like the more recognizably polemical passages of the letters, they serve a political purpose: they are vehicles by which Ruskin's principles of government and order are to be internalized by the reader.

Ruskin's development of this strategy of agreeable socialization can be traced through his letters to the girls at the Winnington School. In one of his early letters, Ruskin sets them a Sunday lesson. After comparing the young pupils to fluttering birds, he prescribes as an antidote to their flightiness a long and involved course of Bible readings on obedience and duty.[28] Two years later, as he increasingly questions his own faith, he refuses the children's request for another Bible study. His accounts to his father of his visits to Winnington over the next few years mention only playful activities: running, swinging, boating, dancing. When he does describe a teaching activity, it, too, is playful: he writes of "making the girls arrange dances to simple music which can be sung to the words of really fine poems." This is the kind of imaginative, pleasurable instruction that is enacted in *Ethics of the Dust*. When Ruskin again sets a scripture lesson for the schoolgirls, it is markedly different in tone and message from the earlier one. Like Ruskin's playfully digressive style in *Fors Clavigera*, this lesson is spirited and fanciful, flitting about from topic to topic like the light-hearted bird that Ruskin had once teased the girls for resembling.[29]

This change in Ruskin's method of instruction can be attributed in part to the example of Margaret Bell's principles of education at Winnington, which favored movement and creativity over traditional rote learning.[30] Ruskin's contact with Bell came at a time when he had begun to question religious dogmatism. Just as Pattison did in the same period, Ruskin found fault with institutionalized religion.[31] Ruskin's correspondence with Bell early in 1863 gives evidence of a continuing dialogue on problems of faith. In his letter of 11 March, it is clear that the most pressing issue in this religious "darkness" is how to exert moral authority without the crutch of dogma. Dispense with religious rituals, Ruskin advises the mistress of Winnington, and "direct *yourself* wholly to the formation of moral habits and happiness in your pupils. . . . declining questions yourself—as too hard for you."[32] The point is not to argue difficult problems of morality, but instead to discover lessons whose very form—like, for example, a lesson in dancing—is a model of obedience or discipline or innocent pleasure. In Ruskin's letters to the Winnington pupils, reading becomes not only a means of instilling values but, as in *Ethics*, an activity which in itself enforces orderly moral behavior.

What Ruskin talks through with Margaret Bell is more than a merely personal change of temper. It is, as he writes to Bishop Colenso, part of a "reformation" in the structure of authority in society.[33] Rituals and institutions had lost their force among a population that was increasingly fragmented geographically and professionally. With the spread of education after the National Education Act of 1870, reading was seen as a general cultural arena, common to laboring as well as administrating classes. A central cultural force that will circulate freely through all levels of society, quietly inculcating a system of values: this is what Arnold dreamed of in "The Literary Influence of Academies." The urgency in nineteenth-century discussions of literature comes from a recognition of this potential cultural power. As one critic has recently remarked, every society, no matter how rational, has "stories . . . [that] determine how we act." The change from the world of feudal hierarchies to modern capitalist societies "is not from primitive infancy to sophisticated adulthood in our ability to recognize fictions as fictions; it is rather a change in the kind of discourse that commands the belief that determines action."[34]

As I argued in chapter 4, Ruskin shared such an antiprogressive reading of cultural history. The fictions he hoped would command belief in his readers reflect this sense that social change should not be equated with increasing cultural sophistication. His idiosyncratic canon includes not only conventionally "great" authors—Plato, Virgil, Dante, Shakespeare (27:314)—but fairy tales and folktales, as well. Linda Austin suggests that through such childish works Ruskin showed his determination in "summoning an audience who already shared his regressive fantasy."[35] At least one contemporary, however, saw his inclusion of fairy tales as a pertinent intervention in cultural debates of the period. R. Menzies Fergusson included in his book of essays *Quiet Folk* a piece called "Fairyland and John Ruskin," in which he reflected on a more general critical "interest in . . . childhood." For Fergusson, as for Ruskin, conjuring childlike tales provided an antidote to a "practical age" in which "the stern fight for wealth and power" dominated public rhetoric. The increasing attention paid to collecting and recording fairy tales in late century showed a dissatisfaction with the scientific narratives of cultural progress and a desire for a more compelling means of promoting national culture. Evoking "the golden days of childhood, when with bated breath we listened intently to the pretty tales told at a mother's knee" was not an exercise in nostalgia, but a sharp political commentary. Incorporating fairy tales in the canon did not just invoke a scene that was a model of the domesticated nationalist utopia Ruskin sketched out in *Fors Clavigera*. It also effectively joined his political utopia with a scene of precritical reading that would reinforce the literary hierarchy promulgated by Victorian critics. Childlike readers listened to canonized tales without debating their merit; they absorbed these moral fables through innocent pleasure in narrative, not through rational reflection on their underlying values. That Fergusson saw the potential political use of this strategy is evident in his borrowing of Matthew Arnold's well-known phrase from *Culture and Anarchy*, as he exhorts every reader to "do what in him lies to intensify this taste for the 'sweetness and light' which linger so lovingly about the innocence of childhood." [36]

If literature was to replace the Bible as the inspired Word for the end of the nineteenth century, then it would be crucial to determine, as it had been for early biblical scholars, which texts would be part of the canon. Ruskin's *Bibliotheca Pastorum* was not the only proposed series that sought to define canonical voices and works. The year after the publication of the first volume of Ruskin's Guild library came the first volumes in John Morley's English Men of Letters series. In 1882 Leslie Stephen undertook the editorship of the proposed *Dictionary of National Biography*. As Frederic Maitland remarks, it was "an unorganised world to which Stephen issued his first circulars." The editorial policy of the *DNB* was to create a cultural map of everyone whose "career presents any feature which justifies its preservation from oblivion." Although much larger in scope than either Morley's or Ruskin's undertaking, the *DNB* nevertheless was a product of the same effort to decide whose stories counted in English society; as Noel Annan notes, its selectivity is evident in its exclusion of businessmen and entrepreneurs, as well as of many notable women.[37] Stephen quietly reinforced the class hierarchy notable in the critical discourse in the period.

At this remove the cultural authority of *Fors Clavigera* may seem slight when compared with the weight still given to the *Dictionary of National Biography*, and perhaps to a lesser degree, to the English Men of

Letters series. But contemporary accounts reveal that Ruskin was not only seen to be a part of this movement to define the sources of English culture. He was recognized as one of its most authoritative and influential voices. In response to Ruskin's version of a list of the best hundred books, an American reviewer spoke out in anger that "the great majority of innocent minded people will . . . accept this theatrical out-burst of perhaps the most eminent living man of letters, as sane criticism, and will conduct their readings in the future accordingly." Ruskin had become, he worried, the "chief-cook of the 'World of Letters.'"[38] In 1880 a *Quarterly Review* critic complained that in *Fors Clavigera* and again in *Fiction, Fair and Foul* Ruskin "asserts the existence of an absolute standard of taste, and yet declares that the multitude must be content to take this on faith from the cultivated few," because a general audience was utterly incapable of understanding on its own the truth of things. The *Quarterly Review* itself hardly held back from authoritative pronouncements on "great" literature. Indeed, what its reviewer really objects to is not Ruskin's exclusivity but his choice of works which "satisfy the conventional prejudices" of a larger public.[39]

Another writer, summing up the influence of Ruskin's career, compared the effect of his work to that of the Victorian writer we now most associate with initiating the modern canon, Matthew Arnold. "The great change," he observed in 1894, "which appears to have been effected in the history of contemporary civilisation in England during the generation preceding our own is to be found mainly in the diffusion of culture . . . among the mass of the middle and lower classes." For this reader of Ruskin, the sage's appeal to the tastes of *le gros public* was not, as it was for the *Quarterly* reviewer, a cause for lament. Ruskin's aesthetic attitudes, he argued, had been instrumental in promoting "the desire for the acquisition of the higher fruits of culture." "Amid the numerous causes which might be adduced for the consummation of this great change" from uncultivated reading to the quest for educated taste, he asserted, "the direct efforts of individual men must be noted, and among these I hold that no two men have been as efficient in their work as Matthew Arnold and Ruskin."[40]

"Efficient" is perhaps not the first word that comes to mind to describe the narrative proceedings of *Fors Clavigera*. Indeed, although large political strategies can be identified in the series as a whole, it has no unified narrative structure in the current sense of that term. There is, however, a characteristic alternation in the work between polemic and story that participates in a more general structure of critical discourse in the period. The tensions between political language and permanent truths that can be located in a single letter of *Fors*, or in the essay of one of Ruskin's contemporaries, are replicated in the tension between fact and fantasy in the work as a whole. Like the Lecturer in *The Ethics of the Dust* who elides the distinction between story and reality, Ruskin the letter writer moves dexterously from scientific fact to mythical fantasy, blending the various modes of discourse in order to question their difference. The distinction between the life we live and the stories we live by is a fine one; in *Fors*, as in the work of current cultural critics, the distinction is nearly effaced.

Ruskin's effort to include *Fors Clavigera* in the literary canon which he was forming proved unsuccessful. A series of ninety-six letters, not easily classified according to subject or genre, was unlikely to find a growing audience at the turn of the new century. Frederic Harrison's reaction to the compiled work is perhaps typical of that of his contemporaries. When faced with the Library Edition of *Fors Clavigera*, Harrison found himself unable to wade through the "unadulterated torrent . . . overlaid with cuttings from the *Daily Telegraph* and provincial prints, stuffed with silly letters from anonymous correspondents and the gossip of aesthetic old ladies." Ruskin's *causerie* no longer tempted him. "The abridged and bowdlerized *Fors* [published in 1896] was trivial and desultory enough, in all conscience. But the 'pure milk' of the Ruskinian word is to me a *purée* which my palate declines to approve."[41]

Ruskin had his own opinion of why *Fors* might not appeal to future readers. It was flawed, he said in the last letter, by its "compromise with the infidelity of this outer world" (29: 527). Rather than addressing only those immutable truths that marked the work of great writers, he had included in his letters ideas and values drawn from his society. He had appealed to "ordinary prudence and kindness" when he should have insisted on Christian inspiration. Ruskin's regrets look forward to Harrison's reaction. Both reveal a critical bias toward texts which are transparently ordered. Ruskin's careful outlines for *Praeterita* suggest a deliberate move away from a digressive, miscellaneous idiom. In a diary entry for 4 October 1886, Ruskin described his approach to his autobiography: "The thirty six chapters of Praeterita being already arranged to the end, require extreme care in packing their contents so as to keep what

I have called essentials only. Far more interesting things might be told, in every case, but not the cardinal ones, so as to fix the readers' attention." [42] The autobiographical passages which had first appeared in *Fors* are withdrawn in *Praeterita* from their connection to larger political arguments. At the end of his career, Ruskin, like Harrison after him, seemed to be leaning toward a clear division of text from context.

Ironically, it is precisely the difficulty of doing so in *Fors Clavigera* that accounts for renewed attention to the work. Ruskin faulted *Fors* for being too invested in current events. At a moment when we have begun to see all writing as in some way a "compromise" with society, the contemporary material in *Fors* becomes as important as the work's "poetic argument." [43] Choosing books that represent timeless truths seems more problematic in the current critical climate than it did when Ruskin wrote *Fors Clavigera*.

That the work is not easily included in a canonical list does not trouble some modern readers as it did Frederic Harrison. In a recent review of Ruskin scholarship, Patrick Connor remarks that its resistance to canonization accounts for much of the appeal of *Fors Clavigera*. The "desire to overthrow the canon of 'great books,'" he argues, "to locate the subversive in the apparently reactionary, has contributed no doubt to the increasing attention paid to Ruskin's later works." [44] In an interesting turn of critical history, our readiness to reevaluate a work like *Fors Clavigera* comes at the very time that Ruskin's late efforts at canon-building are devalued. His failure at self-canonization and his rhetoric of skeptical marginality in *Fors Clavigera* make his seem a relatively contemporary voice in our current debates about critical authority.

In a moment of general cultural crisis, the formation of canons and of the critical authority that they presumed appeared to the Victorians an effective means of reconfiguring social tensions. For Ruskin, this meant preserving traditional structures of authority in an altered social landscape. For his liberal critics, it provided a possible way out of the tension between progress and power. Their attempts to characterize the literary as beyond historical critique did not mark, as some critics have argued, the beginnings of a modernist aesthetic divorced from social concerns. Rather, it signaled a change in the method of political discourse. A population increasingly fragmented, and less likely than in the first half of the century to have been formed by common cultural institutions, might be taught through criticism to see itself as a national audience. The distinction between great literature and mass culture guaranteed that traditional divisions within that audience would be perpetuated, and also, paradoxically, that disparate readers would unite around a common goal. The desire for the acquisition of culture would displace the quest for political power.

This view of Victorian debates about literary value would make them a preliminary chapter to our own critical texts. To distill "truths" from historical conditions, to speak to social issues in a language somehow detached from its social roots: these problems are no clearer now at the end of the twentieth century—and no less contentious—than they were at the end of the nineteenth. At a time of debates about diversity—reminiscent of Victorian discussions of the implications of a diversified political scene—we still look to literature as a catalyst for social change. The position of marginality advocated in recent criticism, seen in this historical context, looks less like a rejection of traditional authority than a recurrence to the authority of the Victorian critic positioned at the margins of contemporary life. Rereading Ruskin in the climate of the 1870s and 1880s can remind us that our critical performances are underwritten by hermeneutic structures with a history of their own.

Notes

Introduction

1. Disraeli, general preface, 1:xv, xvi, xv.
2. Review of *Lothair* (1870), cited in Stewart, ed. *Disraeli's Novels Reviewed*, 264.
3. Gladstone, address, 23, 29, 26. Strauss's work was published in German in 1872; the first English translation (by Mathilde Blind) appeared in 1873.
4. J. Morley, *On Compromise*, 1. For the influence of John Morley's book on late-Victorian liberals, see Hamer, *John Morley*, 246; for its continental influence, see Knickerbocker, *Free Minds*, 175–77.
5. Bagehot, *Physics and Politics, or Thoughts on the Applications of the Principles of "Natural Selection" and "Inheritance" to Political Society* (1872), reprinted in *Collected Works*, 7:48, 107.
6. Draft of the society's constitution; cited in Metcalf, *James Knowles*, 215. For what is still the best account of the society as a symbol of the spirit of the 1870s, see Brown's *Metaphysical Society*. The following description of the society owes much to both Brown and Metcalf.
7. Knowles to Gladstone, 2 Nov. 1876, cited in Metcalf, *James Knowles*, 273.
8. Knowles papers, cited in Metcalf, *James Knowles*, 224; "A Modern Symposium," 322; Ellicot, "Church of England Present and Future," 53.
9. Eagleton, *Function of Criticism*, 61; for the "Committee on Definitions" see Brown, *Metaphysical Society*, 82–83; the debate on religious belief was printed in an open forum, *Nineteenth Century* 1 (1877): 545.
10. J. Morley, *Voltaire*, 355; J. Morley, *Recollections* 1:85; J. Morley, "Valedictory" (1882), reprinted in *Studies in Literature*, 340.
11. Habermas, *Structural Transformation*, 9; J. Morley, *On Compromise*, 1.
12. Eagleton, *Function of Criticism*, 63; J. Morley, *Recollections*, 1:103–4; Beer, "Problems of Description," 45.
13. McGowan, *Representation and Revelation*, 95. In *The Practical Ruskin* Austin makes a point similar to my observation about the historicity of Ruskin's etymologies, but she frames it within a rather different intellectual context: Ruskin felt that "to economize words or money, we must couple them with historical or material signifieds; we misspend when we open the household to unlimited symbolization" (84).
14. On 13 Nov. 1877; see Brown's appendix of the records of society meetings, *Metaphysical Society*, 333. Ruskin's unpublished correspondence with Knowles in 1875 suggests that in addition to his intellectual scruples about the proceedings of the group, he left the society for more personal reasons: his fear that those he attacked in *Fors* would be angry, and his sensitivity to what he felt were slights on his authority as Slade Professor of Art (Ruskin to Knowles, 15 Sept. 1875, and undated letter).

Knowles, in one of the few statements in which he expressed doubts about the Society's effectiveness, wrote back despairing that Ruskin could see individual antagonism as a cause to stay away rather than as a compelling reason to work toward some solution: "Heaven help the world indeed, if such men as make our Metaphysical Society cannot so manage their differences of opinion and feeling as to enable them to meet always amicably being all 'honourable men.' There would be but little chance that ever 'war should cease in all the world'—if that could not be triumphantly accomplished" (Knowles to Ruskin, 5 April 1875, Ruskin Foundation, Ruskin Library, University of Lancaster, MS L. 21).

15. Ruskin to unnamed correspondent, 28 and 31 Jan. 1871, Bodleian Library, Oxford, MS Eng. lett. c.38, fols. 16 and 19.

16. For Ruskin's implied critique of Gladstone and for the Library Edition editors' explanation of his reference to Gladstone's recently published *Edinburgh Review* article, see 27:12.

17. Arnold, *Culture and Anarchy* (1869), reprinted in *Complete Prose Works*, 5:228; Maidment, "Readers Fair and Foul," 57; J. Morley, *Voltaire*, 355.

18. Austin, *Practical Ruskin*, 128, 139.

19. Spear, *Dreams of an English Eden*, 180.

20. Account statement by George Allen, Ruskin Foundation, MS 91.

21. This information is culled from the bibliographical notes in the Library Edition of *Fors Clavigera*, 27:xcii–c; 28:xxiii–xxvi; 29:xxix; 29:xxxii.

22. Allen to J. W. Bunney, 20 Feb. 1876, cited in Hewison, *Art and Society*, 7; circulation figures cited in Ellegård, *Readership of the Periodical Press*, 27, 19; Allen to J. W. Bunney, 20 Feb. 1876, cited in Hewison, *Art and Society*, 7.

23. Ruskin to Joan Severn, 11 March 1873, Ruskin Foundation, MS L. 36; review of *Fors Clavigera* in the *Guardian*, 995; Thompson, *William Morris*, 200, 201; Williams, *Culture and Society*, 128.

24. Anthony, *John Ruskin's Labour*, 201; Spear, *Dreams of an English Eden*, 181; Stoddart, "Formation of the Working Classes"; Hewison, *Art and Society*, 9.

25. Lists of Guild members were published occasionally in the "Notes and Correspondence" in *Fors Clavigera* and later in the separate address of the Master to the members (see the Library Edition, vol. 7). A list of new members in 1882, with Ruskin's notes on their occupations, can be found in Bodleian MS Eng. misc. c.232, fols. 62–68.

26. The *Daily News* had an average circulation of 90,000 in the 1870s, but it had reached a peak circulation of 150,000 during the Franco-Prussian War. The *Daily Telegraph* had an average circulation of 190,000 to 217,000 between 1870 and 1881 (Ellegård, *Readership of the Periodical Press*, 16–17; see also Altick, *English Common Reader*, 355).

27. Altick provides a concise summary of these debates in *English Common Reader*, ch. 15.

28. See, for example, Strahan, "Our Very Cheap Literature," and Hitchman, "Penny Press."

29. Altick, *English Common Reader*, 355.

30. Ruskin refers to the article "Mr. Ruskin's Unique Dogmatism," 1174–75.

31. This letter was printed in the "Notes and Correspondence" of the first edition of letter 14; in the Library Edition it now appears in the editors' note to that letter.

32. Brian Maidment, "Ruskin, *Fors Clavigera* and Ruskinism, 1870–1900," in Hewison, ed., *New Approaches to Ruskin,* 199. Although I disagree with Maidment's notion that Ruskin's letters represent an open dialogue with his readers, I would not go so far as

Jay Fellows, who asserts that Ruskin's rhetorical "pirouettes, despite the fact that they are prompted by public concerns, seem to take place in an area of profound vacancy . . . which would not only eliminate an audience of 'others,' . . . but would even, in its impulse toward privacy, annul the self" (*Failing Distance*, 101). Fellows continues a tradition, discussed later in this book, of reading the late Ruskin through the conventions of lyric. Neglecting in its own way the issue of Ruskin's mediation of his text, such a reading misses his important reconsiderations of the relationship between public and private voice.

33. Review of *Fors Clavigera*, *Guardian*, 1310.
34. Rosenberg, *Darkening Glass*. The "last romantics" is the title of Hough's book on Victorian sages, which includes several extended discussions of Ruskin.
35. Arnold, "The Literary Influence of Academies" (1864), *Complete Prose Works* 3:252. Arnold's essay was originally delivered as a lecture at Oxford. Super speculates that his criticism of Ruskin was even more pointed in the original version; he suggests that when Arnold submitted it for publication in the *Cornhill*, and the magazine's editor recommended that "Two or three pages at the beginning about the limits of criticism might as well be left out," Arnold "may have modified his remarks on Ruskin in deference to Smith's personal friendship for him" (*Complete Prose Works*, 3:463).
36. Arnold, *Complete Prose Works*, 3:252.
37. Ibid., 3:253; Stephen, "Mr. Ruskin's Recent Writings," 692, 690, 701; Brownell, *Victorian Prose Masters*, 217; Connor, "Ruskin Redivivus," 501.
38. C. S. Finley, "Structure of Ruskin's *Fors Clavigera*," 71; F. Harrison, *John Ruskin*, 182.
39. In *Masculine Desire* Dellamora looks at Ruskin's place at the heart of late century aestheticism. See also Stoddart, "Morality of *Poems and Ballads*."
40. Helsinger, for example, looking for a logical unity in the work, concludes that *Fors* is primarily an often illegible account of Ruskin's own obsessions and nightmares: in the end the reader is "no longer certain that his emblems *are* readable, his associations worth tracing out" (*Ruskin and the Art of the Beholder*, 283). Hayman agrees that *Fors* falls short of Ruskin's other works: "It is . . . both symptomatic and sadly ironic that Ruskin should have dismissed his habitual dialectic at a time when he most needed the coherence that it had earlier arranged" ("John Ruskin and the Art of System-Making," 202).
41. John Rosenberg, "Ruskin's Benediction: A Reading of *Fors Clavigera*," in Hewison, ed., *New Approaches to Ruskin*; Sawyer, *Ruskin's Poetic Argument*, 292–308, and "Ruskin and St. George."
42. Rosenberg supplies one possible answer to that question: the chaos of Ruskin's letters is meant to "directly induc[e] in the reader" the "violent fragmentation of meaning in the modern world" ("Ruskin's Benediction," 132). Rosenberg's response, with its insistence on the transparency of Ruskin's style in *Fors*—"one seems to touch the lineaments of thought itself without the intervening medium of words" (*Darkening Glass*, 187)—leads in a very different direction from my argument in chapter 2, which focuses on mediation in *Fors*.
43. Said, *World*, 55; Maidment, "Ruskin, *Fors Clavigera* and Ruskinism," 196.

Chapter I: Exemplary Citizens

1. Both Spear ("'*These* are the Furies of Phlegethon,'" 147) and Maidment ("Ruskin, *Fors Clavigera* and Ruskinism," 197) recognize the importance of the form of *Time and*

Tide for *Fors Clavigera*. Both, however, seem to regard it as a device originating with Ruskin. Maidment in particular classifies it as one of the "experimental genres which Ruskin himself developed." Although I agree with these critics' characterizations of the features of the form, I see it squarely in terms of conventions already laid out by earlier writers. Why this difference matters to our understanding of *Fors* is the focus of this and the following chapter.

2. Rosenberg's phrase, *Darkening Glass*, 167.

3. Ruskin's short series of letters to the *Daily Telegraph* and the *Pall Mall Gazette* on various political topics are appended to volume 17 of the library edition. Spear sees Ruskin's letters to the press in the 1860s as experiments in audience building (*Dreams of an English Eden*, 161).

4. Ruskin did not give the letters titles until they were reissued in volumes in 1882. For the editors' note indicating the paragraph beside which Ruskin wrote "Looking Down from Ingleborough" in his copy of an untitled first edition, see 27:23n.

5. The manuscript version of letter 1 is reproduced in the Library Edition, between pages 12 and 13 of vol. 27.

6. Bloom, introduction, 13, 12.

7. Sawyer, *Ruskin's Poetic Argument*, 312. Sawyer carefully compares the use of recollection in *Praeterita* and *The Prelude* (314–32).

8. Maidment, "Ruskin, *Fors Clavigera* and Ruskinism," 199.

9. For an overview of this change in public debate, see Briggs, *Age of Improvement*, 172–83.

10. Williams, *Cobbett*, 11. The same shift can be seen even earlier in Edmund Burke's *Reflections on the Revolution in France* (1790). Simon During considers the political implications of Burke's epistolary style: "Almost invisibly, freedom moves from reason and politics to self and language—subjective and sociable, rather than rational or bookish, language" ("Literature—Nationalism's Other?" 146). As I read Cobbett, he collapses such distinctions; his personal style integrates rationality and the social self in a way that rejects the paternalistic authority of Burke's politics.

11. Thompson, *Making of the English Working Class*, 688.

12. 15 Feb. and 5 April 1817, *Anti-Cobbett* 1:27, 1:227.

13. Cited in Aspinall, *Politics and the Press*, 31. Vincent looks at the influence of Cobbett's conversational address on the radical press, which tried to close the gap between oral and literary traditions (*Literacy and Popular Culture*, 243–46). For an extended treatment of Cobbett's conversational style, see Nattrass, *William Cobbett*, 135–44.

14. Williams, for example, in his generous survey of Cobbett's radicalism, faults him for rousing the political interest of a class of readers to whom he never considered extending the franchise. Cobbett's "paradox"—in which "a general popular movement was raised in the interest of a reform which would exclude most of its supporters" (*Cobbett*, 17)—sets the stage for the failure of a genuine working class movement in both Williams's and Thompson's accounts of the century (see Thompson, *Making of the English Working Class*, 686–88).

15. Cobbett, *The Political Censor*, Nov. 1796, cited in Wilson, *Paine and Cobbett*, 150.

16. Cobbett, 1 Feb. 1831, *Two-Penny Trash* 1:191.

17. Cobbett cited in Thompson, *Making of the English Working Class*, 686–87; ibid., 688.

18. *The Rights of Man* (1791), reprinted in Thomas Paine, *Political Writings*, 56. For the influence of Paine's pamphlet on Cobbett's politics in 1816, see Wilson, *Paine and*

Cobbett. Modern biographers have discovered that Cobbett's seeming self-disclosures have little to do with his actual experiences. According to Spater, he had spent much of his adolescence trying to get away from the farm life which provided the model of contented labor in the *Political Register* (*William Cobbett* 1:11–15). The open, candid journalist with whom the reader could "sit down at table" (*CWWH* 8:53) seldom spoke with either his wife or his children (Spater, 2:518–19). Despite his claims for the priority of direct experience, Cobbett's fabricated autobiographical revelations clearly posed an ideal of the political everyman.

19. The editor of the Bollingen edition has provided in footnotes to this sermon links to Cobbett's first cheap *Register*, suggesting that Coleridge had him very much in mind here.

20. In speculating on the reason for the exclusion of Cobbett from modern accounts of Romanticism, Gilmartin suggests that Cobbett's "polemical energy and intractable materiality" have continued to elicit responses much like the one Coleridge elaborates here. Gilmartin's acute reading of Cobbett nevertheless simplifies, by contrast, the contemporary reaction to his work. Coleridge's efforts to incorporate Cobbett's periodical strategies in *The Friend* complicates Gilmartin's assertion that "from the lofty perspective of romantic genius," Cobbett's "literary ambitions along the concrete horizontal axis of publication and distribution, rather than the ideal vertical axis of inspiration" may have represented "the most scandalous implication of radical prose" ("'This Is Very Material,'" 85, 91).

21. See the correspondence between Coleridge and Daniel Stuart of 17 Dec. 1808, 26 Jan. 1809, 26 April 1809, 10 Nov. 1809, reprinted in appendix F to *F*, 2:477, 480, 490, 494. For the Bollingen Edition editor's summary of Coleridge's references to the *Register*, see *F*, 1:xlii–xliii. Coleman discusses Coleridge's responses to Cobbett's political positions as articulated in the *Political Register* (*Coleridge and* The Friend, 180–83).

22. Riede, *Oracles and Hierophants*, 202, 203.

23. Butler, *Romantics, Rebels, and Reactionaries*, 71.

24. This passage was written by Wordsworth, who contributed to Coleridge's periodical after the eleventh number; see the editor's introduction to *F*, 1:lxiv ff.

25. Taylor, *Sources of the Self*, 390.

26. Habermas, *Structural Transformation*, 27.

27. *Punch* 18 Dec. 1880.

28. Kaplan, for example, remarks that "the decision to publish his views in serially published 'sermons' was a mistake in judgment which undercut the possibility that his anger would be subordinated to form" (*Thomas Carlyle*, 356). Like other critics, Kaplan reads *Latter-Day Pamphlets* much as *Fors Clavigera* has been read: as uncontrolled commentary on current events.

29. Letter cited in Goldberg and Seigel, introduction, *Carlyle's Latter-Day Pamphlets*, xxxviii. Cobbett himself later adopted the name for a second cheap publication addressed to the working classes, *Two-Penny Trash; or Politics for the Poor*.

30. My reading supports LaValley's observation that "all the categories that provided interesting means of exploration" in Carlyle's earlier works have "hardened" in *Latter-Day Pamphlets*. However, I interpret that rigidity as a deliberate strategy, not, as does LaValley, as a failure of nerve (*Carlyle and the Idea of the Modern*, 282, 213).

31. Carlyle, "Sir Walter Scott" (1838), reprinted in *WTC* 29:81.

32. Vanden Bossche sees more ambivalence in Carlyle's position on authority in *Latter-Day Pamphlets*. While he admits that "Carlyle virtually acknowledges that his time has passed," Vanden Bossche does see a kind of nostalgic creation of a positive authority in the character of the "prime minister modeled on the Carlylean persona" (*Carlyle and the Search for Authority*, 132). I take the pamphlets to be more consistently skeptical about any form of sagelike authority, although I do not mean to suggest that this was Carlyle's final word on the matter. *Frederick the Great*, for example, proposes a very different solution to democratic chaos, one which would be of central importance to Ruskin in *Fors Clavigera*.

33. Eliot, *Middlemarch*, 790–91. For a detailed discussion of the conjunction of scientific and aesthetic theories of the self in the 1870s, see Levine, *Realistic Imagination*, ch. 12.

34. Clifford, "The Philosophy of the Pure Sciences" (1873), cited in Levine, *Realistic Imagination*, 276.

Chapter II: Ruskin's Figurative Perceptions and the Politics of Representation

1. Ruskin to Severn, Nov. 1872; Ruskin Foundation, MS L. 37.

2. Friswell, *Modern Men of Letters*, 107, 99. Friswell, a highly popular journalist in the period, was active in movements for working-class education. *Modern Men of Letters* received particular publicity because of George Sala's suit against Friswell for defamation of character in the work (Sala received £ 500 in damages).

3. Spear's characterization of Ruskin's purpose in *Fors Clavigera* (*Dreams of an English Eden*, 180).

4. Harris, "The 'Figured Page,'" 141. McGowan misses this crucial point about the form of *Fors Clavigera*: "the Ruskin who presented himself as the proponent of clear sight," he observes, "always evidenced an impatience with mediation and indirection, a tendency that became both more pronounced and more desperate during the long decline into madness of Ruskin's later years" (*Representation and Revelation*, 75). I read *Fors* as an experiment foregrounding the necessary (and for Ruskin politically desirable) limitations of mediation.

5. "Mr. Ruskin's *Fors Clavigera*," 13.

6. James Sully, *Sensation and Intuition* (1874), cited in Small, *Conditions for Criticism*, 73. Small provides a lucid overview of the impact new scientific and social theories had on discussions about critical authority.

7. For an account of these struggles at Oxford, see M. Pattison, *Memoirs of an Oxford Don*, and Roll-Hansen, *Academy*.

8. Review of *Lectures on Art*, 143, 144.

9. E. F. S. Pattison, review of *Lectures on Art* and *Catalogue of Examples*, 305.

10. Review of *Lectures on Art*, 143, 144, 145.

11. Stephen, *Essays on Freethinking and Plainspeaking*, 362 (Stephen was a frequent contributor to the *Saturday Review*); Appleton's description of the Academy's purpose in a letter to the journal's publisher, cited in Roll-Hansen, *Academy*, 120.

12. E. F. S. Pattison's portrait is not, however, scathingly dismissive, as is the one in the *Saturday Review*. Pattison was herself "launched" by Ruskin. It was at his recommendation that she went at the age of nineteen to study art at South Kensington. Although

her review places him well outside the critical circle in which she and her husband figured, her continuing admiration for Ruskin is evident.

13. Mark Pattison's description of the Gothic revival in "Age of Reason," 350. Characterizing Ruskin as eccentric amateur might seem to draw him into a recognizably modern position with Pater and Wilde, but from Pattison's perspective such an aesthetic attitude could already be dismissed as dated. As Small points out, a work such as Pater's *Renaissance*, "in the ways in which it attempts to rehabilitate individual authority, and to disregard an institutional authority based on a scholarly consensus . . . looks back to the critical writing of the 1850s" (*Conditions for Criticism*, 95).

14. M. Pattison, "Age of Reason," 350, 351. Although Pattison's article sounds the "doom" of romanticism, it is evident from his argument that the claims of imagination over reason are still all too potent. The enlightenment revival and Ruskin's reaction to it will be explored in ch. 3 of this study.

15. J. Morley, "Carlyle," reprinted in *Critical Miscellanies*, 1 : 156; Brooke, review of *Lectures on Art*, 426. Brooke's comment draws on the prevailing view of Shelley at that time as the incomparable romantic lyricist whose political works were, in the words of John Morley, "accidents." Shelley's "spiritual imagination and winged melodiousness of verse," Morley argued, were "markedly wanting in a keen and omnipresent feeling for the great course of human events" (*Critical Miscellanies* 1 : 215, 214).

16. The "Advertisement" was printed on p. 2 of the first editions of letters 1–20, and thereafter on the cover of each number—see the Library Edition editors' footnote, 27 : 11; J. Morley, *Critical Miscellanies* 1 : 138, 135, 136.

17. As noted in chapter 1, Ruskin does directly compare his enterprise in *Fors* to Carlyle's *Latter-Day Pamphlets*. He would, of course, not have seen Coleridge's production in its original format. He does mention approvingly what is probably the 1818 rifacimento of *The Friend* in a diary entry for 1843 (*Diaries of John Ruskin*, 1 : 242).

18. Rogers, *Historical Gleanings*, vi, 171; Watson, *Biographies of John Wilkes and William Cobbett*, 398, 397. The third study was Bulwer's *Historical Characters*.

19. J. Morley, *Critical Miscellanies*, 1 : 185, 200, 161, 144; Arnold, "Function of Criticism" (1864), reprinted in *Complete Prose Works*, 3 : 275.

20. Shairp, *Studies in Poetry and Philosophy*, 156, 157.

21. Stephen, "Mr. Ruskin's Recent Writings," 689.

22. "To see the object as in itself it really is" first appeared in *On Translating Homer*; Arnold quoted it in the now more familiar context of "The Function of Criticism," reprinted in *Complete Prose Works*, 3 : 258. The full passage Stephen recalls with his military metaphor reads: "How is Cobbett to say this [that the British Constitution was "a colossal machine for the manufacture of Philistines"] and not be misunderstood, blackened as he is with the smoke of a lifelong conflict in the field of political practice? how is Mr. Carlyle to say it and not be misunderstood, after his furious raid into this field with his *Latter-Day Pamphlets*?" (*Complete Prose Works*, 275). Stopford Brooke also echoes Arnold's language in his review of Ruskin's art lectures, quoted above.

23. Stephen, "Mr. Ruskin's Recent Writings," 692, 695. The phrase from *Modern Painters* occurs in Ruskin's description of the pathetic fallacy (5 : 209).

24. "Mr. Ruskin on Mr. Ruskin," 526–27.

25. "Mr. Ruskin's Letter to Young Girls," 1508; "Mr. Ruskin's Will," 435. Unlike the

other critics cited here, the writer of the first of these reviews values Ruskin's "noble moral enthusiasm" above Arnold's disinterestedness.

26. Traill, *Coleridge*, 124. The direct comparison of *Fors* to *Friend* can be found on 121.

27. Taylor, *Sources of the Self*, 49. "The expressivist turn" is Taylor's phrase for the romantic variations on Locke (*Sources of the Self*, ch. 21). My limitation of this argument to specific debates in the 1870s is meant to acknowledge that both positions were, in practice, more complicated. My concern is not to summarize, for example, the romantic entanglement with Locke. Rather, my focus is the way the romantic reaction had been characterized in the course of the late Victorian discussions of authority. As Eagleton notes, "The clear bold light of republican rationalism, and the intimate affective depths of the poetic, come to figure throughout the nineteenth century as effective antinomies" (*Ideology of the Aesthetic*, 61). Eagleton's account, committed to theorizing an embodied version of the aesthetic, simplifies the dichotomy by suggesting that empiricism was on the aesthetic side of this divide. In fact, one of the curious turns in Victorian debates about scientific and aesthetic authority was that by late century, empiricism was claimed as epistemological foundation by both sides.

28. Taylor, *Sources of the Self*, 36. Ruskin uses the metaphor of the web interchangeably with that of the labyrinth in letter 23.

29. Tucker glosses this line in Tennyson to the Greek root of idiocy meaning privacy, the same derivation Ruskin emphasizes in letter 28. One of the implications of the final war chant in *Maud*, according to Tucker, is that "the hero can but perpetuate the discourse that entraps him if he is to speak at all" (*Tennyson and the Doom of Romanticism*, 426–27). Tucker's reading ends in a metaphor that links Tennyson's poem to the images of labyrinth and web in *Fors* as I have interpreted them here. For related interpretations of the constitutive self of the dramatic monologue, see Martin, *Browning's Dramatic Monologues*, 132, and I. Armstrong, *Language as Living Form*, 149.

30. Taylor sketches out how a true "punctual" self, in terms of modern notions of identity, would be interpreted as madness: "An agent free from all frameworks wouldn't know where he stood on issues of fundamental importance, would have no orientation in these issues whatever. . . . In practice, we should see such a person as deeply disturbed" (*Sources of the Self*, 31). Several of Ruskin's contemporaries who were committed to the disinterested self feared the potential for madness in ruthless rationality. Morley, for example, wrote that the "too common drawback to great openness of thought" was "vacillating opinions . . . appearing, shifting, vanishing, in the quicksands of an unstable mind" (*Fortnightly Review*, 1874, cited in Hamer, *John Morley*, 11).

31. Harris, "'Figured Page,'" 141; the index was compiled partly by Ruskin, and partly by the Rev. J. P. Faunthorpe (at Ruskin's request) based on Ruskin's own notes, see the Library Edition editors' bibliographic history of the index, 29:603–8.

32. M. Pattison, 6 June 1869 sermon, reprinted in *Sermons*, 191.

33. Scott, *Ruskin's Guild of St. George*, 6. For a discussion of the connection between Ruskin's work and cultural literacy arguments from Matthew Arnold to Allan Bloom, see Stoddart, "Formation of the Working Classes." I address in detail there issues of class only briefly alluded to in this study.

34. Ruskin quotes Mill's definition from his *Political Economy* in letters 23 and 4 (27:64).

35. Huxley is usually made the representative of this position in *Fors* (see, for example, references to Huxley in letters 35, 50, 64, and 71). For a discussion of Huxley's prominence at this time, and of the extremity of his positions vis-à-vis Darwin's, see

Desmond and Moore, *Darwin*, chapters 34 to 38. Wihl, in his skilful reading of one of Ruskin's key texts in the period, *Aratra Pentilici* (1871), shows how Ruskin in that work also conjoins what he sees as the false mimesis of scientific and of economic representation (*Ruskin and the Rhetoric of Infallibility*, 144).

36. Ruskin works from a French translation of Gotthelf because, he explains, he cannot read the tales in the German original (27:546).

37. Fried, *Courbet's Realism*, 142–43; Rosenberg, "Ruskin's Benediction," 129.

38. M. Pattison, *Sermons*, 191.

Chapter III: Motherhood of the Dust

1. Helsinger, "Ruskin and the Politics of Viewing," 129, 137, 129. In her *Ruskin and the Art of the Beholder*, Helsinger lays out in detail the construction of the position of the spectator in Ruskin's early works.

2. Helsinger, "Ruskin and the Politics of Viewing," 137.

3. "Imagined communities" is, of course, Benedict Anderson's formula for the project of enlightenment nationalism.

4. Gibbons, "J. S. Mill, Liberalism, and Progress," 107. Gibbons considers Mill a "transitional thinker" between classical liberalism and the collectivist theories of the New Liberals. Carlisle pushes Mill much closer to authoritarian enlightenment theories of the state. She argues that, despite his emphasis on individualism, Mill envisions a society in which "citizens themselves do what the government expects them to do": Bentham's panopticon, she ventures "found its fullest and perhaps most influential embodiment" in Mill's work (*John Stuart Mill*, 203–9). Such a reading of Mill would make him an unexpected ally of strongly communal theories like Ruskin's.

5. Hewison records the Wordsworthian echoes in *Modern Painters*, and describes in detail Ruskin's growing sense as he was writing volume 3 of the limitations of Wordsworth's Nature Spirit (*John Ruskin*, 16–20).

6. Ruskin's statement strikingly resembles, for example, a passage from Ernst Moritz Arndt's *Catechism for the Teutonic Warrior and Soldier* (1813): "Where God's sun first appeared to you, where the stars of heaven first twinkled at you, where lightning first revealed to you God's almighty power and where his storm-winds roared through your soul producing holy terror, there is your fatherland." Cited in Hughes, *Nationalism and Society*, 27. Hughes elaborates the importance of Arndt to late nineteenth-century German nationalism.

7. Helsinger, "Politics of Viewing," 139–40. For a related discussion using Ruskin's landscape canvasses in his Oxford teaching collection, see Helsinger's "Lessons of History."

8. Birch examines Ruskin's use of the figure Demeter in another of his late works, *Proserpina*, where he also draws on the darker attributes of the "Earth Mother" (*Ruskin's Myths*, 180–81, 193).

9. Hobsbawm looks at European nationalism in light of these political movements in "Mass-Producing Traditions," 269.

10. Renan, "Qu'est-ce qu'une nation?" Lecture delivered at the Sorbonne, 11 March 1882; reprinted in *Oeuvres complètes d'Ernest Renan*, 6:305. Thom has demonstrated how Renan emphasizes the importance of "forgetting" as a fundamental foundation for nationality. Renan's feudal, symbolic "Germanism," as Thom explains it in the

context of French historicism in the 1870s, has obvious parallels with Ruskin's ideas on nationality and history, as I discuss them in chapters 3 and 4.

11. Mosse, "Mass Politics," 52.

12. Ruskin to Mr. Wood, 9 Aug. 1871, Bodleian MS Eng. lett. c.38, fols. 101–2.

13. This remark caused Carlyle to write that while Ruskin's letters to the press were "full of holy indignation . . . as if it came from my own heart," Ruskin misunderstood Bismarck's deliberate strategy in rejecting the French truce. Carlyle to Ruskin, 10 Oct. 1870; *CCR*, 155. In his otherwise careful introduction to the volume of their collected letters, Cate claims that Ruskin "cannot understand why Carlyle should favor the Germans in the Franco-Prussian War" (56). Nothing in their letters about the events in Europe, nor in their public writings, confirms such a disagreement. Ruskin does remark in 1874 that Germany had gone too far in its military crusades. Although he admired the German model of government, he felt deeply the "cruelty" displayed in Bismarck's occupation of France: "Had Germany in her great strength, held herself on the defensive patiently, contented with crushing back every Frenchman who crossed the Rhine, the humiliation to France would have been greater; but the shame would have been wholesome" (*CCR* 179).

14. Ollier, *Cassell's History*, 1:193. The Franco-Prussian War was the first war covered through daily newspaper accounts from foreign correspondents; this history is compiled largely of these accounts from a variety of papers.

15. A. I. Shand, *On the Trail of War* (1870); cited in Raymond, *British Policy and Opinion*, 402–3.

16. "The German Empire," *Edinburgh Review* (1871) and *Pall Mall Gazette*, 14 April 1871, cited in Raymond, *British Policy and Opinion*, 403, 401; Ollier, *Cassell's History*, 1:v.

17. Ruskin denounced in 1874 the Prussians' harsh occupation of France (28:69) and raged over a slight on the French people attributed to Bismarck (28:112). He hardly, however, as the Library Edition editors curiously insist, "took the French side warmly in the war" (27:12 n.1), although he did contribute to the Mansion House Committee for the relief of Paris after the siege of 1871. His letters to the *Daily Telegraph*, quoted above, expressed his opposition to the Anglo-French Intervention Committee and his optimism about the future of the German state. For a helpful summary of Ruskin's conflicted feelings about the principles of war as opposed to the conduct of armies, see the chapter entitled "Ruskin on War" in Wilenski, *John Ruskin*; for his reactions to the Franco-Prussian War in particular, see 322–27.

18. Ruskin refers to the first edition in six volumes. In a letter to the *Times* and again in the appendix on *Frederick*, he declares that book 21 is "of extant literature the most important piece for us to read and digest in these days of 'raising the poor without gifts'—never asking who first let them fall" (34:501).

19. Wiener, *English Culture*, 55. Wiener provides a helpful if greatly simplified discussion of how the idea of the rural bridged contrary ideologies in English thought.

20. Oakeshott, *On Human Conduct*, 290. Oakeshott clearly outlines the continuing Baconian resonances in British political thought throughout the nineteenth century.

21. For a cogent discussion of the romantic resonances of Ruskin's Guild and its affiliations with Scott, see Spear, *Dreams of an English Eden*, 90–92 and 128ff. Ruskin's debt to the feudalism of Carlyle is a continuing thread in Spear's argument, which need not be rehearsed again here.

22. Eby, *Road to Armageddon*, 12, 7.

23. Sawyer, "Ruskin and St. George," 6; Ruskin, *Diaries of John Ruskin*, 3:872; Spear, *Dreams of an English Eden*, 194.

24. Spencer, *Principles of Sociology*, 1:596; Spencer's emphases. As Suzanne Graver notes, Spencer inverts romantic valuations of traditional and industrial modes of life: "Instead of associating the emergence of an industrial system with the decline of organic community, he observes in modern society the social organism at its highest stage of development" (*George Eliot and Community*, 163). Thom explains the ways that readers in the period glossed the idea of tribal association as an allusion to modern Germany.

25. Cited in Sylvester, *Robert Lowe and Education*, 62; Rachel Waterhouse, *The Birmingham and Midland Institute, 1854–1954*, and W. C. Aitken, minutes of the 1872 annual meeting of the Institute, both cited in F. Court, ed., *British Economic History*, 163.

26. Frederic Harrison's phrase is misquoted by Ruskin; the original phrase is "collective evolution" (Harrison, "Humanity," 871). In this article, against which Ruskin reacts in the June *Fors*, Harrison had nodded approvingly to Spencer's theories: "You could not have the truth about the social organism better stated than in Spencer's little book on 'Sociology,'" he says of Spencer's prolegomena to *The Principles of Sociology*, entitled *Study of Sociology* (1873) (878).

27. F. Harrison, *Order and Progress*, 121, 118.

28. As Peter Gurney has demonstrated in "Middle-Class Embrace," cooperation was a charged term in 1870s and 1880s political debates. Ruskin deals at length with his difference from both middle-class and working-class appropriations of the language of cooperation in *Fors*, letter 79.

29. Spencer, *Social Statics*, 353–54, 277.

30. Collini explores the loaded political import of the term "character" in the Victorian liberal tradition (via Mill, Arnold, Smiles, and Morley) in *Public Moralists*, ch. 3.

31. Spencer, *Social Statics*, 474.

32. Hobsbawm, *Nations and Nationalism*, 26–27.

33. Ruskin's increasing reference to the Christian underpinnings of his model commonwealth partly reflects what he calls a more "distinctly Christian . . . tone" in *Fors* after 1875 (29:86). The Guild had, however, been soundly grounded in New Testament morality even before Ruskin's "reconversion." As Spear explains, he had never divorced his political rhetoric from his personal heritage. "The concept of body politic" was always, Spear says, "connected in Ruskin's thought, as in Carlyle's before him, to the biblical image of the church as 'the body of Christ'" (*Dreams of an English Eden*, 148). For the Old Testament contribution to Ruskin's paternal authority, and for its psychological grounding in his relationship with his own father, see Hewison, *John Ruskin*, 140.

34. Riley, *Will and Political Legitimacy*, 113.

35. Plato, *Dialogues*, 5:222.

36. For this theme in Greek political theory, and for its practical importance to the running of the *polis*, see Finley, "Politics," 24–36.

37. Undated entry in Ruskin diary for 1869–71 and 1873, Ruskin Foundation, MS 16, 14 *verso*.

38. Herbert Spencer, who had elaborated the framework of developmental psychology in his influential *Principles of Psychology* (1855), clearly uses that framework as the basis of his sociological theories of the 1870s.

39. The connection suggested in *Fors* between German authoritarianism and Ruskin's own experiences of home life is made overtly in a letter to Carlyle, 27 June 1874, in which he clearly identifies with the young Friedrich (*CCR* 193). In *Fors*, a few pages after describing the elder Friedrich as "an Evangelical divine of the strictest orthodoxy," Ruskin could be speaking for the chastised Prince when he writes that "I have been horribly plagued and misguided by evangelical people, all my life" (28:68, 70).

40. Spencer, *Principles of Sociology*, 1:740, 742.

41. Letter cited in Duncan, *Life and Letters of Herbert Spencer*, 1:219.

42. Wiltshire, *Social and Political Thought of Herbert Spencer*, 180.

43. Freeden, *New Liberalism*, 40.

44. Hobson, *Social Problem*, 287; Ritchie, *Principles of State Interference*, 11–12.

45. Hilton, "Road Digging and Aestheticism in Oxford," 229; Mosse, "Mass Politics," 39.

46. Gosse, "Rousseau in England in the Nineteenth Century," reprinted in *Aspects and Impressions*, 189. Among modern readers, E. T. Cook and Irving Babbitt in particular have gestured in passing to the similarities between Rousseau's and Ruskin's thinking, but there has been no extended comparison between the writers' works.

47. Both Barnard and Brennan detail the connection between Herder and Rousseau.

48. Eagleton traces this thread from Burke forward in *Ideology of the Aesthetic*, ch. 2. Sawyer connects Ruskin's use of the "girl-woman" figure as "the emblem of an organic society" in his works of the 1860s with Eagleton's discussion of Burke ("Ruskin and the Matriarchal Logos," 137–39). His reading of *The Queen of the Air*, in which he argues that Ruskin "inscribes a hegemonic order in the cosmos itself, which is governed by an indwelling feminine divinity," has obvious links to Ruskin's "Motherhood of the dust" and "Angel of England."

49. Burke, *Reflections on the French Revolution* (1790), reprinted in *Writings and Speeches*, 3:333, 275.

50. Burke, *A Letter to a Member of the National Assembly* (1791), reprinted in ibid., 4:28, 29, 33.

51. Burke, ibid., 4:52.

52. For the now classic study of this convention, see N. Armstrong, *Desire and Domestic Fiction*. Weeks's *Sex, Politics and Society* extends this theme of public/private exchange through the nineteenth century.

53. Kessen, "Rousseau's Children," 158.

54. Anonymous pamphlet of 1871; reprinted in R. Harrison, ed., *English Defence of the Commune*, 155; Wright, *Our New Masters*, 197; Frederic Harrison, "The Revolution of the Commune," and E. S. Beesley, "Cosmopolitan Republicanism," reprinted in R. Harrison, ed., *English Defence of the Commune*, 171, 76–77; Ollier, *Cassell's History*, 2:506.

55. Burke, *Letter to a Member of the National Assembly*, in *Writings and Speeches*, 4:33.

56. In an 1868 letter to C. E. Norton, he relates *La Nouvelle Héloïse* to his troubled relationship with Rose La Touche (*CRN* 115). He wrote to his father in 1862 that there was "no man whom I more entirely resemble than Rousseau. . . . If I were asked whom of all men of any name in past time I thought myself to be grouped with, I should answer unhesitatingly, Rousseau. I judge by," he continues, among other works, "the *Nouvelle Heloise*" (cited in Cook, *Life of John Ruskin*, 2:548–59). A few years later he remarked to his mother on "the intense resemblance . . . in mind" between himself and the eighteenth-century writer (cited in Cook, *Life of John Ruskin*, 2:549).

57. Fuchs, *Pursuit of Virtue*, 13. For a close textual analysis of how this transposition takes place, see Hall, "Concept of Virtue in *La Nouvelle Héloïse*, 20–33.
58. J. Morley, *Rousseau*, 2:37–38.
59. N. Armstrong, *Desire and Domestic Fiction*, 39.
60. J. Morley, *Rousseau*, 1:145.
61. Shklar, *Men and Citizens*, 27.
62. N. Armstrong, *Desire and Domestic Fiction*, 48. As Gossman has observed, "The pleasures of privacy, the intimate communication of individuals, have no place in such a communal world" ("The Worlds of *La Nouvelle Héloïse*," 261).
63. Hall, "The Concept of Virtue," 29.
64. Smiles, *Self-Help*, 36.
65. For Green's extended discussions of Rousseau, see both his early essay, "Popular Philosophy in its Relation to Life" (*North British Review*, March 1868) and the chapter on Rousseau in *Lectures on the Principles of Political Obligation*, both reprinted in *Works*.
66. Green, *Prolegomena to Ethics*, 218, 217; Green, *Works*, 428, 429–30, 436.
67. Oakeshott, *On Human Conduct*, 242.
68. Oakeshott, *On Human Conduct*, 264. Oakeshott points out that this concept of the state is frequently articulated through the kind of military rhetoric Ruskin uses in *Fors* (273).
69. Starobinski, *Jean-Jacques Rousseau*, 148; my translation. Starobinski sees Julie's death as a sign that Rousseau has opted for individual desire over "an absolute of communal interests." It seems to me that, although Rousseau's sympathies are with Julie, her death—like the death of Maggie Tulliver in *The Mill on the Floss*—shows the impossibility of self-development outside of a communal morality. This is not to say that Rousseau, any more than George Eliot, entirely endorses existing morality, but that he, too, sees individual and social experience as inextricably linked.
70. Oakeshott, *On Human Conduct*, 205; C. Morley, *John Ruskin*, 211. According to Morley, Ruskin was "one of the few authentic materialists. . . . He allowed [material reality] to teach him—he embraced it epistemologically—and he found it moral, capable of ideals." Wihl gives a more nuanced explanation of Ruskin's epistemological origins, and convincingly demonstrates in his discussion of Ruskin and Locke that Ruskin's materialism was always tainted by his recognition that "sensibility is confused with judgment from the outset" (*Ruskin and the Rhetoric of Infallibility*, 21).
71. Williams, *Culture and Society*, 146.
72. Review of *Fors Clavigera*, *Republican*, 5.
73. Scudder, "St. George's Company," 47, 48.
74. F. Harrison, "Past and Present," 100; F. Harrison, "The Revolution of the Commune," reprinted in R. Harrison, ed. *English Defence of the Commune*, 169; F. Harrison, "Past and Present," 105.
75. Bhabha, "DissemiNation," in Bhabda, ed., *Nation and Narration*, 303, 297.

Chapter IV: Conjuring the Necromantic Evidence of History

1. Hobson, *John Ruskin, Social Reformer*, 208–9.
2. M. Pattison, "Age of Reason," 351.
3. For a discussion of the change from an earlier notion of history as literature to the enlightenment conception of history as science, see Lukacs, *Historical Consciousness*,

16–22. For the institutional debates surrounding the various Victorian ideas of historiography in this chapter, see Small, *Conditions for Criticism*, 45–53.

4. Stephen, *History of English Thought*, 2:16; Stephen, "Mr. Ruskin's Recent Writings," 691, 690, 697, 692.

5. Carlyle characterized him as the "Evangelist" of the anarchy of the French Revolution (*WTC* 5:188). Stephen continues this strain in his discussion of Rousseau's "revolutionary fanaticism" in *History of English Thought*, 2:163. According to Gosse, Burke's early attack on Rousseau set British opinion for the following century: it would be "difficult, indeed, in the middle of the century, to find a responsible word published by an English writer in praise of Rousseau" (*Aspects and Impressions*, 172).

6. J. Morley, *Rousseau*, 2:128, 54, 239, 124.

7. Stephen, "Mr. Ruskin's Recent Writings," 690.

8. F. Harrison, *John Ruskin*, 185, 182. John Morley had commented of Rousseau: "The exultation of emotion over intelligence was the secret of his most striking production; the same exaltation, by gaining increased mastery over his whole existence, at length passed the limit of sanity and wrecked him. The tendency of the dominant side of a character towards diseased exaggeration is a fact of daily observation" (*Rousseau*, 2:300).

9. F. Harrison, "The Use of History," lecture delivered in 1862, reprinted in *Meaning of History*, 11, 20; F. Harrison, "The Revolution of the Commune," *Fortnightly Review* (1871), reprinted in R. Harrison, ed., *English Defence of the Commune 1871*, 168–69; F. Harrison, *Order and Progress*, 33, 104.

10. Goodwin and Taylor, *Politics of Utopia*, 17.

11. Bhabha, "DissemiNation," 317.

12. M. Pattison, "Age of Reason," 351.

13. As F. W. Knickerbocker put it, John Morley's French studies were "the reinterpretation of French eighteenth-century thinkers as pioneers of mid-nineteenth-century Liberalism" (*Free Minds*, 131).

14. J. Morley, *Diderot and the Encyclopaedists*, 1:8.

15. J. Morley, *On Compromise*, 206. In "Humanity," Frederic Harrison rephrases Morley's contention in Comtist terms; he claims to demonstrate that "the whole course of human civilization is a collective evolution" toward more accurate conceptions (871).

16. Buchanan, "Mr. John Morley's Essays," 327–28; "Spiritual Revolution" is Buchanan's phrase, 327.

17. Buchanan had declared: "From the first hour of his career to the last, Carlyle has been perniciously preaching the Scotch identity—a type of moral force . . . which is separatist without being spiritual, and spacious without being benevolent—to a generation sadly in need of quite another sort of preacher" ("Mr. John Morley's Essays," 328).

18. Bodleian MS Eng. misc. c.229, 20 *verso*, date uncertain.

19. Ibid., 21 *verso*, date uncertain. Hewison cogently explains how Ruskin's attempt to bring together his biblical vision of Venetian politics with the triumph of Venetian architecture created a new synthesis in *The Stones of Venice* between aesthetic and social questions (*John Ruskin*, 130–33).

20. Landow, *Aesthetic and Critical Theories of John Ruskin*, 349.

21. Sawyer, "Ruskin and St. George," 25.

22. Nietzsche, "The Use and Abuse of History," in *Unzeitgemässe Betrachtungen*, 94.

23. Auerbach, *Scenes from the Drama*, 5.

24. Landow, in *Aesthetic and Critical Theories of John Ruskin*, provides an extensive account of Ruskin's use of typology and allegory as it relates to various nineteenth-century exegetical models (321–55). For related accounts of biblical typology in Ruskin's rhetoric, see Landow, *Victorian Types, Victorian Shadows* and Sussman, *Fact into Figure*. In *Ruskin and the Rhetoric of Infallibility*, Wihl qualifies both Landow's and Sussman's discussions by suggesting that Ruskin himself is often unclear about the difference between allegory and *figura* (46–48). As Spear points out, Ruskin's use of the word "type" shifts greatly in his early work: he employs it "more often in its general sense as essence, pattern, or even symbol than in the strictly religious sense" (*Dreams of an English Eden*, 38).

25. Wihl, *Ruskin and the Rhetoric of Infallibility*, 149.

26. In his essay on Proust's treatment of the difference between literal and figurative meaning, Paul de Man focuses precisely on that writer's use of Giotto's figure of Charity (see *Allegories of Reading*). Wihl, in his chapter "Idolatry in Ruskin and Proust," looks at de Man's reading in connection with Ruskin's *Aratra Pentelici*, and recognizes in passing that Proust's use of Charitas is derived from Ruskin's treatment in *Fors* (*Ruskin and the Rhetoric of Infallibility*, 114).

27. Wihl, *Ruskin and the Rhetoric of Infallibility*, 148.

28. Bahti, *Allegories of History*, 155.

29. Bhabha, "DissemiNation," 297.

30. Ibid., 302; J. Morley, "Memorials of a Man of Letters," *Fortnightly Review* (1878), reprinted in *Studies in Literature*, 304–5.

31. See Fox, *Saint George*, 88–89, 75–76. Fox summarizes the uses of the St. George myth from medieval England to the present. St. George was also the subject of one of Ruskin's own childhood puppet plays (2:xxxiii), a fact that suggests that he was caught up in the popularity of the myth at an early age.

32. Girouard remarks on the cluster of associations surrounding the myth of St. George that made it the perfect symbol of empire: "The fact that he was England's traditional patron saint, that he was also accepted as the patron saint of chivalry and that slaying dragons and rescuing those in distress by doing so, beautifully symbolised what imperialists believed the Empire was all about, ensured his popularity" (*Return to Camelot*, 229). St. George has once again become a potent symbol for those who favor strong English nationalism over the cosmopolitan policies of the European Union. Echoes of Ruskin's political ideas can be heard, for example, in a recent debate about whether St. George's Day should be made Britain's national holiday, in the spirit of American Independence Day or French Bastille Day (see Christopher Hill's discussion of St. George's Day in the *Manchester Guardian Weekly*, 5 May 1991, 4).

33. As in his translation of a passage of Plato discussed in ch. 3, so here Ruskin's translation betrays his ideological differences with the more liberal Jowett. In Jowett, the passage reads "in states generally no one has observed that the plays of childhood have a great deal to do with the permanence or want of permanence in legislation. For when plays are ordered with a view to children having the same plays and amusing themselves after the same manner, and finding delight in the same playthings, the more solemn institutions of the state are allowed to remain undisturbed" (Plato, *Dialogues*, 5:366). For Ruskin, children "us[ing] their fancies in the same way" is the "principal" means of maintaining laws; for Jowett, playing is simply one of the factors that helps to

reinforce existing institutions. Jowett does not create the strong, causal link between imagination and civic action that for Ruskin is the whole point of the passage.

34. For a discussion of Friedrich Jahn's and Ernst Moritz Arndt's advocacy of Platonic principles of performance, and the importance of their ideas to later German nationalist thinking, see Mosse, "Mass Politics," 52–54. For a provocative discussion of Ruskin's use of Platonic rituals to produce a healthy nation and to exorcise its profanity, see Casillo, "Parasitism and Capital Punishment in *Fors Clavigera*."

35. C. Morley, *John Ruskin*, 52.

36. Jeffrey Spear, "Political Questing: Ruskin, Morris and Romance," in Hewison, ed., *New Approaches to Ruskin*, 185.

37. Bahti, *Allegories of History*, 155.

38. J. B. Bury, "The Place of Modern History in the Perspective of Knowledge," cited in Heyck, *Transformation of Intellectual Life in Victorian England*, 147. Heyck's chapter on the professionalization of historiography in the 1870s details the move away from the sweeping narratives of national history that were so popular for most of the Victorian period.

Chapter V: The Guidance of Household Gods

1. Paul Sawyer aptly compares this "moment of inspired bizarreness"—when "the movement of molecules [is] dramatized as crinolines pressing themselves into triangles and squares"—to Lewis Carroll's fantastic games in the Alice books (*Ruskin's Poetic Argument*, 246).

2. In explanation of the myth of Pthah, Ruskin tells how it is that he can sketch a better likeness of an eagle in thirty seconds than can a metal-working firm that had taken three years to produce its eagle on exhibition in the Crystal Palace: "For, during the thirty seconds, the eagle is my object,—not myself; and during the three years, the firm's object, in every fibre of bronze it made, was itself, and not the eagle. That is the true meaning of the little Pthah's having no eyes—he can see only himself" (18:245).

3. See Stange, "Art Criticism as a Prose Genre," 44–47, and Helsinger, *Ruskin and the Art of the Beholder*, 5–16.

4. Helsinger, *Ruskin and the Art of the Beholder*, 16.

5. Austin, *Practical Ruskin*, 133. Austin focuses on Ruskin's response to mass readership in *Fiction, Fair and Foul*.

6. For the reputation of Xenophon's *Economist* up to 1876, see the editors' introduction to the volume in the Library Edition (31:xviii). The translation was prepared by W. G. Collingwood and by one of the Library Edition editors, Alexander Wedderburn, who were both students at Oxford when Ruskin taught there in the 1870s.

7. John Kijinski explores the Victorians' use of metaphors of bodily health to describe the process of reading in "John Morley's 'English Men of Letters' Series," 208.

8. F. Harrison, "On the Choice Books," *Fortnightly Review* (1879); reprinted in *Choice of Books*, 7–8. The version of this essay I refer to was revised for republication in book form; it includes material from "Letters on Home Reading," which Harrison had written at about the same period as the *Fortnightly* article (see Harrison's preface to *Choice of Books*, vi).

9. Ruskin's attachment to Byron has been widely recognized. His most eloquent defence

of the poet was published in the *Nineteenth Century* in 1880 (now part 3 of *Fiction, Fair and Foul*), where Ruskin links his own name with those of Byron and Shelley. Linda Austin discusses Ruskin's antipopulist approach to Byron in *Fiction, Fair and Foul* (*Practical Ruskin*, 157–60). Few critics have noted Ruskin's continued admiration of and debt to Shelley.

10. For an exemplary instance of such an attitude, see Altieri, *Canons and Consequences*, 22–23. "Suspicious" is used repeatedly in his discussions of what he sees as a too politicized criticism.

11. Bloom, *Western Canon*, 20, 33, 21.

12. F. Harrison, *Choice of Books*, 74, 92.

13. Nichol, *Lectures to Ladies*, (1869), cited in F. Court, *Institutionalizing English Literature*, 140; for the academic response to German nationalism, see F. Court, *Institutionalizing English Literature*, 135–38.

14. See Cook and Wedderburn's introduction to the existing volumes of the *Bibliotheca Pastorum* (31 : xiv–xv).

15 Maidment, "Ruskin, *Fors Clavigera* and Ruskinism" 204; Ruskin to Elizabeth Blackwell, 31 Dec. 1884, Bodleian MS Eng. Lett. c. 47, fol. 293.

16. Austin, *Practical Ruskin*, 178, Austin takes the phrase "commodity book" from N. N. Feltes, *Modes of Production of Victorian Novels*; Ruskin to Mr. Hills, 18 Nov. 1872, Bodleian MS Eng. lett. c. 38, fol. 323; Ruskin to Allen, 25 Sept. 1882; Bodleian MS Eng. lett. c. 45, fol. 176.

17. M. Pattison, "Books and Critics," 667.

18. Ibid.; for Matthew Arnold's parallel and paradoxical attempt to define what amounted to a critical "classless" class, see Trilling's discussion of *Culture and Anarchy* in *Matthew Arnold*, 252–53; J. Morley, *Recollections*, 1 : 72, 71.

19. M. Pattison, "Age of Reason," 351; Bourdieu, *Distinction*, 31.

20. Gosse, "What Is a Great Poet" (1889), reprinted in *Questions at Issue*, 100–111; letter of 1879, cited in Thwaite, *Edmund Gosse*, 387.

21. See especially the essay "Semiology and Rhetoric" in de Man, *Allegories of Reading* (the "naive" reader on 16); for an example of such attacks on de Man, see Lentricchia, *After the New Criticism*, xiii, and ch. 8, "Paul de Man: The Rhetoric of Authority."

22. Gosse, *Questions at Issue*, ix, 111.

23. Guillory, "Ideology of Canon-Formation," 175; apRoberts, *Arnold and God*, 281; Arnold, *Complete Prose Works*, 11 : 148.

24. Armstrong, *Desire and Domestic Fiction*, 16–17; M. Pattison, "Books and Critics," 674.

25. Accounts of the deliberate creation of national literary taste late in the century can be found in Baldick, *Social Mission*, and Colls and Dodd, *Englishness*.

26. Dickens demonstrated the usefulness of such techniques for polemical writing in his brilliant articles in *Household Words* on crime and poverty. He adopts in these essays a dramatic persona and relates the results of his investigative reporting in the manner of a detective tale. Stone looks briefly at Dickens's methods of periodical writing in his introduction to *Uncollected Writings from Household Words*.

27. Ruskin to S., Bodleian MS Eng. lett. c. 47, fol. 126, 28 July 1884; Scudder, "St. George's Company," 47.

28. Ruskin to the children at Winnington Hall, 27–28 March 1859; reprinted in Burd, ed., *Winnington Letters*, 132–35.

29. Ruskin to the children at Winnington Hall, 24 Nov. 1861; Ruskin to J. J. Ruskin,

11 Dec. 1863; Ruskin to the children at Winnington Hall, 8 May 1864; all reprinted in Burd, ed., *Winnington Letters*, 339–41, 455, 496–99.

30. For a summary of Margaret Bell's innovative methods for women's education, see Burd's introduction to *Winnington Letters*, 31–40.

31. See, for example, his letter to Margaret Bell of 15 Jan. 1863, reprinted in Burd, ed., *Winnington Letters*, 397. The connection between Pattison and Ruskin in this context is, perhaps, not coincidental. The Winnington library contained a copy of *Essays and Reviews*, in which Pattison's look at religious dogma appeared (*Winnington Letters*, 40). Whether Ruskin read it there or not (he did habitually borrow books from the library), it clearly shaped Margaret Bell's thinking on religious matters, and she was a friend with whom Ruskin openly discussed his religious doubts.

32. Ruskin to Bell, 11 March 1863, reprinted in Burd, ed., *Winnington Letters*, 403–4.

33. Ruskin to Colenso, 2 Nov. 1862, reprinted in Burd, ed., *Winnington Letters*, 386. The Bishop was both a friend of Bell's and an occasional visitor at Winnington. See the editor's introduction to *Winnington Letters*, 73–74, and the many references to him scattered throughout Ruskin's letters to Bell.

34. Waswo, "History that Literature Makes," 541, 543.

35. Austin, *Practical Ruskin*, 141. Austin interestingly contends that in the *Bibliotheca*, Ruskin was little concerned with "literary value"; he was, she argues, "a sort of nineteenth-century *annales* historian" invested in a notion of "domestic history."

36. Fergusson, *Quiet Folk*, 56, 59, 56–57, 63. Fergusson's argument about the political use of fairy tales anticipates current strains of criticism; Zipes, for example, considers at length the role of fairy tales in the "internalization of values" (*Fairy Tales*, 9).

37. Maitland, *Life and Letters of Leslie Stephen*, 366; editorial statement, cited in Annan, *Leslie Stephen*, 84; Annan, *Leslie Stephen*, 88.

38. Royce, "Ruskin vs. Gibbon and Grote," 954, 956. The writer was outraged that Ruskin deliberately passed over Gibbon and Grote in his revision of previous canons; for Ruskin's letter to the *Pall Mall Gazette* outlining his choice of books, see 34:585.

39. Courthope, "The Progress of Taste," 72.

40. Waldstein, *Work of John Ruskin*, 12.

41. F. Harrison, *Realities and Ideals*, 364–65. In his book on Ruskin published six years earlier for Morley's English Men of Letters series, Harrison had remarked that *Fors* "flows on in one fascinating *causerie*" (*John Ruskin*, 184).

42. Ruskin's outlines for *Praeterita* were preserved in his diaries for 1885 and 1886, Bodleian MS Eng. misc. c. 232, reprinted in *Diaries of John Ruskin*, 3:1136.

43. The phrase is from the title of Paul Sawyer's *Ruskin's Poetic Argument*.

44. Connor, "Ruskin Redivivus," 501.

Bibliography

A transcript of Ruskin's diaries was made by E. T. Cook and Alexander Wedderburn while they were preparing the Library Edition of his works. It is more complete than the edition of his diaries published by Evans and Whitehouse. The transcript is now in the Bodleian Library, Bodleian MS Eng. misc. c. 209–49. A similar transcript of letters to and from Ruskin was made, and published in part in vols. 36 and 37 in the Library Edition. The original transcript is held in the Bodleian Library, Bodleian MS Eng. lett. c. 32–52. Many letters not included in the Bodleian typescript are to be found in the Ruskin Foundation Collection, Ruskin Library, University of Lancaster.

Altick, Richard. *The English Common Reader: A Social History of the Mass Reading Public, 1800–1900*. Chicago: Univ. of Chicago Press, 1957.

Altieri, Charles. *Canons and Consequences. Reflections on the Ethical Force of Imaginative Ideals*. Evanston: Northwestern Univ. Press, 1990.

Anderson, Benedict. *Imagined Communities: Reflections on the Origin and Spread of Nationalism*. London: Verso, 1983.

Annan, Noel. *Leslie Stephen: The Godless Victorian*. New York: Random House, 1984.

Anthony, P. D. *John Ruskin's Labour: A Study of Ruskin's Social Theory*. Cambridge: Cambridge Univ. Press, 1983.

Anti-Cobbett, or The Weekly Patriotic Register. 1817.

apRoberts, Ruth. *Arnold and God*. Berkeley: Univ. of California Press, 1983.

Armstrong, Isobel. *Language as Living Form in Nineteenth-Century Poetry*. Sussex: Harvester, 1982.

Armstrong, Nancy. *Desire and Domestic Fiction: A Political History of the Novel*. New York: Oxford Univ. Press, 1987.

Arnold, Matthew. *The Complete Prose Works of Matthew Arnold*. Ed. R. H. Super. 11 vols. Ann Arbor: Univ. of Michigan Press, 1960–77.

Aspinall, A. *Politics and the Press, c. 1780–1850*. London: Home & Van Thal, 1949.

Auerbach, Erich. *Scenes from the Drama of European Literature*. Trans. Ralph Manheim. New York: Meridian, 1959.

Austin, Linda. *The Practical Ruskin: Economics and Audience in the Late Work*. Baltimore: Johns Hopkins Univ. Press, 1991.

Babbitt, Irving. *Rousseau and Romanticism*. Boston: Houghton Mifflin, 1919.

Bagehot, Walter. *The Collected Works of Walter Bagehot*. Ed. Norman St. John-Stevas. 15 vols. London: Economist, 1965–86.

Bahti, Timothy. *Allegories of History: Literary Historiography after Hegel*. Baltimore: Johns Hopkins Univ. Press, 1992.

Baldick, Chris. *The Social Mission of English Criticism, 1848–1922.* Oxford: Oxford Univ. Press, 1983.

Barnard, F. M. "National Culture and Political Legitimacy: Herder and Rousseau." *Journal of the History of Ideas* 44 (1983): 231–53.

Beer, Gillian. "Problems of Description in the Language of Discovery." In *One Culture: Essays in Science and Literature*, ed. George Levine, 35–58. Madison: Univ. of Wisconsin Press, 1987.

Bhabha, Homi K., ed. *Nation and Narration.* London: Routledge, 1990.

Birch, Dinah. *Ruskin's Myths.* Oxford: Clarendon, 1988.

Bloom, Harold. Introduction to *John Ruskin*, ed. Harold Bloom, 1–14. New York: Chelsea House, 1986.

———. *The Western Canon: The Books and School of the Ages.* New York: Riverhead, 1994.

Bourdieu, Pierre. *Distinction: A Social Critique of the Judgement of Taste.* Trans. Richard Nice. Cambridge: Harvard Univ. Press, 1984.

Bradley, John, and Ian Ousby, eds. *The Correspondence of John Ruskin and Charles Eliot Norton.* Cambridge: Cambridge Univ. Press, 1987.

Brennan, Timothy. "The National Longing for Form." In *Nation and Narration*, ed. Bhabha, 44–70.

Briggs, Asa. *The Age of Improvement, 1783–1867.* 1959. London: Longmans, 1984.

Brooke, Stopford. Review of *Lectures on Art*, by John Ruskin. *Macmillan's* 22 (1870): 423–34.

Brown, Alan Willard. *The Metaphysical Society: Victorian Minds in Crisis, 1869–1880.* New York: Columbia Univ. Press, 1947.

Brownell, W. C. *Victorian Prose Masters.* New York: Scribner's, 1902.

Buchanan, Robert. "Mr. John Morley's Essays." *Contemporary Review* 17 (1871): 319–37.

Bulwer, William Henry Lytton, Sir. *Historical Characters: Talleyrand, Cobbett, Mackintosh, Canning.* London: Bentley, 1868.

Burd, Van Akin, ed. *The Winnington Letters: John Ruskin's Correspondence with Margaret Alexis Bell and the Children at Winnington Hall.* London: Allen & Unwin, 1968.

Burke, Edmund. *The Writings and Speeches of the Right Honourable Edmund Burke.* Beaconsfield Ed. 12 vols. New York: Taylor, 1901.

Butler, Marilyn. *Romantics, Rebels, and Reactionaries; English Literature and Its Background, 1760–1830.* New York: Oxford Univ. Press, 1981.

Carlisle, Janice. *John Stuart Mill and the Writing of Character.* Athens: Univ. of Georgia Press, 1991.

Carlyle, Thomas. *The Works of Thomas Carlyle.* Centenary ed. 30 vols. London: Chapman & Hall, 1897–99.

Casillo, Robert. "Parasitism and Capital Punishment in *Fors Clavigera*." *Victorian Studies* 29 (1986): 537–67.

Cate, George Allen, ed. *The Correspondence of Thomas Carlyle and John Ruskin.* Stanford: Stanford Univ. Press, 1982.

Cobbett, William. *A Grammar of the English Language.* London: Bensley, 1823.

———. *Two-Penny Trash; or Politics for the Poor.* London: published by the author, 1830–32.

———. *Weekly Political Register.* London: Bagshaw, 1802–35.

Coleman, Deirdre. *Coleridge and* The Friend *(1809–1810).* Oxford: Clarendon, 1988.

Coleridge, Samuel Taylor. *Biographia Literaria*. 1817. Ed. James Engell and W. Jackson Bate. 2 vols. Bollingen Ed. Princeton: Princeton Univ. Press, 1983.

————. *Collected Letters of Samuel Taylor Coleridge*. Ed. Earl Leslie Griggs. 6 vols. Oxford: Clarendon, 1956–71.

————. *The Friend*. 1809–10. Ed. Barbara E. Rooke. Bollingen Ed. 2 vols. Princeton: Princeton Univ. Press, 1969.

————. *Lay Sermons*. 1817. Ed. R. J. White. Bollingen Ed. Princeton: Princeton Univ. Press, 1972.

————. *The Watchman*. 1796. Ed. L. Patton. Bollingen Ed. Princeton: Princeton Univ. Press, 1969.

Collini, Stefan. *Public Moralists: Political Thought and Intellectual Life in Britain 1850–1930*. Oxford: Clarendon, 1991.

Colls, Robert, and Philip Dodd. *Englishness: Politics and Culture, 1880–1920*. London: Croom Helm, 1986.

Connor, Patrick. "Ruskin Redivivus." *Art History* 7 (1984): 498–503.

Cook, E. T. *The Life of John Ruskin*. 2 vols. London: Allen, 1911.

Court, Franklin. *Institutionalizing English Literature: The Culture and Politics of Literary Study, 1750–1900*. Stanford: Stanford Univ. Press, 1992.

Court, W. H. B., ed. *British Economic History 1870–1954, Commentary and Documents*. Cambridge: Cambridge Univ. Press, 1965.

[Courthope, W. J.]. "The Progress of Taste." *Quarterly Review* 149 (1880): 46–83.

Dellamora, Richard. *Masculine Desire: The Sexual Politics of Victorian Aestheticism*. Chapel Hill: Univ. of North Carolina Press, 1990.

de Man, Paul. *Allegories of Reading: Figural Language in Rousseau, Nietzsche, Rilke, and Proust*. New Haven: Yale Univ. Press, 1979.

Desmond, Adrian, and James Moore. *Darwin*. Harmondsworth UK: Penguin, 1991.

Disraeli, Benjamin. General preface. 1870. Vol. 1. *Collected Works of the Right Honourable B. Disraeli*. 10 vols. London: Longmans, 1870–71.

Duncan, David. *Life and Letters of Herbert Spencer*. New York: Appleton, 1908.

During, Simon. "Literature—Nationalism's Other? The Case for Revision." In *Nation and Narration*, ed. Bhabha, 138–53.

Eagleton, Terry. *The Function of Criticism from The Spectator to Post-Structuralism*. London: Verso, 1984.

————. *The Ideology of the Aesthetic*. Oxford: Blackwell, 1990.

Eby, Cecil. *The Road to Armageddon: The Martial Spirit in English Popular Literature, 1870–1914*. Durham: Duke University Press, 1987.

Eliot, George. *Middlemarch*. 1871–1872. Harmondsworth UK: Penguin, 1965.

Ellegård, Alvar. *The Readership of the Periodical Press in Mid-Victorian Britain*. Göteborgs Universitets Arsskrift 63.3 (1957).

Ellicot, C. J. "The Church of England Present and Future." *Nineteenth Century* 1 (1877): 50–71.

Fellows, Jay. *The Failing Distance: The Autobiographical Impulse of John Ruskin*. Baltimore: Johns Hopkins Univ. Press, 1975.

Feltes, N. N. *Modes of Production of Victorian Novels*. Chicago: Univ. of Chicago Press, 1986.

Fergusson, R. Menzies. *Quiet Folk*. London: Simpkin, 1889.

Finley, C. Stephen. "The Structure of Ruskin's *Fors Clavigera*." *Prose Studies* 9.3 (1986): 71–85.

Finley, M. I. "Politics." In *The Legacy of Greece: A New Appraisal*, ed. M. I. Finley, 24–36. Oxford: Clarendon, 1981.

Fitch, Raymond. *The Poison Sky: Myth and Apocalypse in Ruskin*. Athens: Ohio Univ. Press, 1982.

Fox, David Scott. *Saint George: The Saint with Three Faces*. Windsor Forest UK: Kensal Press, 1983.

Freeden, Michael. *The New Liberalism: An Ideology of Social Reform*. Oxford: Clarendon, 1978.

Fried, Michael. *Courbet's Realism*. Chicago: Univ. of Chicago Press, 1990.

Friswell, J. Hain. *Modern Men of Letters Honestly Criticised*. London: Hodder & Stoughton, 1870.

Fuchs, Jeanne Thomas. *The Pursuit of Virtue: A Study of Order in* La Nouvelle Héloïse. New York: Peter Lang, 1993.

Gay, Peter. *The Party of Humanity: Essays in the French Enlightenment*. New York: Knopf, 1964.

Gibbins, John. "J. S. Mill, Liberalism, and Progress." In *Victorian Liberalism: Nineteenth Century Political Thought and Practice*, ed. Richard Bellamy, 91–109. London: Routledge, 1990.

Gilmartin, Kevin. "'This Is Very Material': William Cobbett and the Rhetoric of Radical Opposition." *Studies in Romanticism* 34 (1995): 81–101.

Girouard, Mark. *The Return to Camelot: Chivalry and the English Gentleman*. New Haven: Yale Univ. Press, 1981.

Gladstone, W. E. Address. Liverpool Collegiate Institution. 1872. London: Murray, 1873.

Goldberg, M. K., and Jules P. Seigel. Introduction to *Carlyle's Latter-Day Pamphlets*, xix–lxv. N.p.: Canadian Federation for the Humanities, 1983.

Goodwin, Barbara, and Keith Taylor. *The Politics of Utopia: A Study in Theory and Practice*. London: Hutchinson, 1982.

Gosse, Edmund. *Aspects and Impressions*. New York: Scribner's, 1922.

———. *Questions at Issue*. London: Heinemann, 1893

Gossman, Lionel. "The Worlds of *La Nouvelle Héloïse*." *Studies in Voltaire and the Eighteenth Century* 41 (1966): 235–76.

Graver, Suzanne. *George Eliot and Community: A Study in Social Theory and Fictional Form*. Berkeley: Univ. of California Press, 1984.

Green, Thomas Hill. *Prolegomena to Ethics*. Ed. A. C. Bradley. Oxford: Clarendon, 1899.

———. *Works of Thomas Hill Green*. Ed. R. L. Nettleship. 3 vols. London: Longmans, Green, 1890.

Guillory, John. "The Ideology of Canon Formation: T. S. Eliot and Cleanth Brooks." *Critical Inquiry* 10 (1983): 173–98.

Gurney, Peter. "The Middle-Class Embrace: Language, Representation, and the Contest Over Cooperative Forms in Britain, c. 1860–1914." *Victorian Studies* 37 (1994): 253–86.

Habermas, Jürgen. *The Structural Transformation of the Public Sphere: An Inquiry into a Category of Bourgeois Society*. Trans. Thomas Burger. Cambridge: MIT Press, 1989.

Hall, H. Gaston. "The Concept of Virtue in *La Nouvelle Héloïse*." *Yale French Studies* 28 (1961–62): 20–33.

Hamer, D. A. *John Morley: Liberal Intellectual in Politics.* Oxford: Clarendon, 1968.

Harris, Daniel A. "The 'Figured Page': Dramatic Epistle in Browning and Yeats." *Yeats Annual* 1 (1982): 133–94.

Harrison, Frederic. *The Choice of Books.* London: Macmillan, 1886.

———. "Humanity: A Dialogue." *Contemporary Review* 27 (1876): 862–85.

———. *John Ruskin.* English Men of Letters. London: Macmillan, 1902.

———. *The Meaning of History, and Other Historical Pieces.* London: Macmillan, 1911.

———. *Order and Progress: Thoughts on Government, Studies of Political Crises.* 1875. Ed. Martha Vogeler. Rutherford NJ: Farleigh Dickinson Univ. Press, 1975.

———. "Past and Present." *Fortnightly Review* 26 (1876): 93–105.

———. *Realities and Ideals, Social, Political, Literary and Artistic.* London: Macmillan, 1908.

Harrison, Royden, ed. *The English Defence of the Commune 1871.* London: Merlin, 1971.

Hayman, John. "John Ruskin and the Art of System-Making." *English Studies* 4 (1974): 197–202.

Hazlitt, William. *The Complete Works of William Hazlitt.* Centenary ed. Ed. P. P. Howe. 21 vols. London: Dent, 1930–34.

Helsinger, Elizabeth. "Lessons of History: Ruskin's Switzerland." In *Creditable Warriors: 1830–1876,* ed. Michael Cotsell, 187–208. Atlantic Highlands NJ: Ashfield Press, 1990.

———. *Ruskin and the Art of the Beholder.* Cambridge: Harvard Univ. Press, 1982.

———. "Ruskin and the Politics of Viewing." *Nineteenth-Century Contexts* 18 (1994): 125–46.

Hewison, Robert. *Art and Society: Ruskin in Sheffield, 1876.* London: Brentham Press, 1981.

———. *John Ruskin: The Argument of the Eye.* London: Thames & Hudson, 1976.

———. "Notes on the Construction of the Stones of Venice." In *Studies in Ruskin: Essays in Honor of Van Akin Burd,* ed. Robert Rhodes and Del Ivan Janik, 131–52. Athens: Ohio Univ. Press, 1982.

———, ed. *New Approaches to Ruskin.* London: Routledge & Kegan Paul, 1981.

Heyck, T. W. *The Transformation of Intellectual Life in Victorian England.* London: Croom Helm, 1982.

Hill, Christopher. *Manchester Guardian Weekly,* 5 May 1991: 4.

Hilton, Tim. "Road Digging and Aestheticism in Oxford, 1875." *Studio International* 188 (1974): 226–29.

Hitchman, Francis. "The Penny Press." *Macmillan's* 43 (1881): 385–98.

Hobsbawm, Eric. "Mass-Producing Traditions, Europe 1870–1914." In *The Invention of Tradition,* ed. Eric Hobsbawm and Terence Ranger, 263–308. Cambridge: Cambridge Univ. Press, 1983.

———. *Nations and Nationalism since 1870: Programme, Myth, Reality.* Rev. ed. Cambridge: Cambridge Univ. Press, 1993.

Hobson, J. A. *John Ruskin, Social Reformer.* London: Nisbet, 1898.

———. *The Social Problem, Life and Work.* London: Nisbet, 1901.

Hough, Graham. *The Last Romantics.* London: Duckworth, 1949.

Hughes, Michael. *Nationalism and Society: Germany 1800–1945.* London: Arnold, 1988.

Kaplan, Fred. *Thomas Carlyle: A Biography.* Cambridge: Cambridge Univ. Press, 1983.

Kessen, William. "Rousseau's Children." *Daedalus* 107 (1978): 155–66.

Kijinski, John. "John Morley's 'English Men of Letters' Series and the Politics of Reading." *Victorian Studies* 34 (1991): 205–25.

Knickerbocker, F. W. *Free Minds: John Morley and His Friends.* Cambridge: Harvard Univ. Press, 1943.

Landow, George. *The Aesthetic and Critical Theories of John Ruskin.* Princeton: Princeton Univ. Press, 1971.

————. *Victorian Types, Victorian Shadows: Biblical Typology in Victorian Literature, Art, and Thought.* Boston: Routledge & Kegan Paul, 1980.

LaValley, Albert J. *Carlyle and the Idea of the Modern: Studies in Carlyle's Prophetic Literature and Its Relation to Blake, Nietzsche, Marx, and Others.* New Haven: Yale Univ. Press, 1968.

Lentricchia, Frank. *After the New Criticism.* London: Athlone Press, 1980.

Levine, George. *The Realistic Imagination: English Fiction from Frankenstein to Lady Chatterley.* Chicago: Univ. of Chicago Press, 1981.

Lukacs, John. *Historical Consciousness, or the Remembered Past.* New York: Harper & Row, 1968.

Maidment, Brian. "Readers Fair and Foul: John Ruskin and the Periodical Press." In *The Victorian Periodical Press: Samplings and Soundings,* ed. Joanne Shattock and Michael Wolff, 29–58. Toronto: Toronto Univ. Press, 1982.

Maitland, Frederic. *The Life and Letters of Leslie Stephen.* London: Duckworth, 1906.

Martin, Loy. *Browning's Dramatic Monologues and the Post-Romantic Subject.* Baltimore: Johns Hopkins Univ. Press, 1985.

McGowan, John. *Representation and Revelation: Victorian Realism from Carlyle to Yeats.* Columbia: Univ. of Missouri Press, 1986.

Metcalf, Priscilla. *James Knowles: Victorian Editor and Architect.* Oxford: Clarendon, 1980.

"A Modern Symposium." *Saturday Review* 42 (1877): 322.

Morley, Catherine. *John Ruskin, Late Work, 1870–1890: The Museum and Guild of St. George, an Educational Experiment.* New York: Garland, 1984.

Morley, John. *Critical Miscellanies.* 1877. 3 vols. London: Macmillan, 1886.

————. *Diderot and the Encyclopaedistes.* 2 vols. 1878. London: Macmillan, 1897.

————. *On Compromise.* London: Chapman Hall, 1874.

————. *Recollections.* 2 vols. New York: Macmillan, 1917.

————. *Rousseau.* 2d ed. 2 vols. London: Macmillan, 1878.

————. *Studies in Literature.* London: Macmillan, 1897.

————. *Voltaire.* 1872. London: Macmillan, 1923.

Mosse, George. "Mass Politics and the Political Liturgy of Nationalism." In *Nationalism: The Nature and Evolution of an Idea,* ed. Eugene Kamenka, 39–54. Canberra: Australian National Univ. Press, 1973.

"Mr. Ruskin on Mr. Ruskin." Review of *Fors Clavigera,* by John Ruskin. *Saturday Review* 38 (1874): 526–28.

"Mr. Ruskin's Fors Clavigera." Review of *Fors Clavigera,* by John Ruskin. *Saturday Review* 31 (1871): 13–15.

"Mr. Ruskin's Letter to Young Girls." Review of *Letter to Young Girls,* by John Ruskin. *Spectator* 49 (1876): 1,507–8.

"Mr. Ruskin's Unique Dogmatism." Review of *Fors Clavigera,* by John Ruskin. *Spectator* 50 (1877) 1,174–75.

"Mr. Ruskin's Will." Review of *Fors Clavigera,* by John Ruskin. *Spectator* 50 (1877): 435–36.

Nattrass, Leonora. *William Cobbett: The Politics of Style.* Cambridge: Cambridge Univ. Press, 1995.

Nietzsche, Friedrich. *Unzeitgemässe Betrachtungen.* 1873–76. Trans. William Arrowsmith et al. New Haven: Yale University Press, 1990.

Oakeshott, Michael. *On Human Conduct.* Oxford: Clarendon, 1975.

Ollier, Edmund. *Cassell's History of the War Between France and Germany, 1870–1871.* 2 vols. London: Cassell, Petter & Galpin, 1873–74.

Paine, Thomas. *Political Writings.* Ed. Bruce Kuklick. Cambridge: Cambridge Univ. Press, 1989.

Pattison, E. F. S. Review of *Lectures on Art* and *Catalogue of Examples,* by John Ruskin. *Academy* 1 (1870): 305–6.

Pattison, Mark. "The Age of Reason." *Fortnightly Review* n.s., 21 (1877): 343–61.

———. "Books and Critics." *Fortnightly Review* n.s., 21 (1877): 659–79.

———. *Memoirs of an Oxford Don.* 1885. London: Cassell, 1988.

———. *Sermons.* London: Macmillan, 1880.

Plato. *The Dialogues of Plato.* Trans. Benjamin Jowett. 2d ed. 5 vols. Oxford: Clarendon Press, 1875.

Raymond, Dora. *British Policy and Opinion During the Franco-Prussian War.* New York: Columbia Univ. Press, 1921.

Renan, Ernest. *Oeuvres complètes d'Ernest Renan.* 40 vols. Paris: Calmann-Levy, 1947–61.

Review of *Fors Clavigera,* by John Ruskin. *Guardian* 26 (16 Aug. 1871): 995.

Review of *Fors Clavigera,* by John Ruskin. *Guardian* 26 (1 Nov. 1871): 1,310.

Review of *Fors Clavigera,* by John Ruskin. *Republican* (19 Aug. 1871): 5.

Review of *Lectures on Art,* by John Ruskin. *Saturday Review* 30 (1870): 143–45.

Riede, David. *Oracles and Hierophants: Constructions of Romantic Authority.* Ithaca: Cornell Univ. Press, 1991.

Riley, Patrick. *Will and Political Legitimacy.* Cambridge: Harvard Univ. Press, 1982.

Ritchie, D. G. *The Principles of State Interference.* 1891. London: Sonnenschein, 1902.

Rogers, James E. Thorold. *Historical Gleanings: A Series of Sketches.* London: Macmillan, 1869.

Roll-Hansen, Diderik. *The Academy, 1869–1879: Victorian Intellectuals in Revolt.* Anglistica, vol. 8. Copenhagen: Rosenkilde & Bagger, 1957.

Rosenberg, John. *The Darkening Glass: A Portrait of Ruskin's Genius.* New York: Columbia Univ. Press, 1961.

Rousseau, Jean-Jacques. *Oeuvres complètes de J. J. Rousseau.* Ed. V. D. Musset-Pathay. 25 vols. Paris: Dupont, 1823–26.

Royce, G. Monroe. "Ruskin vs. Gibbon and Grote." *New Englander and Yale Review* 45 (1886): 954–63.

Ruskin, John. *The Brantwood Diary of John Ruskin.* Ed. Helen Gill Viljoen. New Haven: Yale Univ. Press, 1971.

———. *The Diaries of John Ruskin.* Ed. Joan Evans and John Howard Whitehouse. 3 vols. Oxford: Clarendon, 1958.

———. *The Works of John Ruskin.* Ed. E. T. Cook and Alexander Wedderburn. 39 vols. London: Allen, 1903–12.

Said, Edward. *The World, the Text, and the Critic.* Cambridge: Harvard Univ. Press, 1983.

Sawyer, Paul. "Ruskin and St. George: The Dragon-Killing Myth in *Fors Clavigera.*" *Victorian Studies* 23 (1979): 5–28.

———. "Ruskin and the Matriarchal Logos." In *Victorian Sages and Cultural Discourse: Renegotiating Gender and Power,* ed. Thaïs E. Morgan, 129–41. New Brunswick: Rutgers Univ. Press, 1990.

————. *Ruskin's Poetic Argument: The Design of the Major Works*. Ithaca: Cornell Univ. Press, 1985.

Scott, Edith Hope. *Ruskin's Guild of St. George*. London: Methuen, 1931.

Scudder, H. E. "St. George's Company." Review of *Fors Clavigera*, by John Ruskin. *Atlantic Monthly* 42 (1878): 39–51.

Shairp, J. C. *Studies in Poetry and Philosophy*. 1868. Boston: Houghton, Osgood, 1880.

Sherburne, James Clark. *John Ruskin, or the Ambiguities of Abundance: A Study in Social and Economic Criticism*. Cambridge: Harvard Univ. Press, 1972.

Shklar, Judith. *Men and Citizens: A Study of Rousseau's Social Theory*. Cambridge: Cambridge Univ. Press, 1969.

Small, Ian. *Conditions for Criticism: Authority, Knowledge and Literature in the Late Nineteenth Century*. Oxford: Clarendon Press, 1991.

Smiles, Samuel. *Self-Help*. 1859. Centenary Ed. London: John Murray, 1958.

Spater, George. *William Cobbett: The Poor Man's Friend*. 2 vols. Cambridge: Cambridge Univ. Press, 1982.

Spear, Jeffrey. *Dreams of an English Eden: Ruskin and His Tradition in Social Criticism*. New York: Columbia Univ. Press, 1984.

————. "'These are the Furies of Phlegethon: Ruskin's Set of Mind and the Creation of *Fors Clavigera*." In *The Ruskin Polygon: Essays on the Imagination of John Ruskin*, ed. Faith M. Holland and John Dixon Hunt, 137–58. Manchester: Manchester Univ. Press, 1982.

Spencer, Herbert. *The Principles of Sociology*. 3 vols. Rev. ed., 1885. New York: Appleton, 1898.

————. *Social Statics: The Conditions of Human Happiness Specified, and the First of Them Developed*. 1851. New York: Appleton, 1873.

Stange, G. Robert. "Art Criticism as a Prose Genre." In *The Art of Victorian Prose*, ed. George Levine and William Madden, 39–52. New York: Oxford Univ. Press, 1968.

Starobinski, Jean. *Jean-Jacques Rousseau, la transparence et l'obstacle*. 2d ed. Paris: Gallimard, 1971.

Stephen, Leslie. *Essays on Freethinking and Plainspeaking*. London: Longmans, 1873.

————. *History of English Thought in the Eighteenth Century*. 2 vols. 1876. New York: Harcourt, 1962.

————. "Mr. Ruskin's Recent Writings." Review of *Fors Clavigera*, by John Ruskin. *Fraser's Magazine* n.s., 9 (1874): 688–701.

Stewart, R. W., ed. *Disraeli's Novels Reviewed, 1826–1968*. Metuchen NJ: Scarecrow Press, 1975.

Stoddart, Judith. "The Formation of the Working Classes: John Ruskin's *Fors Clavigera* as a Manual of Cultural Literacy." In *Culture and Education in Victorian England*, ed. Patrick Scott and Pauline Fletcher, 43–58. Lewisburg PA: Bucknell Univ. Press, 1990.

————. "The Morality of *Poems and Ballads*: Swinburne and Ruskin." In *The Whole Music of Passion: New Essays on Swinburne*, ed. Rikki Rooksby and Nicholas Shrimpton, 92–106. Aldershot UK: Scolar Press, 1993.

Stone, Harry. Introduction. *Uncollected Writings from Household Words, 1850–1859*. 2 vols. Bloomington: Indiana Univ. Press, 1968.

Strahan, Alexander. "Our Very Cheap Literature." *Contemporary Review* 14 (1870): 439–60.

Sussman, Herbert. *Fact into Figure: Typology in Carlyle, Ruskin, and the Pre-Raphaelite Brotherhood.* Columbus: Ohio State Univ. Press, 1979.

Sylvester, D. W. *Robert Lowe and Education.* Cambridge: Cambridge Univ. Press, 1974.

Taylor, Charles. *Sources of the Self: The Making of Modern Identity.* Cambridge: Harvard Univ. Press, 1989.

Thom, Martin. "Tribes within Nations: The Ancient Germans and the History of Modern France." In *Nation and Narration,* ed. Bhabha, 23–43.

Thompson, E. P. *The Making of the English Working Class.* Rev. ed. Harmondsworth UK: Penguin, 1980.

———. *William Morris: Romantic to Revolutionary.* Rev. ed. New York: Pantheon, 1976.

Thwaite, Ann. *Edmund Gosse, Literary Landscape 1849–1928.* 1984. New York: Oxford Univ. Press, 1984.

Traill, H. D. *Coleridge.* English Men of Letters. New York: Harper, 1884.

Trilling, Lionel. *Matthew Arnold.* Rev. ed. London: Unwin, 1949.

Tucker, Herbert. *Tennyson and the Doom of Romanticism.* Cambridge: Harvard Univ. Press, 1988.

Vanden Bossche, Chris R. *Carlyle and the Search for Authority.* Columbus: Ohio State Univ. Press, 1991.

Vincent, David. *Literacy and Popular Culture: England 1750–1914.* Cambridge: Cambridge Univ. Press, 1989.

Waldstein, Charles. *The Work of John Ruskin, Its Influence upon Modern Thought and Life.* London: Methuen, 1894.

Waswo, Richard. "The History that Literature Makes." *New Literary History* 19 (1988): 541–64.

Watson, J. S. *Biographies of John Wilkes and William Cobbett.* Edinburgh: Blackwood, 1870.

Weeks, Jeffrey. *Sex, Politics and Society: The Regulation of Sexuality since 1800.* London: Longmans, 1981.

Wiener, Martin. *English Culture and the Decline of the Industrial Spirit, 1850–1980.* Cambridge: Cambridge Univ. Press, 1981.

Wihl, Gary. *Ruskin and the Rhetoric of Infallibility.* New Haven: Yale Univ. Press, 1985.

Wilenski, R. H. *John Ruskin: An Introduction to Further Study of His Life and Work.* 1935. New York: Russell & Russell, 1967.

Williams, Raymond. *Cobbett.* New York: Oxford Univ. Press, 1983.

———. *Culture and Society, 1780–1950.* London: Chatto & Windus, 1958.

Wilson, David A. *Paine and Cobbett: The Transatlantic Connection.* Kingston: McGill-Queen's Univ. Press, 1988.

Wiltshire, David. *The Social and Political Thought of Herbert Spencer.* Oxford: Oxford Univ. Press, 1978.

Wright, Thomas. *Our New Masters.* 1873. Rpt. New York: Kelley, 1969.

Zipes, Jack. *Fairy Tales and the Art of Subversion: The Classical Genre for Children and the Process of Civilization.* London: Heinemann, 1983.

Index

Victorian Literature and Culture Series

ALLAN C. DOOLEY
Author and Printer in Victorian England

SIMON GATRELL
Thomas Hardy and the Proper Study of Mankind

JEFFREY SKOBLOW
Paradise Dislocated: Morris, Politics, Art

MATTHEW ROWLINSON
Tennyson's Fixations: Psychoanalysis and the Topics of the Early Poetry

BEVERLY SEATON
The Language of Flowers: A History

BARRY MILLIGAN
Pleasures and Pains: Opium and the Orient in Nineteenth-Century British Culture

GINGER S. FROST
Promises Broken: Courtship, Class, and Gender in Victorian England

LINDA DOWLING
The Vulgarization of Art: The Victorians and Aesthetic Democracy

TRICIA LOOTENS
Lost Saints: Silence, Gender, and Victorian Literary Canonization

MATTHEW ARNOLD
The Letters of Matthew Arnold, vols. 1–3
Edited by Cecil Y. Lang

EDWARD FITZGERALD
Edward FitzGerald, Rubáiyát of Omar Khayyám: *A Critical Edition*
Edited by Christopher Decker

CHRISTINA ROSSETTI
The Letters of Christina Rossetti, vol. 1
Edited by Antony H. Harrison

BARBARA LEAH HARMON
The Feminine Political Novel in Victorian England

JOHN RUSKIN
The Genius of John Ruskin: Selections from His Writings
Edited by John D. Rosenberg

ANTONY H. HARRISON
Victorian Poets and the Politics of Culture: Discourse and Ideology

JUDITH STODDART
Ruskin's Culture Wars: Fors Clavigera *and the Crisis of Victorian Liberalism*